I0439002

OCS Study
MMS 2002-010

Economic Impact of Recreational Fishing and Diving Associated with Offshore Oil and Gas Structures in the Gulf of Mexico

Final Report

 **U.S. Department of the Interior**
Minerals Management Service
Gulf of Mexico OCS Region

OCS Study
MMS 2002-010

Economic Impact of Recreational Fishing and Diving Associated with Offshore Oil and Gas Structures in the Gulf of Mexico

Final Report

Authors

Robert L. Hiett
J. Walter Milon

Prepared under MMS Contract
1435-01-97-CT-30868
by
QuanTech, Inc.
Rosslyn, Virginia 22209

Published by

U.S. Department of the Interior
Minerals Management Service
Gulf of Mexico OCS Region

New Orleans
March 2002

DISCLAIMER

This report was prepared under contract between the Minerals Management Service (MMS) and QuanTech, Inc. This report has been technical reviewed by the MMS, and it has been approved for publication. Approval does not signify that the contents necessarily reflect the views and policies of the MMS, not does mention of trade names or commercial products constitute endorsement of recommendation for use. It is, however, exempt from review and compliance with the MMS editorial standards.

REPORT AVAILABILITY

Extra copies of this report may be obtained from the Public Information Office (Mail Stop 5034) at the following address:

U.S. Department of the Interior
Minerals Management Service
Gulf of Mexico OCS Region
Public Information Office (MS 5034)
1201 Elmwood Park Boulevard
New Orleans, Louisiana 70123-2394

Telephone: (504) 736-2519 or
1-800-200-GULF

CITATION

Suggested citation:

Hiett, R. L. and J. W. Milon. 2002. Economic Impact of Recreational Fishing and Diving Associated with Offshore Oil and Gas Structures in the Gulf of Mexico: Final Report. OCS Study MMS 2002-010. U.S. Dept. of the Interior, Minerals Management Service, Gulf of Mexico OCS Region, New Orleans, LA. 98 pp.

TABLE OF CONTENTS

LIST OF TABLES

Chapter 1
Executive Summary

Introduction

The purpose of this research project by QuanTech, Inc., of Rosslyn, Virginia, was to estimate demand, expenditures, and economic impact associated with recreational fishing and diving near offshore Gulf of Mexico-based oil and gas structures and artificial reefs created from such structures. The primary research approach involved a series of sample surveys of recreational fishermen and divers along the Gulf coast including the states of Alabama, Mississippi, Louisiana, and Texas. Data collection began in January 1999 and continued throughout the calendar year.

Objectives

There were three study objectives addressed by this research. First, QuanTech was asked to assess the recreational demand for fishing and diving associated with offshore oil and gas-related structures and with artificial reefs resulting from the "rigs to reef" programs in Texas, Louisiana, Mississippi, and Alabama. Secondly, the study was to assess the economic impacts resulting from this recreational demand on the economies of Texas, Louisiana, Mississippi, and Alabama. Finally, an objective was to analyze the incremental expenses associated with recreational fishing and diving that would not have been incurred if anglers had no offshore structure fishing or diving opportunities.

Overview of Study Approach

QuanTech's data collection methodology for meeting these project objectives combined in-person interviewing of recreational fishermen and divers in the field with follow-up telephone interviewing from a central dialing facility. The research design involved three basic data collection methods. The first was *in-person field interviews* in which trained data collectors stationed along coastal areas of the Gulf of Mexico visited predetermined boat launch sites and conducted interviews with fishermen and divers as they returned from the day's activities. Respondents were eligible if they were fishing in any saltwater area of the Gulf of Mexico, including sounds, rivers, bays, and other estuarine areas. Offshore was defined as "from the water's edge". The second method involved a telephone *follow-up interview* to collect detailed expenditures information from qualified respondents identified during the field interviewing. The third method involved a *telephone interview* with an independent sample of charter boat operators, party boat operators, and dive shops. The in-person field interviews were conducted with private boat fishermen, charter boat fishermen, party boat fishermen, and divers. Telephone follow-up interviews were conducted with subsamples from these same groups. Separate telephone interviews were conducted with charter boat operators, party boat operators, and dive shops.

The field interviews were used to estimate the proportion of fishing and diving trips taken near Gulf of Mexico oil and gas structures or artificial reefs created from such structures. The follow-up telephone interviews were used to estimate trip-related costs and capital expenditures associated with recreational fishing and diving. The independent surveys of charter boat operators, party boat operators, and dive shops were used to assess subjective estimates of the importance of oil and gas structures to recreational fishing and diving in the Gulf.

A key methodological issue was that of converting proportions and mean values per individual recreational fishing and diving trip into total estimates of demand and economic impact. Such estimates require knowledge of the total number of fishing and diving trips taken. The approach in this study was not to attempt to make such estimates of total demand as part of this project but to rely on estimates developed independently by the National Marine Fisheries Service (NMFS) of the U.S. Department of Commerce. The NMFS conducts an annual survey of marine recreational fishing in Alabama, Mississippi, and Louisiana with sample sizes considerably larger than the level of effort available for the MMS study. The NMFS survey is referred to as the Marine Recreational Fishery Statistics Survey (MRFSS) and has been conducted in the Gulf of Mexico since 1980 (National Marine Fisheries Service, 1992). In addition, Texas conducts its own survey of recreational fishing and NMFS incorporates the Texas data into its own estimates. The approach taken in this study, therefore, was to rely upon estimates of total fishing trips and numbers of participants provided by NMFS and to apply those estimates to the results of the 1999 MMS data collection to meet the project objectives.

Demand Estimates

The first objective of the study was to estimate demand by recreational fishermen and divers associated with oil and gas structures in the Gulf of Mexico and with artificial reefs constructed from such structures. These demand estimates were generated by the process of combining results of the field survey with data obtained from the National Marine Fisheries Service MRFSS. Overall, it is estimated that a total of 980,264 fishing trips were taken within 300 feet of an oil or gas structure or an artificial reef created from such structures during 1999 out of a total of 4,484,080 marine recreational fishing trips in the Gulf from Alabama through Texas. In addition, there were 83,780 dive trips near oil and gas structures out of a total of 89,464 dive trips taken from Alabama through Texas. These results are summarized separately by mode in the following paragraphs.

Private Boat Fishing

A total of 8,660 interviews were obtained in the field with private boat fishermen as they returned from their fishing trips. Analysis of data for these respondents indicated that, overall, the proportion of private boat trips taken within 300 feet of oil or gas structures was 20.2 percent. That is, of the 4.1 million private boat fishing trips[1] taken in these states during 1999, 823,075 were within 300 feet of an oil or gas structure. This information is shown separately by state in Table 1-1.

Table 1-1. Total Estimated Private Boat Fishing Trips Near Oil and Gas Structures

State	Total Trips	Proportion of Trips Near Oil/Gas Structures	Trips Near Oil/Gas Structures
Alabama	505,635	.414	209,333
Mississippi	507,545	.197	99,986
Louisiana	2,067,076	.166	343,135
Texas[2]	986,250	.173	170,621
Total	**4,066,506**	**.202**	**823,075**

---

[1] Data available at http://remora.ssp.nmfs.gov/.

[2] Information from Texas is not available through the MRFSS but was provided by the Texas Parks and Wildlife Department based upon state surveys.

Charter Boat Fishing

A total of 1,287 interviews were obtained in the field with charter boat fishermen as they returned from their fishing trips. Charter boats were defined as those operating under charter for a specific price and time. Charter boats are operated by a licensed captain and crew, with the fishermen consisting of preformed groups. Analysis of data for these respondents indicated that, overall, the proportion of charter boat trips taken within 300 feet of oil or gas structures was 32.3 percent. That is, of the 298,023 charter boat fishing trips taken in these states during 1999, 96,337 were within 300 feet of an oil or gas structure. This information is shown separately by state in Table 1-2.

Table 1-2. Total Estimated Charter Boat Fishing Trips Near Oil and Gas Structures

State	Total Trips	Proportion of Trips Near Oil/Gas Structures	Trips Near Oil/Gas Structures
Alabama	71,394	.210	14,993
Mississippi	49,426	.217	10,725
Louisiana	73,770	.231	17,041
Texas	103,433	.518	53,578
Total	298,023	.323	96,337

Party Boat Fishing

A total of 378 interviews were obtained in the field with party boat fishermen as they returned from their fishing trips. A party boat was defined as one on which fishing space and privileges are provided for a fee. Fishermen on party boat trips, also referred to as head boat trips, usually do not know the other fishermen on the boat. Analysis of data for these respondents indicated that, overall, the proportion of party boat trips taken within 300 feet of oil or gas structures was 50.9 percent. That is, of the 119,551 party boat fishing trips taken in these states during 1999, 60,852 were within 300 feet of an oil or gas structure. This information is shown separately by state in Table 1-3.

Table 1-3. Total Estimated Party Boat Fishing Trips Near Oil and Gas Structures

State	Total Trips	Proportion of Trips Near Oil/Gas Structures	Trips Near Oil/Gas Structures
Alabama	15,386	.000	0
Mississippi	0	--	0
Louisiana	7,913	1.000	7,913
Texas	96,252	.550	52939
Total	119,551	.509	60,852

Dive Trips

A total of 150 interviews were obtained in the field with divers as they returned from their trips. Analysis of data for these respondents indicated that, overall, the proportion of dive trips taken within 300 feet of oil or gas structures was 93.6 percent. That is, of the 89,464 dive trips taken in these states during 1999, 83,780 were within 300 feet of an oil or gas structure. This information is shown separately by state in Table 1-4.

3

Table 1-4. Total Estimated Dive Trips Near Oil and Gas Structures

State	Total Trips	Proportion of Trips Near Oil/Gas Structures	Trips Near Oil/Gas Structures
Alabama	11,124	.489	5,440
Mississippi	11,166	1.000	11,166
Louisiana	45,476	1.000	45,476
Texas	21,698	1.000	21,698
Total	89,464	.936	83,780

Economic Impact

Trip expenditure data were collected during follow-up phone interviews with oil and gas structure users who were engaged in recreational fishing from private boats, charter or party boats, or who participated in recreational diving. Average trip expenditure data for oil and gas structure users were combined with estimates of the total number of trips to oil and gas structures to produce estimates of the annual expenditures associated with trips near oil and gas structures for each mode in the four Gulf of Mexico states. Trip and equipment data were evaluated to estimate the economic impact in coastal counties of each state.

Overall, the survey accounted for a total of $172.9 million in trip related costs for fishing and diving near oil and gas structures in the Gulf states from Alabama through Texas. Of this number, $13.2 million were trip expenditures for diving with the balance of $159.7 million associated with trip expenses for recreational fishing.

Annual equipment expenditure data were also collected during the follow-up phone interviews with oil and gas structure users. These data were extrapolated by multiplying the average expenditures for each mode and state times the estimated number of participants using oil and gas structures. Because equipment expenditures may not be solely related to trips to oil and gas structures, the expenditure and corresponding impact estimates may overstate the economic activity generated by fishers and divers who participated in trips near oil and gas structures.

The survey accounted for a total of $640.0 million in equipment costs associated with recreational fishing and diving activities by those who visited oil or gas structures in the Gulf states from Alabama through Texas during the survey year. Of this number, $0.6 million was equipment expenditures for diving with the balance associated with equipment expenditures for recreational fishing.

The expenditure data, distributed according to whether the respondent lived in coastal or noncoastal areas and according to the location of the expenditure, were then used in the IMPLAN (Impact analysis for PLANning) input-output modeling framework to produce estimates of economic impacts generated by oil and gas structure users in each state. These impacts include total output, employment, and personal income (value added) effects in the coastal regions of each state.

This analysis indicated that there was a total of $324.6 million in economic output in coastal counties of the Gulf region associated with fishing and diving activities near oil and gas structures during the year. The value added component of this was $164.1 million with employment estimated at 5,560 full time equivalents.

Incremental Effects

As noted previously, a third major objective was to estimate incremental expenses associated with recreational fishing and diving that would not have been incurred if anglers had no offshore structure fishing or diving opportunities. In order to estimate this *incremental* effect of oil/gas structures on angler expenditures in the Gulf of Mexico region, it is necessary to statistically account for the variety of factors that may influence these decisions. In evaluating incremental effects, it is important to recognize that statistical procedures can only establish an *association* between expenditures and fishing near oil/gas structures; they can not determine causation.

The sample data indicated that the difference in annual trip and equipment expenditures between users and nonusers of oil and gas structures was $3,232 per angler across the Gulf region. After correcting for nonnormality in the distribution of expenditures and self-selection in the choice of fishing sites, predicted values from a Selection model indicated that the difference in expenditures between the two groups was much smaller. The predicted average expenditures for users were $4,691 with a 95 percent confidence interval of $4,198 to $5,183. For non-users, predicted average expenditures were $3,159 with a 95 percent confidence interval of $2,721 to $3,597. The resulting difference of $1,532 per angler is the most reliable estimate of the difference in annual expenditures between users and non-users of oil and gas structures across the Gulf of Mexico region.

Commercial Industry Perceptions

Telephone interviews were conducted at the end of 1999 with captains and owners of for hire fishing vessels and with operators of dive shops along coastal states. A series of questions was asked to determine their use of oil and gas structures and artificial reefs created from such structures for fishing and diving activities. Results indicated that use of such structures was extensive for both groups. Some 70.0 percent of the for hire fishing industry representatives and 84.6 percent of the dive shop operators indicated that they considered the presence of oil and gas structures in the Gulf to be very important to their industries. The vast majority (85.0 percent of for hire operators and 100.0 percent of dive shops) said their industry would be hurt by the removal of such structures and wanted them left in place after they are no longer used for oil and gas extraction.

Conclusions

In summary, it can be concluded as a result of this study that there is substantial recreational activity associated with the presence of oil and gas structures in the Gulf of Mexico from Alabama through Texas and these activities have a considerable economic impact. Because the presence of oil and gas structures is important to recreational fishing and diving, consideration should be given to assuring the continued availability of at least some of these structures across the range of the Gulf Coast area, even after they are no longer used for oil or gas extraction. Decisions on structure removal must take into account the effects on recreational activities and the economic value they represent. It is noted that the process by which fishermen and divers select the specific oil and gas structures to visit is not well understood. Both the incremental value that was established in this research and the fact that fishermen and divers visit multiple structures on each trip suggest that there is a decision process which underlies the selection of particular structures for recreational activities. If a decision about removal of a specific structure is being considered, it would be extremely useful to have in hand a set of variables which are known to be associated with structure selection. Decision-making processes for structure removal should include consideration of the needs of recreational fishermen and divers. Moreover, fishing and diving interests across the Gulf should be kept informed about the processes of structure removal and given opportunity to participate in such decisions.

Chapter 2
Study Methodology

Introduction

QuanTech's data collection methodology for meeting the objectives of the project combined in-person interviewing of recreational fishermen and divers in the field with follow-up telephone interviewing from a central dialing facility. The research design involved three basic data collection methods. The first was *in-person field interviews* in which trained data collectors stationed along coastal areas of the Gulf of Mexico visited predetermined boat launch sites and conducted interviews with fishermen and divers as they returned from the day's activities. The second method involved a telephone *follow-up interview* to collect detailed expenditures information from qualified respondents identified during the field interviewing. The third method involved a *telephone interview* with an independent sample of charter boat operators, party boat operators, and dive shops. The in-person field interviews were conducted with private boat fishermen, charter boat fishermen, party boat fishermen, and divers. Telephone follow-up interviews were conducted with subsamples from these same groups. Separate telephone interviews were conducted with charter boat operators, party boat operators, and dive shops.

The purpose of the field interviews was to obtain an estimate of the proportion of fishing and diving trips that were taken near Gulf of Mexico oil and gas structures or artificial reefs created from such structures. The purpose of the follow-up interviews was to obtain estimates of trip-related costs and capital expenditures associated with recreational fishing and diving. The independent surveys of charter boat operators, party boat operators, and dive shops was to obtain subjective estimates of the importance of oil and gas structures to recreational fishing and diving in the Gulf.

A key methodological issue was that of converting proportions and mean values per individual recreational fishing and diving trip into total estimates of demand and economic impact. Such estimates require knowledge of the total number of fishing and diving trips taken. The approach in this study was not to attempt to make such estimates of total demand as part of this project but to rely on estimates developed independently by the National Marine Fisheries Service (NMFS) of the U.S. Department of Commerce. The NMFS conducts an annual survey of marine recreational fishing in Alabama, Mississippi, and Louisiana with sample sizes considerable larger than the level of effort available for the MMS study. The NMFS survey is referred to as the Marine Recreational Fishery Statistics Survey (MRFSS) and has been conducted in the Gulf of Mexico since 1980. In addition, Texas conducts its own survey of recreational fishing and NMFS incorporates the Texas data into its own estimates.

The approach taken in this study, therefore, was to rely upon estimates of total fishing trips and numbers of participants provided by NMFS and to apply those estimates to the results of the 1999 QuanTech data collection to meet the project objectives. Detailed information on total numbers of trips derived from the MRFSS is provided in Chapter 3.

Project Background

It has been well documented in the literature that the number of offshore oil and gas structures in the Gulf of Mexico is extensive. According to Dauterive (2000) 5,862 oil and gas structures had been installed in the Gulf of Mexico by 1999, of which 1,879 had been retired. This left in place, as of the end of 1999, 3,983 such structures. Both the practical experience of many fishermen and the scientists who have studied the issue confirm that these structures act as artificial reefs, creating a habitat that allows marine species to expand their normal ranges and to exist in open ocean settings where they had been unable to exist previously (Driessen, 1989).

There have been a number of research efforts to evaluate the use of oil and gas structures by recreational fishermen. Ditton and Auyong in 1983 conducted a study of use of 164 major offshore petroleum structures by recreational and commercial fishermen. Gordon (1993) used an intercept approach to interview recreational fishermen in the central Gulf of Mexico region to determine travel patterns and destination points.

The survey project broadest in scope was the use by the National Marine Fisheries Service (NMFS) of its Marine Recreational Fishery Statistics Survey (MRFSS) to collect oil and gas structure-related recreational fishing data. The NMFS in 1984 used the Gulf of Mexico portion of the MRFSS to collect data showing the incidence of Gulf fishing near such structures (Witzig, 1986). This study, which is frequently cited because it covered the entire Gulf of Mexico and was conducted throughout a single calendar year, indicated that, while there was considerable variation in use of oil and gas structures for recreational fishing throughout the year, approximately 37 percent of trips overall by coastal Louisiana residents were near oil or gas structures. This figure was 28 percent for Texas coastal residents. The survey also indicated that, as fishermen traveled farther offshore to fish, the proportion fishing near oil and gas structures increased. In Louisiana, among those fishing more than three miles from shore in a private boat, 54 percent were near an oil or gas structure.

Since 1984 there has been no Gulf-wide survey covering recreational fishing near oil and gas structures or artificial reefs created from such structures.

There have also been limited efforts to assess the value of recreational fishing and diving near oil and gas structures in the Gulf of Mexico. Most of these have focused on the analytical methods available to determine the value of oil and gas structures to recreational fishing and diving. Such work includes studies by Roberts, Thompson, and Pawlyk (1985) who looked at contingent valuation of recreational diving; Bockstael, Graefe, Strand, and Rockland (1985) who reviewed literature on non-market goods valuation to assess problems associated with economic analysis of artificial reefs; and Milon (1991) who performed an evaluation of methods that can be applied to artificial habitat development projects.

There has been no Gulf-wide evaluation of the value of recreational fishing and diving associated with oil and gas structures or of their economic impact.

The current project was designed to address these deficiencies through the conduct of a large-scale sample survey covering the Gulf Coast from Alabama through Texas during the entire calendar year of 1999.

Preparation for Field Work

Before data collection could begin in the field, it was necessary to develop questionnaires for each target group, to develop and implement sampling plans, to hire and train field interviewers, and to develop data handling protocols. Work in each of these areas is described in the following paragraphs.

Questionnaire Development

A total of four questionnaires were developed for the field component of the project, although many of the same questions were asked in each. They included questionnaires for:

8

- Field Interview/Private Fishermen
- Field Interview/Charter Fishermen
- Field Interview/Party Boat Fishermen
- Field Interview/Diver

Copies of questionnaires used in the study are provided as Appendix A. A standard process was followed in the development of these data collection instruments. The program manager and the senior economist prepared lists of information required to perform the necessary economic assessment and impact analysis. Draft questionnaires were developed and reviewed by project staff and field interviewers knowledgeable about fishing along the Gulf coast. Updates to the questionnaires were made as a result of this review.

Once a draft of each questionnaire was prepared, a supporting statement for a request for Office of Management and Budget (OMB) clearance was developed and submitted through MMS and the Department of Interior to OMB. OMB clearance was obtained in January 1999 and data collection began immediately thereafter.

To facilitate interviewing and to standardize procedures, a written list of procedures was developed which interviewers were to follow in the field. These procedures covered such important issues as:

- Project Background
- Overview of Study Method and Design
- Sampling Methods
- Field Activities

The field sampling methods included detailed procedures for visiting the primary assigned site for conducting interviews and the use of alternate sites in the event no fishermen or divers were observed at the primary sites. The field activities included such issues as proper use of all data collection and administrative forms, screening of respondents, and eligibility requirements. Special attention was given to the importance of obtaining telephone numbers from respondents to allow for follow-up telephone interviews to obtain the needed expenditures information. A copy of these procedures is provided as Appendix D.

Sampling Plans

One of the more complex tasks was the development of quotas of interviews to be obtained by time of year by state. The guiding philosophy was that interviews should be distributed approximately in proportion to actual fishing effort as indicated by the NMFS' MRFSS. Using the target number of total interviews specified for the MMS-funded study, a sample allocation by state and month for private boats and charter boats was developed so that the number of interviews obtained would approximate the distribution geographically and seasonally of total recreational fishing trips based upon the MRFSS. For party boats (also referred to as head boats) the total projected interviews was 400. This was distributed by state based upon the number of known party boats operating in each state and equally from May through December, with no interviews allocated during the winter and early spring months. The resulting allocation of interviews is shown in Table 2-1. It should be noted that the unit of analysis was the individual fisherman. If, for example, several people fished together in a private or for-hire boat, an interview was attempted separately with each person who fished. The design also allowed individual fishermen as well as charter and party boats to be encountered multiple times during the course of the data collection year.

Table 2-1. Allocation of Field Interviews by Mode of Fishing, State, and Time of Year

State	Month	Private Boat Quota	Charter Boat Quota	Party Boat Quota
Alabama				
	Jan - Feb	76	26	0
	Mar - Apr	55	104	0
	May - Jun	230	60	19
	Jul - Aug	283	75	19
	Sep - Oct	107	48	19
	Nov - Dec	102	44	19
	Total	**853**	**357**	**76**
Mississippi	Jan - Feb	62	7	0
	Mar - Apr	104	126	0
	May - Jun	166	38	3
	Jul - Aug	217	11	3
	Sep - Oct	195	107	3
	Nov - Dec	96	23	3
	Total	**840**	**312**	**12**
Louisiana	Jan - Feb	290	31	0
	Mar - Apr	305	51	0
	May - Jun	588	62	19
	Jul - Aug	578	64	19
	Sep - Oct	582	50	19
	Nov - Dec	477	74	19
	Total	**2820**	**332**	**76**
Texas	Jan - Feb	205	31	0
	Mar - Apr	217	50	0
	May - Jun	417	61	59
	Jul - Aug	410	64	59
	Sep - Oct	413	49	59
	Nov - Dec	338	75	59
	Total	**2000**	**330**	**236**

It should be noted that no specific allocation of interviews was assigned for recreational divers. It was assumed that recreational divers would depart from the same marinas and boat launch sites used by private boats and boats in the for-hire industry. Field interviewers were provided with diver questionnaires and instructed to interview all recreational divers encountered during their regular interviewing assignments at boat launch sites and marinas. The ratio of divers to marine recreational fishermen could then be calculated directly from the results of the sample of total interviews obtained. The total number of diving trips taken in the Gulf of Mexico could then be estimated by applying this ratio to the total private boat fishing trips as reported by the NMFS based upon the MRFSS. This procedure was necessary because the MRFSS does not make any estimate of diver trips.

Before interviewing in the field could begin, it was necessary to convert the target quotas into numbers of assignments that would be required to obtain the interviews by state and time of year. For Alabama, Mississippi, and Louisiana, QuanTech used historical data from the NMFS' MRFSS consisting of both interviewer productivity estimates and lists of sites at which private boat and charter boat fishing took place.

A detailed review of historical MRFSS data was undertaken and interviewing locations (sites) at which no or minimal interviews had been obtained in prior years were removed from the site list. The list of interviewing sites included in the study is shown by state in Appendix E.

Because the NMFS' MRFSS was not conducted in Texas in prior years, it was necessary to develop a list of marinas and boat launch sites comparable to those in Alabama through Louisiana and to develop a procedure for randomly sampling these sites. To assure that the needed expertise was available to address the special characteristics of fishing in Texas, QuanTech subcontracted with the Texas A&M Research Foundation for field data collection services. The foundation developed a list of marinas and boat launch sites using local information and data obtained from the Texas Parks and Wildlife Department from that agency's annual survey of marine recreational fishermen. The Texas A&M Research Foundation then randomly sampled interviewing locations to generate sufficient assignments to achieve the quotas required by QuanTech. A listing of Texas interviewing locations is also included in Appendix E.

Once the site listing was completed and the number of assignments necessary to achieve quota for a wave determined, the actual assignments were generated monthly by selecting a random sample of sites which were then assigned to either weekday or weekend strata and distributed to field staff members who visited sites and obtained interviews within the required time.

Field Interviewers

Because of its long history of field data collection along coastal areas of the Gulf of Mexico, QuanTech had in place at the beginning of the project trained and experienced interviewers in Alabama, Mississippi, and Louisiana. To facilitate interviewing in Texas, a subcontract agreement was made with Texas A&M Research Foundation to provide qualified staff in that state. As a result of their training and experience in working on the MRFSS, all interviewers had previously been trained and had demonstrated knowledge of local fisheries. Each interviewer was mailed a comprehensive set of materials covering all field tasks and was briefed on the project and its unique requirements by the QuanTech Program Manager and Field Task Leader. The Texas A&M Research Foundation conducted its own training session, which included verification of fish knowledge, project procedures, and the ability to conduct interviews.

The number of interviewers who worked on the project throughout the year by state was:

Alabama	1
Mississippi	2
Louisiana	2
Texas	4

Interviewers were provided with a complete set of materials to assist in the field interviewing. Each was provided with a set of written instructions regarding all their duties and how to conduct himself or herself on site. They were given copies of questionnaires and forms on which to record all information provided by the respondents. Interviewers were provided with lists of interviewing sites. They were provided with clipboards, pencils, maps, and other administrative materials to facilitate the interviewing process. In order to get the forms back into the central contractor offices as quickly as possible, each interviewer was provided with a facsimile machine and a toll free number to use. Forms were sent to QuanTech daily for immediate quota tracking and data editing.

Data Handling Protocols

Before data collection work began in January 1999 QuanTech established detailed procedures for processing questionnaires. Interviewers were instructed to conduct interviews at boat access sites specified by QuanTech, completing all interview forms in accordance with the instructions provided. All coding of forms was accomplished in the field. All forms were 100 percent edited by the interviewers for completeness and accuracy. Once this was done, they were sent by facsimile to QuanTech offices using toll free telephone numbers provided for that purpose.

As questionnaires were received at QuanTech, a staff member reviewed each set of forms obtained at a particular site and assigned a unique control number. All coding on each form was then edited a second time to make certain that the information was legible, complete, and accurate.

QuanTech programmers created a double key entry protocol using the Statistical Analysis System (SAS). Under this protocol, two different persons keyed in each form and a series of programs were run which compared the first and second entry and identified discrepancies that were corrected by review of the original hard copy form. In addition, other error checking was performed to identify problems with the data so corrections could be made prior to creating final data sets.

Methodological Results

In general QuanTech was successful in obtaining field interviews following the protocols specified for the study. As shown in Table 2-2, a total of 8,660 interviews were obtained from recreational fishermen and divers across the geographic range from Alabama through Texas.

Table 2-2. Total Field Interviews Obtained

State	Private Boat	Charter Boat	Party Boat	Diver	Total
Alabama	1,085	458	71	90	1,704
Mississippi	1,132	304	22	42	1,500
Louisiana	2,794	329	83	10	3,216
Texas	1,834	196	202	8	2,240
Total	**6,845**	**1,287**	**378**	**150**	**8,660**

Cooperation with the survey in the field was extremely high. These 8,660 field interviews were obtained during the course of 296 individual assignments throughout 1999. Only 167 eligible respondents in the field declined to participate by not providing the information requested (1.9 percent). In addition, there were 18 respondents not interviewed because of language difficulties (0.2 percent).

Preparation for Follow-up Telephone Interviewing

Telephone follow-up interviewing began as field forms were received at QuanTech offices and continued until all follow-up interviewing was completed in January 2000. As with the field interview, before telephone follow-up data collection could begin, it was necessary to develop questionnaires, to develop sampling plans, to hire and train interviewers, and to develop data handling protocols. Work in each of these areas is described in the following paragraphs.

Questionnaire Development

A total of four telephone follow-up questionnaires were developed. They included:

- Telephone Follow-up Interview/Private Fishermen
- Telephone Follow-up Interview/Charter Fishermen
- Telephone Follow-up Interview/Party Boat Fishermen
- Telephone Follow-up Interview/Divers

Copies of the telephone follow-up questionnaires used in the study are provided as Appendix B. As with the field questionnaires, the program manager and the senior economist developed the instruments that were then submitted to OMB for review.

Once OMB clearance was obtained, preparation of the questionnaires for telephone interviewing was undertaken. Because of the large sample sizes for the private boat component of the survey, this questionnaire was programmed onto a Computer Assisted Telephone Interviewing (CATI) system. With this system, questions are displayed on a monitor and the interviewer reads the question and records the responses provided by the respondents. Skip patterns in questions are automatically determined by the CATI system. On-line error checking also takes place to eliminate invalid responses and other data errors.

Because the sample sizes were smaller for the telephone follow-up interviewing in the charter, party boat, and diver modes, these interviews were conducted using hard copy questionnaires rather than a CATI system.

Sampling Plans

As field interviews were returned to QuanTech and keyed into data files, they were reviewed to determine whether the fishermen or divers had participated in recreational activities within 300 feet of an oil or gas structure or an artificial reef created from such a structure. All of the respondents who reported fishing or diving near a structure or reef and who gave a telephone number for follow-up purposes were sampled to be interviewed by telephone. In addition, a random sample of fishermen and divers who did not fish near an oil or gas structure or artificial reef was drawn equal to the number of those who did fish near oil and gas structures. That is, for each 100 fishermen and divers who fished near an oil or gas structure and gave a phone number, an additional 100 fishermen and divers were selected at random who did not fish near such a structure. This sampling was continuous throughout the year.

Interviewing Staff

QuanTech maintains a staff of telephone interviewers who are trained and experienced in conducting marine recreational fishery surveys. These staff members are recruited and trained on the basis of their ability to conduct complex interviews, to speak well, to respond to questions about the survey, and to record responses accurately. Before telephone interviewing began, QuanTech held a briefing session with the telephone interviewing staff. This involved a presentation on the project and its objectives as well as a question by question review of the data collection forms. Practice interviews were conducted before data collection began.

Data Handling

There were two general procedures followed for handling the data obtained during the follow-up telephone interviews. For those respondents who had been fishing in the private boat mode, the CATI system was used which automatically created data files containing results of the interviews. These files had already been edited preliminarily due to the fact that the CATI system was programmed to eliminate out of range responses and to correctly handle all skip patterns. The CATI data was then imported into SAS for further editing and analysis.

For those respondents who had been charter and party boat fishing or who had been diving, hard copy questionnaires were used. These were individually edited for accuracy and were keyed into Excel files. The Excel files were edited by sorting and comparison of selected fields to identify range errors and erroneous skip patterns. Data was then converted into SAS files for further editing and analysis.

Methodological Results

The sampled phone numbers for the follow-up telephone interviews were provided to QuanTech interviewers. Numbers were dialed up to 14 times (as required by OMB) in order to contact the fishermen and divers and complete an interview. All telephone interviews were conducted from QuanTech's dialing facility under the direct supervision of an experienced telephone center manager.

As shown in Table 2-3, a total of 6,845 private boat interviews were obtained in the field, with 2,196 of those sampled for their follow-telephone interviews. Nonresponse rates were relatively high, despite considerable effort to reach respondents and complete the interviews. Telephone interviewers dialed all numbers up to 14 different times to obtain an interview. Directory assistance was used to check wrong numbers and nonworking numbers. In spite of these efforts, only 609 completed follow-up telephone interviews were obtained with private boat fishermen (27.7 percent).

14

Table 2-3. Results of Telephone Follow-up Interview Attempts for Private Boat Fishermen

	Number	Number
Total Interviews Obtained in Field		6,845
Total Interviews Sampled for Telephone Follow-up		2,196
Refusals	171	
Language Barrier	6	
Nonworking Numbers	147	
Wrong Numbers	154	
No Contact in Maximum Attempts	788	
Other Incomplete	321	
Total Noncontacts	1,587	
Completed Telephone Interviews		**609**

For the charter boat fishermen a total of 1,287 interviews were obtained in the field, with 317 sampled for the follow-up telephone interviewing (Table 2-4). Nonresponse rates were considerably lower for the charter boat fishermen, with only 150 noncontacts among this group. A total of 167 completed interviews was obtained with the charter boat fishermen in the sample, a response rate of 52.6 percent.

Table 2-4. Results of Telephone Follow-up Interview Attempts for Charter Boat Fishermen

	Number	Number
Total Interviews Obtained in Field		1,287
Total Interviews Sampled for Telephone Follow-up		317
Refusals	31	
Language Barrier	1	
Nonworking Numbers	24	
Wrong Numbers	10	
No Contact in Maximum Attempts	70	
Other Incomplete	14	
Total Noncontacts	150	
Completed Telephone Interviews		**167**

For the party boat fishermen a total of 378 interviews were obtained in the field, with 86 sampled for the follow-up telephone interviewing (Table 2-5). Nonresponse rates were moderately high for the party boat fishermen, with 49 noncontacts among this group. A total of 37 completed interviews was obtained with the party boat fishermen in the sample (43.0 percent).

Table 2-5. Results of Telephone Follow-up Interview Attempts for Party Boat Fishermen

	Number	Number
Total Interviews Obtained in Field		378
Total Interviews Sampled for Telephone Follow-up		86
Refusals	6	
Language Barrier	0	
Nonworking Numbers	4	
Wrong Numbers	5	
No Contact in Maximum Attempts	33	
Other Incomplete	1	
Total Noncontacts	49	
Completed Telephone Interviews		**37**

For the divers a total of 150 interviews were obtained in the field, with 125 sampled for the follow-up telephone interviewing (Table 2-6). Nonresponse rates were relatively high for the divers, with 99 noncontacts among this group. Only 26 completed interviews was obtained with the divers in the sample (20.8 percent).

Table 2-6. Results of Telephone Follow-up Interview Attempts for Divers

	Number	Number
Total Interviews Obtained in Field		150
Total Interviews Sampled for Telephone Follow-up		125
Refusals	22	
Language Barrier	0	
Nonworking Numbers	16	
Wrong Numbers	15	
No Contact in Maximum Attempts	27	
Other Incomplete	19	
Total Noncontacts	99	
Completed Telephone Interviews		**26**

The extremely high cooperation rates experienced in the field interviewing suggest that considerable confidence can be taken in the analyses based upon that data, particularly the estimates of numbers of trips taken, including trips reported near oil and gas structures. The response rates for the telephone follow-up interviews, however, were far lower than desired. Because the focus of the follow-up interviews was on economic information, there may have been a predisposition of fishermen and divers not to participate. Intensive telephone surveys by fisheries agencies may also be contributing to "respondent fatigue", resulting in lower cooperation rates. It seems clear on the present study that the number of wrong phone numbers and nonworking numbers provided by respondents is a form of passive refusal. That is, the respondent may find it easier to give a wrong phone number than to tell the interviewer he doesn't want to receive a follow-up call. In any event, the results of the economic analysis, which is based upon the telephone survey portion of the project, should be interpreted cautiously because of this potential for nonresponse bias.

Preparation for Business Telephone Interviews

Telephone interviewing with these groups began at the end of calendar year 1999 and was completed during the first week of February 2000. The purpose of these interviews was to obtain a more subjective evaluation of the importance of oil and gas structures to recreational fishing and diving activities. Copies of the questionnaires are shown in Appendix C. Tasks for the accomplishment of these surveys are described in the following paragraphs.

Questionnaire Development

A total of three telephone survey questionnaires were developed for the business interviews. They included the following:

- Telephone Interview with Charter Boat Operators
- Telephone Interview with Party Boat Operators
- Telephone Interview with Dive Shop Operators

As with the field and telephone follow-up questionnaires, the program manager and the senior economist developed the instruments that were submitted to OMB for review.

Because of the small sample sizes for this survey component, hard copy questionnaires were used rather than a CATI system.

Sampling Plans

The sample frames for these surveys were developed using a variety of sources. A listing of known charter boats and party boats was obtained from the Gulf States Marine Fisheries Commission (GSMFC). These lists were randomly sampled and attempts made to contact boat operators in the for hire fisheries. The results were not satisfactory, with many of the phone numbers disconnected and with many boats no longer operating. QuanTech staff then supplemented these lists by using telephone directory listings, performing Internet searches, and contacting local tourism agencies. A similar approach was used to identify dive shops. Searches of telephone directories, diver magazines, and the Internet were carried out to identify potential respondents to the dive shop operator survey.

Interviewing Staff

QuanTech telephone interviewers performed the surveys of charter boat operators, dive shops, and party boat operators from QuanTech's dialing facility in Virginia. Before telephone interviewing began, QuanTech held a briefing session with the telephone interviewing staff. This involved a presentation on the project and its objectives as well as a question by question review of the data collection forms. Practice interviews were conducted before data collection began.

Data Handling

Since these surveys were carried out using hard copy questionnaires, completed forms were edited for accuracy and were keyed into data files. These files were edited by sorting and comparison of selected fields to identify range errors and erroneous skip patterns.

Methodological Results

For the charter boat operator survey, a total of 232 numbers were sampled for inclusion in the survey. The results of dialing are shown in Table 2-7. The large number of refusals may be attributed to the fact that charter boat operators are heavily surveyed by NMFS and may resent being asked to participate in additional data collection efforts.

Table 2-7. Dialing Results for Charter Boat Operators Survey

Dialing Result	Number
Nonworking Number	33
Wrong Number	9
Answering Machine	12
No Answer	34
Busy	7
Refusal	51
Other Noncomplete	26
Complete Interview	60
Total	**232**

For the party boat operator survey, only 16 vessel names were identified in the Gulf for inclusion in the survey. The results of dialing are shown in Table 2-8. Only two completed interviews could be obtained from this group, primarily because of the small size of the frame coupled with an inability to reach respondents. Because the two completed interviews were too few to allow separate analysis, results for this group were combined with the charter operators to create a "for hire" database.

Table 2-8. Dialing Results for Party Boat Operators Survey

Dialing Result	Number
Nonworking Number	0
Wrong Number	2
Answering Machine	5
No Answer	3
Busy	2
Refusal	0
Other Noncomplete	5
Complete Interview	2
Total	**16**

For the dive shop operator survey, a total of 25 numbers were sampled for inclusion in the survey. The results of dialing are shown in Table 2-9. A total of 13 completes was obtained, a moderately high response rate.

Table 2-9. Dialing Results for Dive Shop Operators Survey

Dialing Result	Number
Nonworking Number	1
Wrong Number	0
Answering Machine	3
No Answer	3
Busy	1
Refusal	4
Other Noncomplete	0
Complete Interview	13
Total	**25**

Data Analysis

There were two major components of the data analysis undertaken during the course of project. The first was the development of estimates of total recreational trips with the number of participants associated with these trips. The second was the economic analysis that was undertaken to estimate both economic impact as well as demand attributable to the presence of oil and gas structures in the Gulf of Mexico. Methodological issues associated with accomplishment of these two tasks are described in the following paragraphs. Chapter 3 of this report provides the estimates of total trips and participants while results of the economic analysis are provided in Chapters 4 and 5. Results of the for hire industry and dive shop operator surveys are provided in Chapter 6.

Trip and Participant Estimation

As noted previously, the procedures for calculating total recreational trips and participants involved combining the estimates of total marine recreational fishing trips reported by the National Marine Fisheries Service (NMFS) through its conduct of the Marine Recreational Fishery Statistics Survey (MRFSS) with the results of the 1999 Minerals Management Service survey conducted under this contract.

Published NMFS' estimates were obtained of total marine fishing trips for private and charter boat recreational fishing for all Gulf of Mexico areas (Gulf, sounds, rivers, and bays combined) by state for 1996 – 1998 (the last complete year for which data was available at the time of analysis). This data served as the basis of the data analysis. These published estimates are reported by NMFS for both coastal residents and noncoastal residents and were available for Alabama, Mississippi, and Louisiana. For each state, QuanTech multiplied the total estimated trips for a mode of fishing (private boats, for example) by the proportion of fishermen within that strata who reported that they fished within 300 feet of an oil or gas structure. This resulted in an estimate of the total number of recreational trips which were taken near oil or gas structures. Separate estimates were generated for both coastal and noncoastal residents.

A different approach was required for Texas, where NMFS does not conduct the MRFSS. The State of Texas conducts its own survey of marine recreational fishermen in Texas, and provides results to NMFS. This estimate of total trips in both the private boat and the charter boat modes was obtained by QuanTech and used to perform calculations similar to those for Alabama, Mississippi, and Louisiana to estimate the total number of recreational trips near oil and gas structures.

For Alabama, Mississippi, and Louisiana the same procedures were used to estimate total charter boat trips as for private boats. NMFS' estimates of total trips were averaged over the prior three years and multiplied by the proportion of respondents to the 1999 MMS survey who said they fished within 300 feet of an oil or gas structure.

Party boat information is also not obtained by NMFS through the MRFSS. However, NMFS conducts a separate party boat survey throughout the Gulf and results of that survey were provided to QuanTech for use in estimating total party boat fishing trips by state.

There were no published estimates of the number of recreational diving trips in Alabama through Texas that could be used. Because QuanTech interviewed both divers and private boat fishermen at the same boat docks and marinas, which were randomly sampled, it was assumed that the ratio of divers to private boat fishermen obtained during interviewing could be applied to the estimates of total private boat trips to derive an estimate of total dive trips.

By applying ratios and proportions obtained from the 1999 MMS survey to total recreational trip information published by NMFS, QuanTech was also able to allocate both the total numbers of trips taken by recreational participants near oil and gas structures in the Gulf of Mexico from Alabama through Texas for both coastal and noncoastal residents.

In addition to calculating the total recreational trips near oil and gas structures, it was also necessary to estimate the total number of people who participated in these activities. This was necessary for the economic analysis because the economic models distinguish between expenditures associated with an individual trip and capital costs where the outlay may be used across many different trips.

In a fashion similar to that used for estimating total trips, QuanTech obtained from NMFS its estimates of total participants in marine recreational fishing. Using the ratios of total trips to total participants obtained from the NMFS data, QuanTech estimated the total participants associated with recreational trips for each strata of the 1999 MMS study, including private boat fishing, charter boat fishing, party boat fishing, and divers. This was done separately for coastal and noncoastal residents by state.

Economic Analysis

The economic analyses relied primarily on expenditures information obtained from the telephone follow-up interviews and the total estimates of trips and participants developed as part of this project. Total expenditures by category were calculated from the telephone follow-up data by strata and, using the IMPLAN model, total economic impact was estimated.

Two issues which affected the economic analyses were the problem of small sample sizes and outliers in the data. As was noted earlier in this chapter, the number of completed follow-up interviews, which obtained the data needed for the economic analysis, was small for party boat participants and divers. As a result, care must be exercised in the application of data for these strata. In addition, it was observed during the data analysis that some of the answers to questions about expenditures seemed unusually large. These were addressed by the analysts on a case by case basis.

Chapter 3
Estimates of Recreational Fishing and Diving Trips
Near Gulf of Mexico Oil and Gas Structures

Introduction

A primary objective of the study was to develop estimates of the demand of recreational fishermen, charter and head boat users, and recreational divers for offshore-structure-related recreational activities. In this chapter, demand estimates are presented which show the total number of fishing and diving trips by recreational users as well as the number and proportion of these trips which were near oil or gas structures.

The basic approach to estimating demand for the key user groups was to rely upon total reported fishing trips obtained from the National Marine Fisheries Service (NMFS). NMFS has conducted its Marine Recreational Fishery Statistical Survey (MRFSS) in Alabama, Mississippi, and Louisiana since 1979 and reports on both the total number of fishing trips taken annually from these states and the number of individuals who participate in marine recreational fishing. The State of Texas does not participate in the MRFSS, but does perform its own recreational fishery surveys and obtains similar data.

Once estimates of total fishing trips were obtained from NMFS, proportions of reported trips near oil and gas structures based upon the 1999 MMS study were used to calculate the number of these trips which would have been near the oil and gas structures.

In the following section is described in detail the methods of estimating total recreational trips in the Gulf of Mexico from Alabama, Mississippi, Louisiana, and Texas. This is followed by a section that provides detailed information on the estimates of total trips taken near oil and gas structures.

Total Trips

The Marine Recreational Fishery Statistical Survey (MRFSS) is a large-scale survey of salt water sport fishermen which is conducted by NMFS year round along the Gulf Coast (except Texas). The survey uses a telephone survey of households in coastal counties to determine the average number of fishing trips taken per household in each two-month period of the year. Because many people fish who do not live in one of the coastal counties covered by the telephone survey, the MRFSS uses results of an on-site intercept survey of marine recreational fishermen to estimate the proportion of anglers who fish but do not live in one of the coastal counties covered by the telephone survey of households. The number of trips estimated from the household survey is then inflated by this proportion to obtain an estimate of total trips. It is also possible to allocate this total number of trips into the different types of fishing, including private and charter boat fishing. Table 3-1 provides information on the total estimated private boat and charter boat trips based upon the MRFSS for Alabama, Mississippi, and Louisiana.

As noted previously, the State of Texas performs its own survey of saltwater sport fishermen. Data from that survey is shown in Table 3-1. Another type of fishing that is not available through the MRFSS is that of party boat (head boat) fishing. A separate survey of head boats is undertaken by NMFS throughout the Southeast. Estimated total angler days of fishing for party boats is shown in Table 3-1. It should be noted that, according to the NMFS estimates, there are no party boats operating in Mississippi.

Table 3-1. Total Estimated Marine Recreational Fishing and Diving Trips For Alabama, Mississippi, Louisiana, and Texas

State	Private Boat Trips	Charter Boat Trips	Party Boat Trips	Dive Trips	Total Trips
Alabama	505,635	71,394	15,386	11,124	603,539
Mississippi	507,545	49,426	0	11,166	568,137
Louisiana	2,067,076	73,770	7,913	45,476	2,194,235
Texas	986,250	103,433	96,252	21,698	1,207,633
Total	**4,066,506**	**298,023**	**119,551**	**89,464**	**4,573,544**

As noted in Chapter 2, there was no specific quota for interviewing divers in the field component of the MMS survey. Interviewers were instructed to approach all boats as they returned from their recreational activities during the course of an assignment and attempt an interview. If the members of the party had been recreational diving, they were administered the diver questionnaire.

Using this sampling approach, a total of 150 divers were interviewed during the course of 1999 field work. This represents 2.2 percent of the 6,845 private boat interviews obtained. By applying this ratio to the total number of private boat trips, it is estimated that there were 89,464 diver trips during 1999 in the Gulf of Mexico from Alabama through Texas. The resulting estimated total dive trips is also shown in Table 3-1.

Fishing and Diving Near Oil and Gas Structures

During the field interview, each eligible respondent was asked the key question, "Was any of your fishing (or diving) today with 300 feet of an oil or gas rig or within 300 feet of an artificial reef created from an oil or gas rig?" Responses to this question are provided in detail in the following sections.

Private Boat Fishing

Respondents who had been fishing from a private boat were asked, "Was any of your private boat fishing today within 300 feet of an oil or gas rig or within 300 feet of an artificial reef created from an oil or gas rig?" Results are shown separately by state in Table 3-2.

Table 3-2. Private Boat Fishing Near Oil/Gas Structures

State	Yes		No		Total	
	Number	Percent	Number	Percent	Number	Percent
Alabama	449	41.4	636	58.6	1,085	100.0
Mississippi	223	19.7	909	80.3	1,132	100.0
Louisiana	464	16.6	2,330	83.4	2,794	100.0
Texas	318	17.3	1,516	82.7	1,834	100.0
Total	**1,454**	**21.2**	**5,391**	**78.8**	**6,845**	**100.0**

Overall, for the sample of private boat fishermen interviewed, 21.2 percent reported that they fished within 300 feet of an oil or gas structure or an artificial reef created from an oil or gas structure. Considerable variation from state to state was observed, however, and the results by state were somewhat counterintuitive. The state with the largest number of oil and gas structures offshore is Louisiana. However, the proportion of private boat fishermen reporting activities near oil and gas structures was lowest for this state (16.6 percent).

The coastal geography of Louisiana is considerably different from the surrounding states. Louisiana is characterized by an extensive network of bays and other estuarine areas across the entire state. While there are many oil and gas structures throughout these near shore areas, the bays and estuaries offer a variety of habitat conducive to successful fishing other than oil and gas structures. A possible explanation for the lower proportion of fishing reported near oil and gas structures, therefore, may be that much of the Louisiana fishing takes place in these bays and other estuarine areas where fishing is often successful without reliance on habitat provided by the oil and gas structures.

To understand this phenomenon better, the data for each state was examined by area of fishing effort. One of the questions asked during the field interview was whether the fishing was in the Gulf (open waters) or inshore (a sound, river, bay, or other estuarine area). Tables 3-3 and 3-4 show the proportions of anglers who reported fishing near an oil or gas structure separately for those who fished in Gulf waters versus those who fished inshore.

Table 3-3. Private Boat Fishing Near Oil/Gas Structures (Gulf Fishermen)

State	Yes		No		Total	
	Number	Percent	Number	Percent	Number	Percent
Alabama	430	49.9	432	50.1	862	100.0
Mississippi	217	32.4	453	67.6	670	100.0
Louisiana	370	59.4	253	40.6	623	100.0
Texas	300	51.8	279	48.2	579	100.0
Total	**1,317**	**48.2**	**1,417**	**51.2**	**2,734**	**100.0**

23

Table 3-4. Private Boat Fishing Near Oil/Gas Structures (Inshore Fishermen)

State	Yes		No		Total	
	Number	Percent	Number	Percent	Number	Percent
Alabama	19	8.5	204	91.5	223	100.0
Mississippi	6	1.3	456	98.7	462	100.0
Louisiana	94	4.3	2,077	95.7	2,171	100.0
Texas	18	1.4	1,237	98.6	1,255	100.0
Total	137	3.3	3,974	96.7	4,111	100.0

A comparison of Tables 3-3 and 3-4 confirm that fishing near oil and gas structures is much more likely for Gulf fishermen than for those who fish in the inshore areas. For example, 48.2 percent of Gulf fishermen reported fishing within 300 feet of an oil or gas structure (Table 3-3). Conversely, only 3.3 percent of inshore fishermen reported activity within 300 feet of an oil or gas structure (Table 3-4).

The reason that Louisiana has a lower proportion of fishing near oil and gas structures appears to be that the incidence of fishing in Gulf waters by Louisiana anglers is lower than for other states. This is confirmed by Table 3-5, which shows that only 22.3 percent of Louisiana fishermen said they fished in the Gulf, compared to 79.5 percent of Alabama fishermen and 59.2 percent of Mississippi fishermen. Only 31.6 percent of Texas fishermen said they fished in the Gulf. These lower incidences of Gulf fishing in Louisiana and Texas are probably attributable to coastal geography with more bays, bayous, sounds, and river areas. It should be noted that the proportions of anglers fishing in Gulf waters appears to vary considerably from year to year. According to MRFSS data for 1998, only 9.8 percent of all Louisiana private boat fishing trips was in the Gulf versus inshore areas. In 1997, however, the figure was 22.3 percent, precisely the same result obtained by QuanTech in its 1999 survey.

Table 3-5. Respondents Who Fish in Gulf by State

State	Gulf		Inshore		Total	
	Number	Percent	Number	Percent	Number	Percent
Alabama	862	79.4	223	20.6	1,085	100.0
Mississippi	670	59.2	462	40.8	1,132	100.0
Louisiana	623	22.3	2,171	77.7	2,794	100.0
Texas	579	31.6	1,255	68.4	1,834	100.0
Total	2,734	39.9	4,111	60.1	6,845	100.0

Charter Boat Fishing

Interviews were conducted directly with anglers who went fishing on charter boats. Interviewers consulted with captains or mates to obtain detailed location and similar information with which charter boat patrons may not have been familiar. Respondents who had been fishing from a chartered boat were also asked, "Was any of your charter boat fishing today within 300 feet of an oil or gas rig or within 300 feet of an artificial reef created from an oil or gas rig?" Results are shown separately by state in Table 3-6.

Table 3-6. Charter Boat Fishing Near Oil/Gas Structures

State	Yes		No		Total	
	Number	Percent	Number	Percent	Number	Percent
Alabama	96	21.0	362	79.0	458	100.0
Mississippi	66	21.7	238	78.3	304	100.0
Louisiana	76	23.1	253	76.9	329	100.0
Texas	101	51.8	94	48.2	195	100.0
Total	339	26.4	947	73.6	1,286	100.0

Overall, for the sample of charter boat fishermen interviewed, 26.4 percent reported that they fished within 300 feet of an oil or gas structure or an artificial reef created from an oil or gas structure. The proportion fishing near oil and gas structures in Alabama, Mississippi, and Louisiana were very similar, ranging from 21.0 percent in Alabama to 23.1 percent in Louisiana. The rate for Texas was double that for the other states (51.8 percent).

As with private boat fishing, data for each state was examined by the location of the charter fishing effort. One of the questions asked during the field interview was whether the fishing was in the Gulf or inshore (a sound, river, or bay). Tables 3-7 and 3-8 show the proportions of charter fishermen with activity near an oil or gas structure separately for those who fished in Gulf waters versus those who fished inshore.

Table 3-7. Charter Boat Fishing Near Oil/Gas Structures (Gulf Fishermen)

State	Yes		No		Total	
	Number	Percent	Number	Percent	Number	Percent
Alabama	96	21.6	349	78.4	445	100.0
Mississippi	65	21.7	234	78.3	299	100.0
Louisiana	61	40.4	90	59.6	151	100.0
Texas	101	59.7	68	40.2	169	100.0
Total	323	30.4	741	69.6	1,064	100.0

Table 3-8. Charter Boat Fishing Near Oil/Gas Structures (Inshore Fishermen)

State	Yes		No		Total	
	Number	Percent	Number	Percent	Number	Percent
Alabama	0	0.0	11	100.0	11	100.0
Mississippi	1	20.0	4	80.0	5	100.0
Louisiana	15	8.4	163	91.6	178	100.0
Texas	0	0.0	26	100.0	26	100.0
Total	16	7.3	204	92.7	220	100.0

These tables suggest that the availability of oil and gas structures is moderately important for charter anglers who fish in Gulf waters. Overall, 30.4 percent of Gulf charter boat fishermen reported fishing within 300 feet of an oil or gas structure (Table 3-7). Conversely, only 7.3 percent of inshore charter boat fishermen report activity within 300 feet of an oil or gas structure (Table 3-8). It should be noted that inshore charter fishing is a somewhat rare event, primarily occurring only in Louisiana. As indicated in Table 3-8, only 220 charter anglers reported that they fished in inshore areas, with most of these (178) occurring in Louisiana.

As indicated in Table 3-9, Alabama, Mississippi, and Texas are much more likely to have charter fishermen taking trips into the Gulf than Louisiana. This appears to be an important factor in the extent to which there is fishing near oil and gas structures, with more Gulf fishing associated with higher levels of fishing near such structures.

Table 3-9. Respondents Who Fish in Gulf by State

State	Gulf		Inshore		Total	
	Number	Percent	Number	Percent	Number	Percent
Alabama	445	97.2	13	2.8	458	100.0
Mississippi	299	98.4	5	1.6	304	100.0
Louisiana	151	45.9	178	54.1	329	100.0
Texas	170	86.7	26	13.3	196	100.0
Total	1,065	82.8	222	17.2	1,287	100.0

Party Boat Fishing

Respondents who had been fishing from a party boat were also asked, "Was any of your party boat fishing today within 300 feet of an oil or gas rig or within 300 feet of an artificial reef created from an oil or gas rig?" Results are shown separately by state in Table 3-10.

Table 3-10. Party Boat Fishing Near Oil/Gas Structures

State	Yes		No		Total	
	Number	Percent	Number	Percent	Number	Percent
Alabama	0	0.0	71	100.0	71	100.0
Mississippi	2	9.1	20	90.9	22	100.0
Louisiana	83	100.0	0	0.0	83	100.0
Texas	111	55.0	91	45.0	202	100.0
Total	196	51.9	91	48.1	378	100.0

Overall, for the sample of party boat fishermen interviewed, 51.9 percent reported that they fished within 300 feet of an oil or gas structure or an artificial reef created from an oil or gas structure. The highest proportions were observed in Louisiana (100.0 percent) and Texas (55.0 percent). This is somewhat different than for private boat and charter boat fishing in those states where the proportions fishing near oil and gas structures was lower than for Alabama and Mississippi.

As with private and charter boat fishing, data for each state was examined by the location of the charter fishing effort. One of the questions asked during the field interview was whether the fishing was in the Gulf or inshore (a sound, river, or bay). Tables 3-11 and 3-12 show the proportions of party boat fishermen with activity near an oil or gas structure separately for those who fished in Gulf waters versus those who fished inshore.

Table 3-11. Party Boat Fishing Near Oil/Gas Structures (Gulf Fishermen)

State	Yes		No		Total	
	Number	Percent	Number	Percent	Number	Percent
Alabama	0	0.0	71	100.0	71	100.0
Mississippi	2	9.1	20	90.9	22	100.0
Louisiana	83	100.0	0	0.0	83	100.0
Texas	107	56.9	81	43.1	188	100.0
Total	192	52.7	172	47.3	364	100.0

Table 3-12. Party Boat Fishing Near Oil/Gas Structures (Inshore Fishermen)

State	Yes		No		Total	
	Number	Percent	Number	Percent	Number	Percent
Alabama	0	--	0	--	0	--
Mississippi	0	--	0	--	0	--
Louisiana	0	--	0	--	0	--
Texas	4	28.6	10	71.4	14	100.0
Total	4	28.6	10	71.4	14	100.0

These tables suggest that the availability of oil and gas structures are particularly important for party boat anglers who fish in Gulf waters in Texas and Louisiana. Overall, 52.7 percent of Gulf party boat fishermen reported fishing with 300 feet of an oil or gas structure (Table 3-11). Table 3-12 shows that inshore party boat fishing is almost nonexistent throughout the range of the study. Only four trips were reported to be in inshore waters, and these occurred in Texas.

This information is confirmed in Table 3-13, which shows that 96.3 percent of all party boat trips were taken into Gulf.

Table 3-13. Respondents Who Fish in Gulf by State

State	Gulf		Inshore		Total	
	Number	Percent	Number	Percent	Number	Percent
Alabama	71	100.0	0	0.0	71	100.0
Mississippi	22	100.0	0	0.0	22	100.0
Louisiana	83	100.0	0	0.0	83	100.0
Texas	188	93.1	14	6.9	202	100.0
Total	364	96.3	14	3.7	378	100.0

Recreational Diving

Respondents who had been diving were also asked, "Was any of your diving today within 300 feet of an oil or gas rig or within 300 feet of an artificial reef created from an oil or gas rig?" Results are shown separately by state in Table 3-14.

Table 3-14. Diving Near Oil/Gas Structures

State	Yes		No		Total	
	Number	Percent	Number	Percent	Number	Percent
Alabama	44	48.9	46	51.1	90	100.0
Mississippi	41	100.0	0	0.0	41	100.0
Louisiana	10	100.0	0	0.0	10	100.0
Texas	8	100.0	0	0.0	8	100.0
Total	**103**	**69.1**	**46**	**30.9**	**149**	**100.0**

The number of interviews obtained with divers during the course of the project was relatively small. As noted in Chapter 2, the approach was to interview divers along with recreational fishermen at boat launch sites sampled over the course of the study. Of the 149 divers interviewed, 69.1 percent reported that they engaged in recreational diving near an oil or gas structure. For Mississippi, Louisiana, and Texas, all of the divers interviewed said their diving was near oil and gas structures. Care should be taken in interpreting this data, however, because of the small number of observations.

Estimates of Total Trips

In order to determine the total number of fishing and diving trips taken near oil and gas structures in the Gulf of Mexico, the total trips (Table 3-1) were multiplied by the proportion reporting activity near oil and gas structures. Results are shown in Tables 3-15 through 3-18.

These tables indicate that there were a total of 980,264 fishing trips of all types taken within 300 feet of an oil or gas structure or within 300 feet of an artificial reef created from such a structure. The largest percentage of these trips was in Louisiana (37.5 percent) with 28.3 percent in Texas, 22.9 percent in Alabama, and 11.3 percent in Mississippi.

In addition, there were an estimated 83,780 dive trips to oil and gas structures. The largest percentage were in Louisiana (54.3 percent), with 25.9 percent in Texas, 13.3 percent in Mississippi, and 6.5 percent in Alabama.

Table 3-15. Estimated Total Number of Private Boat Fishing Trips Near Oil/Gas Structures

State	Total Trips	Percent Near Oil/Gas Structures	Estimated Number of Trips
Alabama	505,635	41.4	209,333
Mississippi	507,545	19.7	99,986
Louisiana	2,067,076	16.6	343,135
Texas	986,250	17.3	170,621
Total	**4,066,506**	**20.2**	**823,075**

Table 3-16. Estimated Total Number of Charter Boat Fishing Trips Near Oil/Gas Structures

State	Total Trips	Percent Near Oil/Gas Structures	Estimated Number of Trips
Alabama	71,394	21.0	14,993
Mississippi	49,426	21.7	10,725
Louisiana	73,770	23.1	17,041
Texas	103,433	51.8	53,578
Total	298,023	32.3	96,337

Table 3-17. Estimated Total Number of Party Boat Fishing Trips Near Oil/Gas Structures

State	Total Trips	Percent Near Oil/Gas Structures	Estimated Number of Trips
Alabama	15,386	0.0	0
Mississippi	0	0.0	0
Louisiana	7,913	100.0	7,913
Texas	96,252	55.0	52,939
Total	119,551	50.9	60,852

Table 3-18. Estimated Total Number of Dive Trips Near Oil/Gas Structures

State	Total Trips	Percent Near Oil/Gas Structures	Estimated Number of Trips
Alabama	11,124	48.9	5,440
Mississippi	11,166	100.0	11,166
Louisiana	45,476	100.0	45,476
Texas	21,698	100.0	21,698
Total	89,464	93.6	83,780

One of the requirements of the project was to estimate key economic values within state by county area. In order to accomplish this, it was necessary to further allocate estimates of total trips by whether the recreational participant resided in a coastal or noncoastal area. These allocations are shown in Tables 3-19 through 3-22.

A particularly interesting finding of the research, and as shown in Tables 3-19 through 3-22, is that the vast majority of trips near oil and gas structures for private boat fishing and for diving was by coastal residents. For charter boat fishing and party boat fishing, the vast majority of trips near oil and gas structures was taken by noncoastal residents. While the availability of oil and gas structures is important for all recreational groups, it appears they may be an especially important component of the for-hire fishing industry along the Gulf coast.

Table 3-19. Estimated Number of Coastal and Noncoastal Private Boat Fishing Trips Near Oil/Gas Structures

State	Total Number of Trips Near Oil/Gas Structures	Share of Total Trips Near Oil/Gas Structures		Estimated Number of Trips Near Oil/Gas Structures	
		Coastal Residents (percent)	Noncoastal Residents (percent)	Coastal Residents	Noncoastal Residents
Alabama	209,333	85	15	178,561	30,772
Mississippi	99,986	85	15	85,088	14,898
Louisiana	343,135	94	6	322,204	20,931
Texas	170,621	90	10	153,730	16,891
Total	823,075			739,582	83,493

Table 3-20. Estimated Number of Coastal and Noncoastal Charter Boat Fishing Trips Near Oil/Gas Structures

State	Total Number of Trips Near Oil/Gas Structures	Share of Total Trips Near Oil/Gas Structures		Estimated Number of Trips Near Oil/Gas Structures	
		Coastal Residents (percent)	Noncoastal Residents (percent)	Coastal Residents	Noncoastal Residents
Alabama	14,993	19	81	2,879	12,114
Mississippi	10,725	16	84	1,695	9,030
Louisiana	17,041	44	56	7,549	9,492
Texas	53,578	28	72	15,109	38,469
Total	96,337			27,231	69,106

31

Table 3-21. Estimated Number of Coastal and Noncoastal Party Boat Fishing Trips Near Oil/Gas Structures

State	Total Number of Trips Near Oil/Gas Structures	Share of Total Trips Near Oil/Gas Structures		Estimated Number of Trips Near Oil/Gas Structures	
		Coastal Residents (percent)	Noncoastal Residents (percent)	Coastal Residents	Noncoastal Residents
Alabama	-	19	81	-	-
Mississippi	-	16	84	-	-
Louisiana	7,913	44	56	3,505	4,408
Texas	52,939	28	72	14,929	38,010
Total	60,852			18,434	42,418

Table 3-22. Estimated Number of Coastal and Noncoastal Dive Trips Near Oil/Gas Structures

State	Total Number of Trips Near Oil/Gas Structures	Share of Total Trips Near Oil/Gas Structures		Estimated Number of Trips Near Oil/Gas Structures	
		Coastal Residents (percent)	Noncoastal Residents (percent)	Coastal Residents	Noncoastal Residents
Alabama	5,440	85	15	4,640	800
Mississippi	11,166	85	15	9,502	1,664
Louisiana	45,476	94	6	42,702	2,774
Texas	21,698	90	10	19,550	2,148
Total	83,780			76,394	7,386

Number of Oil/Gas Structures Visited

Those respondents who indicated that they were fishing or diving near an oil or gas structure were asked to indicate the number of different structures visited during the trip. Results are shown in Table 3-23. The number of oil and gas structures visited was highest for fishermen in Louisiana and Texas. For divers, the average number of structures visited was highest for Mississippi.

Table 3-23. Average Oil/Gas Structures Visited Per Recreational Trip

State	Private Boat	Charter Boat	Party Boat	Dive Trip
Alabama	1.19	1.24	-	1.50
Mississippi	1.37	1.18	-	2.24
Louisiana	3.01	2.57	3.37	2.10
Texas	2.10	2.21	2.03	2.00

Using the means shown in Table 3-23, the total estimated oil and gas structures visited was calculated by multiplying the mean per visit times the total visits. These results are shown in Tables 3-24 through 3-27.

These tables indicate that the number of rigs visited by recreational fishermen and divers during the course of a year is substantial. Overall, there were 1,777,227 oil or gas structure-visits by recreational private boat fishermen, with another 193,449 structure-visits by charter boat fishermen. There were 134,133 structure-visits by party boat fishermen. In addition, there were 172,068 visits to oil and gas structures and reefs created from such structures by recreational divers.

The fact that multiple structures are regularly visited on recreational fishing and diving trips is highly significant. It is clear that fishermen and divers take advantage of the variety offered by multiple sites, either because one location is crowded, because fishing is not productive, because a change in species is desired, or even because a change in scenery is wanted. This finding strongly suggests the importance to fishing and diving of maintaining the availability of multiple structures within close proximity.

Table 3-24. Total Oil/Gas Structures Visited by Private Boat Fishermen

State	Total Trips Near Structures	Average Structures Per Trip	Total Structures Visited on All Trips
Alabama	209,333	1.19	249,106
Mississippi	99,986	1.37	136,981
Louisiana	343,135	3.01	1,032,836
Texas	170,621	2.10	358,304
Total	**823,075**	**2.16**	**1,777,227**

Table 3-25. Total Oil/Gas Structures Visited by Charter Boat Fishermen

State	Total Trips Near Structures	Average Structures Per Trip	Total Structures Visited on All Trips
Alabama	14,993	1.24	18,591
Mississippi	10,725	1.18	12,656
Louisiana	17,041	2.57	43,795
Texas	53,578	2.21	118,407
Total	**96,337**	**2.01**	**193,449**

33

Table 3-26. Total Oil/Gas Structures Visited by Party Boat Fishermen

State	Total Trips Near Structures	Average Structures Per Trip	Total Structures Visited on All Trips
Alabama	0	-	0
Mississippi	0	-	0
Louisiana	7,913	3.37	26,667
Texas	52,939	2.03	107,466
Total	**60,852**	**2.20**	**134,133**

Table 3-27. Total Oil/Gas Structures Visited by Divers

State	Total Trips Near Structures	Average Structures Per Trip	Total Structures Visited on All Trips
Alabama	5,440	1.50	8,160
Mississippi	11,166	2.24	25,012
Louisiana	45,476	2.10	95,500
Texas	21,698	2.00	43,396
Total	**83,780**	**2.05**	**172,068**

As with the number of recreational trips taken, it was necessary for the economic analysis to calculate the number of participants in marine recreational activities as well as to allocate both the number of participants and structure visits across coastal and noncoastal areas by state. Information on numbers of marine recreational participants published by the NMFS was used to convert trip estimates into participants. The results of these calculations are shown separately by type of activity in Tables 3-28 through 3-31.

Table 3-28. Estimated Number of Coastal and Noncoastal Private Boat Fishing Participants Using Oil/Gas Structures

State	Estimated Number of Trips Near Oil/Gas Structures		Average Number of Trips to Oil/Gas Structures		Number of Participants Using Oil/Gas Structures	
	Coastal Residents	Noncoastal Residents	Coastal Residents	Noncoastal Residents	Coastal Residents	Noncoastal Residents
Alabama	178,561	30,772	15.3	2.9	11,652	10,630
Mississippi	85,088	14,898	26.5	2.0	3,213	7,449
Louisiana	322,204	20,931	9.0	3.2	35,921	6,506
Texas	153,730	16,891	9.2	5.5	16,627	3,081
Total	739,582	83,493			67,413	27,666

Table 3-29. Estimated Number of Coastal and Noncoastal Charter Boat Fishing Participants Using Oil/Gas Structures

State	Estimated Number of Trips Near Oil/Gas Structures		Average Number of Trips to Oil/Gas Structures		Number of Participants Using Oil/Gas Structures	
	Coastal Residents	Noncoastal Residents	Coastal Residents	Noncoastal Residents	Coastal Residents	Noncoastal Residents
Alabama	2,879	12,114	4.4	0.5	662	22,613
Mississippi	1,695	9,030	15.6	8.1	109	1,121
Louisiana	7,549	9,492	10.4	7.2	727	1,327
Texas	15,109	38,469	8.6	1.6	1,765	24,730
Total	27,231	69,106			3,262	49,792

Table 3-30. Estimated Number of Coastal and Noncoastal Party Boat Fishing Participants Using Oil/Gas Structures

State	Estimated Number of Trips Near Oil/Gas Structures		Average Number of Trips to Oil/Gas Structures		Number of Participants Using Oil/Gas Structures	
	Coastal Residents	Noncoastal Residents	Coastal Residents	Noncoastal Residents	Coastal Residents	Noncoastal Residents
Alabama	-	-	0.3	0.6	-	-
Mississippi	-	-	1.0		-	-
Louisiana	3,505	4,408	1.2	1.7	2,921	2,645
Texas	14,929	38,010	17.7	0.6	845	60,816
Total	18,434	42,418			3,766	63,461

Table 3-31. Estimated Number of Coastal and Noncoastal Dive Participants Using Oil/Gas Structures

State	Estimated Number of Trips Near Oil/Gas Structures		Average Number of Trips to Oil/Gas Structures		Number of Participants Using Oil/Gas Structures	
	Coastal Residents	Noncoastal Residents	Coastal Residents	Noncoastal Residents	Coastal Residents	Noncoastal Residents
Alabama	4,640	800	15.3	2.9	303	276
Mississippi	9,502	1,664	26.5	2.0	359	832
Louisiana	42,702	2,774	9.0	3.2	4,761	862
Texas	19,550	2,148	9.2	5.5	2,115	392
Total	76,394	7,386			7,537	2,362

Summary

The results of the survey of recreational fishermen and divers show that there is both a substantial amount of recreational fishing and diving in the Gulf of Mexico states from Alabama through Texas and significant usage of oil and gas structures for these recreational activities. The estimates developed for this project are that there were 4,484,080 recreational fishing trips and 89,464 recreational diving trips taken from Alabama through Texas during 1999. Results also indicated that more than one fifth of these activities were within 300 feet of an oil or gas structure or an artificial reef created from such a structure. The incidence was lowest for private boat fishing (21.2 percent). For charter boat fishing, 30.4 percent of the trips were near an oil or gas structure, and 51.9 percent of party boat trips were near such a structure. For divers, 69.1 percent of the trips were reported to be near an oil or gas structure. Both fishermen and divers tended to visit multiple structures on each trip. During the year, it is estimated that fishermen in all modes had 2,104,809 oil/gas structure-visits, while divers reported an additional 172,068 structure-visits.

Chapter 4
Expenditures and Economic Impacts Associated With Recreational Fishing and Diving Trips Near Oil and Gas Structures in the Gulf of Mexico

Introduction

Recreational trips by fishermen and divers to oil and gas structures in the Gulf of Mexico result in economic expenditures for these trips and economic impacts in the coastal counties near these structures. An objective of this study was to identify the economic consequences of the demand for oil and gas structures by recreational fishermen, charter and head boat users, and recreational divers in Alabama, Mississippi, Louisiana and Texas. In this chapter, expenditure estimates are presented that show the type and magnitude of expenditures by recreational users of oil and gas structures in each state. These expenditure estimates are also used to develop estimates of the economic impacts of recreational uses of oil and gas structures in each state.

The basic approach is to combine estimates of the number of trips by recreational users as presented in Chapter 3 with trip and equipment related expenditure data collected from respondents during the follow-up phone interviews described in Chapter 2. For the purpose of this analysis, expenditures were classified according to the residency status of oil and gas structure users. *Coastal residents* were defined as users whose primary residence was within the counties in each state defined as coastal counties for the Marine Recreational Fisheries Statistics Survey (MRFSS). *Non-coastal residents* are users who reside outside these counties, either in the same state where the respondent was intercepted for this survey or from outside the state. Expenditures by non-coastal residents were distributed according to whether trip and equipment expenditures were incurred in coastal counties (as defined for the MRFSS) or outside of a coastal county.

The expenditure data, distributed according to user's residency status and the location where the expenditures were incurred, were then used in the IMPLAN (Impact analysis for PLANning) input-output modeling framework to produce estimates of economic impacts generated by oil and gas structure users in each state.[3] These impacts include total output, employment, and personal income (value added) effects in the coastal and non-coastal regions of each state.

In addition, the trip and equipment related expenditure data were evaluated using an expenditure function econometric analysis to determine the extent to which total expenditures by oil and gas structure users were influenced by decisions to take trips to these structures. This analysis, which is reported in Chapter 5, is used to estimate the incremental effect of oil and gas structures on the total expenditures related to recreational fishing and diving in each state. This analysis is distinct from the economic impact analysis described in this chapter that focuses only on expenditures in the coastal counties of each state.

Annual Trip and Equipment Expenditures

Trip expenditure data were collected during follow-up phone interviews with oil and gas structure users who were engaged in recreational fishing from private boats, charter or party boats, or who participated in recreational diving. Average trip expenditure data for oil and gas structure users in

---

[3] IMPLAN is a proprietary software package maintained by the Minnesota IMPLAN Group (MIG), Inc., Stillwater, MN.

each mode and state were combined with estimates of the total number of trips to oil and gas structures in each mode and state as reported in Chapter 3. This produced estimates of the annual expenditures associated with trips near oil and gas structures for each mode in the four Gulf of Mexico states. The total trip expenditures were distributed according to whether trip expenditures were incurred in the coastal counties (as defined for the MRFSS) or outside the coastal counties of each state.

Annual equipment expenditure data were also collected during the follow-up phone interviews with oil and gas structure users. These expenditures included both new and used equipment although only new equipment expenditures were used for the impact estimates. This reflects the fact that purchases of used goods do not create economic impacts in the current year since the good was produced in a prior year. Unlike trip expenses, these expenditures were not directly related to the number of trips near oil and gas structures. Therefore, the sample data were extrapolated by multiplying the average expenditures for each mode and state times the estimated number of participants using oil and gas structures in each mode and state as presented in Chapter 3. It should be noted that these equipment expenditures may not be solely related to trips to oil and gas structures since the equipment could be used for other types of fishing and diving activities. Therefore, the expenditure and corresponding impact estimates may overstate the economic activity generated by fishers and divers who participated in trips near oil and gas structures.

The following sections present the estimation results stemming from these calculations. Statistical data on average trip expenditures and annual equipment expenditures for the sample of users in the phone interviews are presented in Appendix F.

Private Boat Fishing

Annual trip and equipment expenditures associated with oil and gas structure users by private boat recreational fishermen in Alabama, Mississippi, Louisiana and Texas are reported in Tables 4-1 to 4-4, respectively. The results across the four states show that total annual expenditures for private boat fishing trips to oil and gas structures by coastal residents were higher than for non-coastal residents. Non-coastal residents generally incurred higher per trip expenditures than coastal residents for items such as fuel and lodging (see Appendix F). But, the fact that coastal residents accounted for a large majority of the total private boat trips to oil and gas structures (Chapter 3) resulted in many more occasions to spend money.

In general, the largest trip expense items for coastal residents were fuel (gasoline for the vehicle and boat), groceries and food stuffs (restaurants and bars), and bait. Lodging costs were also a significant component of total trip costs in all states reflecting the fact that many private boat trips were multi-day trips. Louisiana had the highest total trip expenditures across the four states due to the large number of Louisiana coastal residents who fished near oil/gas structures.

Lodging costs were a major expense item for non-coastal residents as well but fuel, groceries and food stuffs, and baits were also important. Non-coastal private boat fishermen who used oil and gas structures in the four states typically incurred a larger share of their total expenses in the coastal counties they were visiting than in the non-coastal counties where they resided. The primary expenses incurred outside the coastal counties were gasoline for the car and food products. Across the four states, Texas had the highest annual trip expenditures by non-coastal private boaters who fished near oil/gas structures.

Tables 4-1 to 4-4 also show that the annual equipment expenditures of private boaters who fished near oil/gas structures varied considerably from state to state. For both coastal and non-coastal residents, typically the main expenditure was for boats. It should be noted, however, that the total value of a boating package (boat, motor, trailer, and equipment) was recorded as a *boat* purchase if a respondent could not separate the costs of each item. Also, it should be noted that the number of non-coastal private boat respondents who fished near oil/gas structures in each state was relatively low (the highest was 13 in Louisiana). Therefore, a large equipment purchase by one or two respondents can have a significant impact on the sample average and inflate the overall estimates when extrapolated to the population of all private boaters who fished near oil/gas structures in a state. Other significant equipment purchases in all states included fishing tackle (rods and reels, lures, etc.) and boat repairs.

In Alabama and Louisiana, equipment expenditures by coastal private boaters were significantly higher than those of non-coastal residents. The primary expenditure in both states was for "boats" although boat repairs were also important.

In Mississippi and Texas, on the other hand, equipment expenditures by non-coastal residents were larger than those of coastal residents. In Mississippi, this result was driven by the fact that 1 of the 3 non-coastal respondents reported a new boat purchase of $16,000 outside of the coastal region resulting in an average for the sample of $5,333. Without this single purchase, the estimated total of $39,727,771 in new boat purchases outside the coastal region would have been $0. In Texas, there were also high value equipment purchases reported by several of the 7 non-coastal respondents. This resulted in relatively higher expenditures for non-coastal residents as compared to coastal residents when the sample averages were extrapolated to all non-coastal participants.

Table 4-1. Annual Trip and Equipment Expenditures for Private Boat Fishing Near Oil/Gas Structures in Alabama (in $)

| | Annual Expenditures | | |
| | Coastal Resident | Non-Coastal Resident | |
Expense		Near-Coast	Away-Coast
Trip Related			
Charter/Party Fees	0	0	0
Baits	2,296,944	276,948	0
Tackles	937,446	0	0
Other Rentals	0	0	0
Groceries	1,992,579	184,632	123,088
Transportation	0	0	0
Gasoline	823,613	0	1,569,370
Fuel Costs	4,064,293	307,720	0
Clothing	0	0	0
Food Stuffs	1,345,295	0	153,860
Other Trip Expenses	342,918	0	30,772
Lodging Costs	1,680,097	615,439	0
Car Rental	0	0	0
Boat Rental	60,873	0	0
Launch Fees	85,222	0	0
Docking Fees	0	0	0
Trip Repairs	405,821	0	0
Dive Fees	0	0	0
Guide Fees	0	0	0
Fishing Licenses	217,114	0	0
Air Fees	0	0	0
Totals	14,252,215	1,384,738	1,877,089
Equipment Related			
Motors	4,634,214	0	0
Auxillary Equipment	0	0	0
Boats	16,530,243	0	0
Trailers	397,218	0	0
Rods and Reels	2,129,091	0	0
Lines	317,510	0	6,378
Lures	522,475	0	372,061
Other Fishing Equipment	101,953	0	0
Camping Equipment	43,429	0	0
Boat Outfitting - Diving	0	0	0
Dive Equipment	0	0	0
Other Dive Equipment	0	0	0
Boat Outfitting - Fishing	0	0	0
Books	71,234	0	233,867
Capital Repairs	1,237,997	0	0
Dive Lessons	0	0	0
Memberships	80,106	0	0
Licenses	184,442	0	204,102
Totals	26,249,912	0	816,408

Table 4-2. Annual Trip and Equipment Expenditures for Private Boat Fishing Near Oil/Gas Structures in Mississippi (in $)

| | Annual Expenditures | | |
| | Coastal Resident | Non-Coastal Resident | |
Expense		Near-Coast	Away-Coast
Trip Related			
Charter/Party Fees	0	0	0
Baits	1,176,039	148,979	0
Tackles	622,966	0	0
Other Rentals	0	0	0
Groceries	1,650,101	263,196	0
Transportation	0	0	0
Gasoline	179,141	0	516,958
Fuel Costs	6,199,275	595,917	49,660
Clothing	379,858	0	0
Food Stuffs	1,537,663	446,937	59,592
Other Trip Expenses	395,052	0	14,898
Lodging Costs	413,285	288,026	0
Car Rental	0	0	0
Boat Rental	30,389	19,864	0
Launch Fees	54,699	19,864	0
Docking Fees	48,622	0	0
Trip Repairs	0	0	0
Dive Fees	0	0	0
Guide Fees	0	0	0
Fishing Licenses	838,725	0	0
Air Fees	0	0	0
Totals	**13,525,815**	**1,782,784**	**641,107**
Equipment Related			
Motors	2,294,923	0	0
Auxillary Equipment	0	0	0
Boats	0	0	39,727,771
Trailers	0	0	0
Rods and Reels	991,407	1,241,493	0
Lines	201,609	0	0
Lures	1,187,049	148,979	0
Other Fishing Equipment	353,418	0	0
Camping Equipment	89,502	0	0
Boat Outfitting - Diving	0	0	0
Dive Equipment	0	0	0
Other Dive Equipment	0	0	0
Boat Outfitting - Fishing	0	0	0
Books	44,636	0	99,319
Capital Repairs	1,210,572	0	0
Dive Lessons	0	0	0
Memberships	88,355	0	0
Licenses	72,290	0	121,666
Totals	**6,533,760**	**1,390,472**	**39,948,756**

Table 4-3. Annual Trip and Equipment Expenditures for Private Boat Fishing Near Oil/Gas Structures in Louisiana (in $)

| | Annual Expenditures | | |
| | Coastal Resident | Non-Coastal Resident | |
Expense		Near-Coast	Away-Coast
Trip Related			
Charter/Party Fees	0	0	0
Baits	4,370,172	484,639	12,881
Tackles	903,078	172,280	45,083
Other Rentals	0	0	0
Groceries	6,307,933	1,122,236	173,890
Transportation	1,134,520	0	0
Gasoline	2,212,315	0	753,283
Fuel Costs	11,517,650	1,603,655	225,413
Clothing	0	0	0
Food Stuffs	5,890,429	526,501	342,950
Other Trip Expenses	553,646	0	111,097
Lodging Costs	3,208,423	925,805	0
Car Rental	0	0	0
Boat Rental	136,142	0	0
Launch Fees	939,383	0	0
Docking Fees	471,960	0	0
Trip Repairs	0	0	0
Dive Fees	0	0	0
Guide Fees	0	0	0
Fishing Licenses	952,997	0	0
Air Fees	0	0	0
Totals	38,598,650	4,835,115	1,664,597
Equipment Related			
Motors	4,553,335	0	0
Auxillary Equipment	0	0	500,435
Boats	47,557,057	0	600,522
Trailers	1,416,593	0	1,000,870
Rods and Reels	6,655,458	0	350,304
Lines	2,596,919	20,017	80,070
Lures	2,539,749	25,022	190,165
Other Fishing Equipment	1,135,804	0	200,174
Camping Equipment	379,445	0	645,561
Boat Outfitting - Diving	0	0	0
Dive Equipment	0	0	0
Other Dive Equipment	0	0	0
Boat Outfitting - Fishing	0	0	0
Books	217,548	0	147,628
Capital Repairs	4,682,346	0	975,848
Dive Lessons	0	0	0
Memberships	1,091,283	0	17,015
Licenses	770,526	0	87,076
Totals	73,596,064	45,039	4,795,668

Table 4-4. Annual Trip and Equipment Expenditures for Private Boat Fishing Near Oil/Gas Structures in Texas (in $)

| | Annual Expenditures | | |
| | Coastal Resident | Non-Coastal Resident | |
Expense		Near-Coast	Away-Coast
Trip Related			
Charter/Party Fees	0	0	0
Baits	3,644,671	808,378	0
Tackles	1,313,106	241,307	0
Other Rentals	0	0	0
Groceries	3,606,238	603,267	965,227
Transportation	0	0	0
Gasoline	1,504,147	0	627,639
Fuel Costs	8,685,718	1,737,409	0
Clothing	224,189	337,830	518,810
Food Stuffs	2,174,632	3,069,423	0
Other Trip Expenses	720,607	0	84,457
Lodging Costs	2,129,794	3,317,969	0
Car Rental	0	0	0
Boat Rental	144,121	0	0
Launch Fees	278,635	0	0
Docking Fees	0	0	0
Trip Repairs	32,027	0	0
Dive Fees	0	0	0
Guide Fees	0	0	0
Fishing Licenses	80,067	0	48,261
Air Fees	0	0	0
Totals	24,537,954	10,115,583	2,244,395
Equipment Related			
Motors	0	0	10,122,746
Auxillary Equipment	0	0	3,080,836
Boats	7,620,842	0	6,161,672
Trailers	0	0	1,760,478
Rods and Reels	4,456,461	880,239	880,239
Lines	561,864	44,012	154,922
Lures	1,617,697	17,605	198,054
Other Fishing Equipment	4,731,850	0	0
Camping Equipment	441,662	0	220,060
Boat Outfitting - Diving	0	0	0
Dive Equipment	0	0	0
Other Dive Equipment	0	0	0
Boat Outfitting - Fishing	0	0	5,281,433
Books	303,102	0	25,087
Capital Repairs	3,406,863	220,060	0
Dive Lessons	0	0	0
Memberships	174,587	0	59,416
Licenses	408,754	0	81,862
Totals	23,723,681	1,161,915	28,026,803

Charter Boat Fishing

Annual trip and equipment expenditures associated with oil and gas structures by charter boat recreational fishermen in Alabama, Mississippi, Louisiana and Texas are reported in Tables 4-5 to 4-8, respectively. These trip and equipment expenditures were much smaller than for private boat fishing due to the smaller number of trips by charter boat anglers to oil/gas structures.

The results across the four states show that annual expenditures by non-coastal residents were generally higher than for coastal residents. This was due to the fact that charter boat trips were typically taken by non-coastal residents across the four states.

In general, the largest trip related expense items for coastal residents were for food products (groceries and food stuffs) and for charter fees. Note, however, that charter fees for coastal residents in Alabama and Mississippi were $0. Because the expenditure survey asked for money *actually paid* by each respondent, it is most likely that these fishers accompanied someone else who paid for the charter boat trip. For equipment related expenditures, the largest expense categories for coastal residents were for fishing tackle (rods and reels, line, lures and other fishing equipment).

By contrast, the largest expense items for non-coastal residents were for charter fees, food products, and gasoline used in travelling to the charter fishing site. Charter fees, food products, and other trip expenses were typically purchased near the coast whereas gasoline for their vehicle was purchased away from the coast. In all four states, non-coastal charter boat fishermen who used oil and gas structures incurred a larger share of their total expenses in the coastal counties they were visiting than in the non-coastal counties where they resided.

Tables 4-5 to 4-8 also show that annual equipment expenditures by non-coastal residents who fished at oil and gas structures from charter boats were less than the trip related expenditures across all four states. As with the coastal residents, the largest equipment expenditures were for fishing tackle. But, non-coastal residents generally incurred these expenditures away from the coastal counties.

Table 4-5. Annual Trip and Equipment Expenditures Associated with Charter Boat Fishing Near Oil/Gas Structures in Alabama (in $)

Expense	Coastal Resident	Non-Coastal Resident Near-Coast	Away-Coast
		Annual Expenditures	
Trip Related			
Charter/Party Fees	0	6,915,271	0
Baits	10,795	129,220	0
Tackles	0	0	0
Other Rentals	0	0	0
Groceries	14,393	446,212	0
Transportation	0	0	0
Gasoline	6,207	0	1,353,778
Fuel Costs	0	0	0
Clothing	0	0	0
Food Stuffs	7,197	2,019,057	0
Other Trip Expenses	0	4,038	0
Lodging Costs	0	646,098	0
Car Rental	0	0	0
Boat Rental	0	0	0
Launch Fees	0	0	0
Docking Fees	0	0	0
Trip Repairs	0	0	0
Dive Fees	0	0	0
Guide Fees	0	0	0
Fishing Licenses	0	0	0
Air Fees	0	0	0
Totals	38,592	10,159,897	1,353,778
Equipment Related			
Motors	0	0	0
Auxillary Equipment	0	0	0
Boats	0	0	0
Trailers	0	0	0
Rods and Reels	51,286	0	2,261,344
Lines	21,921	0	56,534
Lures	17,371	0	0
Other Fishing Equipment	0	188,445	0
Camping Equipment	0	0	1,130,672
Boat Outfitting - Diving	0	0	0
Dive Equipment	0	0	0
Other Dive Equipment	0	0	0
Boat Outfitting - Fishing	0	0	0
Books	2,482	0	293,975
Capital Repairs	0	0	0
Dive Lessons	0	0	0
Memberships	0	0	0
Licenses	6,618	0	158,294
Totals	99,678	188,445	3,900,819

Table 4-6. Annual Trip and Equipment Expenditures for Charter Boat Fishing Near Oil/Gas Structures in Mississippi (in $)

| | Annual Expenditures | | |
| | Coastal Resident | Non-Coastal Resident | |
Expense		Near-Coast	Away-Coast
Trip Related			
Charter/Party Fees	0	169,321	0
Baits	3,389	0	0
Tackles	338,910	0	0
Other Rentals	0	0	0
Groceries	9,038	903,045	0
Transportation	112,970	0	0
Gasoline	0	0	305,116
Fuel Costs	0	0	0
Clothing	0	0	507,963
Food Stuffs	310,668	225,761	237,049
Other Trip Expenses	178,493	0	11,288
Lodging Costs	0	948,197	0
Car Rental	0	0	33,864
Boat Rental	0	0	0
Launch Fees	0	0	0
Docking Fees	0	0	0
Trip Repairs	0	0	0
Dive Fees	0	0	0
Guide Fees	0	0	0
Fishing Licenses	181,317	16,932	50,796
Air Fees	0	0	0
Totals	1,134,784	2,263,257	1,146,077
Equipment Related			
Motors	0	0	0
Auxillary Equipment	0	0	0
Boats	0	0	0
Trailers	0	0	0
Rods and Reels	2,170	0	81,304
Lines	11,033	0	21,447
Lures	796	0	7,710
Other Fishing Equipment	0	0	280
Camping Equipment	21,704	0	0
Boat Outfitting - Diving	0	0	0
Dive Equipment	0	0	0
Other Dive Equipment	0	0	0
Boat Outfitting - Fishing	0	0	0
Books	3,653	0	5,747
Capital Repairs	0	0	0
Dive Lessons	0	0	0
Memberships	30,747	0	2,804
Licenses	8,211	0	11,214
Totals	78,314	0	130,506

Table 4-7. Annual Trip and Equipment Expenditures for Charter Boat Fishing Near Oil/Gas Structures in Louisiana (in $)

| | Annual Expenditures | | |
| | Coastal Resident | Non-Coastal Resident | |
Expense		Near-Coast	Away-Coast
Trip Related			
Charter/Party Fees	466,079	785,111	0
Baits	105,688	33,899	6,780
Tackles	11,160	0	0
Other Rentals	98,467	0	0
Groceries	92,888	0	84,071
Transportation	0	0	0
Gasoline	81,974	0	257,500
Fuel Costs	0	0	0
Clothing	49,234	0	4,068
Food Stuffs	200,217	6,780	94,918
Other Trip Expenses	16,739	6,780	20,340
Lodging Costs	190,370	75,935	0
Car Rental	0	0	0
Boat Rental	0	0	0
Launch Fees	0	0	0
Docking Fees	0	0	0
Trip Repairs	0	0	0
Dive Fees	0	0	0
Guide Fees	0	0	0
Fishing Licenses	11,488	27,120	27,120
Air Fees	0	0	0
Totals	1,324,304	935,624	494,796
Equipment Related			
Motors	0	0	0
Auxillary Equipment	0	0	0
Boats	0	0	0
Trailers	0	0	0
Rods and Reels	131,129	0	113,727
Lines	9,985	0	1,895
Lures	21,707	0	14,216
Other Fishing Equipment	89,104	0	0
Camping Equipment	20,854	0	0
Boat Outfitting - Diving	0	0	0
Dive Equipment	0	0	0
Other Dive Equipment	0	0	0
Boat Outfitting - Fishing	0	0	0
Books	4,329	0	3,222
Capital Repairs	0	0	0
Dive Lessons	0	0	0
Memberships	1,896	0	0
Licenses	8,215	0	3,033
Totals	287,219	0	136,093

Table 4-8. Annual Trip and Equipment Expenditures for Charter Boat Fishing Near Oil/Gas Structures in Texas (in $)

Expense	Coastal Resident	Non-Coastal Resident Near-Coast	Away-Coast

Trip Related

Expense	Coastal Resident	Near-Coast	Away-Coast
Charter/Party Fees	1,759,119	7,373,226	0
Baits	16,188	0	0
Tackles	118,714	0	0
Other Rentals	0	0	0
Groceries	447,874	577,035	0
Transportation	0	0	0
Gasoline	75,923	0	1,233,893
Fuel Costs	0	0	0
Clothing	0	0	0
Food Stuffs	248,219	1,154,070	0
Other Trip Expenses	46,406	294,929	0
Lodging Costs	0	512,920	0
Car Rental	0	0	801,438
Boat Rental	0	0	0
Launch Fees	0	0	0
Docking Fees	0	0	0
Trip Repairs	0	0	0
Dive Fees	0	0	0
Guide Fees	0	0	0
Fishing Licenses	0	153,876	0
Air Fees	0	0	0
Totals	2,712,443	10,066,056	2,035,331

Equipment Related

Expense	Coastal Resident	Near-Coast	Away-Coast
Motors	0	0	0
Auxillary Equipment	0	0	0
Boats	0	0	0
Trailers	0	0	0
Rods and Reels	570,329	0	618,252
Lines	88,102	0	28,852
Lures	2,269	0	267,909
Other Fishing Equipment	3,781	0	0
Camping Equipment	239,979	0	123,650
Boat Outfitting - Diving	0	0	0
Dive Equipment	0	0	0
Other Dive Equipment	0	0	0
Boat Outfitting - Fishing	0	0	0
Books	43,736	0	164,867
Capital Repairs	0	0	0
Dive Lessons	0	0	0
Memberships	32,140	0	0
Licenses	69,070	0	358,586
Totals	1,049,406	0	1,562,116

Party Boat Fishing

Annual trip and equipment expenditures associated with oil and gas structure trips in Louisiana and Texas by party boat recreational fishermen are reported in Tables 4-9 and 4-10, respectively. Since there were no party boat trips near oil/gas structures in Alabama or Mississippi, no expenditure results are reported.

The results for the two states show that annual party boat trip expenditures were considerably smaller than for private boat fishing due to the smaller number of trips by party boats to oil/gas structures. Both coastal and non-coastal resident expenditures for party boat trips in Louisiana were dominated by party boat fees and lodging costs. The other major expenditures were for gasoline to drive to the party boat site and for food products (groceries and purchased meals). Non-coastal party boat fishermen who used oil and gas structures in Louisiana typically incurred a larger share of their non-party boat fee expenses outside the coastal counties they were visiting than in the non-coastal counties where they resided.

Similarly in Texas, party boat fees dominated the total trip expenses for coastal and non-coastal residents. Groceries and purchased meals were also a large share of coastal and non-coastal resident trip expenses. With the exception of gasoline for their vehicles, non-coastal residents spent the majority of their party boat trip expenses in Texas coastal counties.

Table 4-9 also shows that annual equipment expenditures by non-coastal residents who fished near oil and gas structures from party boats in Louisiana were higher than those of coastal residents. These expenditures were primarily for fishing tackle. Table 4-10 shows that annual equipment expenditures in Texas by party boat anglers were primarily incurred by coastal residents. Again these expenditures were mostly for fishing tackle. The relatively high expenditure of $4.5 million for fishing lures occurs because 1 of the 2 non-coastal party boat respondents reported annual expenditures of $150. This same individual reported camping equipment purchases of $13,700 but this response was not extrapolated to all non-coastal residents because it was not clear these expenditures were related to party boat fishing.

Table 4-9. Annual Trip and Equipment Expenditures for Party Boat Fishing Near Oil/Gas Structures in Louisiana (in $)

| | Annual Expenditures | | |
| Expense | Coastal Resident | Non-Coastal Resident | |
		Near-Coast	Away-Coast
Trip Related			
Charter/Party Fees	215,586	359,949	0
Baits	0	58,767	29,384
Tackles	3,505	0	2,938
Other Rentals	0	0	0
Groceries	70,109	0	51,421
Transportation	0	0	0
Gasoline	60,995	0	51,127
Fuel Costs	0	0	0
Clothing	0	0	0
Food Stuffs	77,120	58,767	308,528
Other Trip Expenses	13,321	0	0
Lodging Costs	127,949	14,692	0
Car Rental	0	0	0
Boat Rental	0	0	0
Launch Fees	0	0	0
Docking Fees	0	0	0
Trip Repairs	0	0	0
Dive Fees	0	0	0
Guide Fees	0	0	0
Fishing Licenses	0	0	0
Air Fees	0	0	0
Totals	568,585	492,175	443,399
Equipment Related			
Motors	0	0	0
Auxillary Equipment	0	0	0
Boats	0	0	0
Trailers	0	0	0
Rods and Reels	0	0	528,905
Lines	0	0	88,151
Lures	0	0	176,302
Other Fishing Equipment	0	0	44,957
Camping Equipment	17,527	0	0
Boat Outfitting - Diving	0	0	0
Dive Equipment	0	0	0
Other Dive Equipment	0	0	0
Boat Outfitting - Fishing	0	0	0
Books	6,135	0	0
Capital Repairs	0	0	0
Dive Lessons	0	0	0
Memberships	0	0	22,038
Licenses	37,976	0	19,393
Totals	61,638	0	879,745

Table 4-10. Annual Trip and Equipment Expenditures for Party Boat Fishing Near Oil/Gas Structures in Texas (in $)

Expense	Coastal Resident	Non-Coastal Resident Near-Coast	Away-Coast
Trip Related			
Charter/Party Fees	3,632,674	1,425,383	0
Baits	253,790	190,051	0
Tackles	74,644	0	0
Other Rentals	0	0	0
Groceries	223,932	285,077	0
Transportation	0	0	0
Gasoline	105,248	0	826,722
Fuel Costs	0	0	0
Clothing	0	0	0
Food Stuffs	179,146	1,615,434	190,051
Other Trip Expenses	149,288	0	0
Lodging Costs	0	0	0
Car Rental	0	0	0
Boat Rental	0	0	0
Launch Fees	0	0	0
Docking Fees	0	0	0
Trip Repairs	0	0	0
Dive Fees	0	0	0
Guide Fees	0	0	0
Fishing Licenses	0	0	0
Air Fees	0	0	0
Totals	4,618,721	3,515,944	1,016,773
Equipment Related			
Motors	0	0	0
Auxillary Equipment	0	0	0
Boats	0	0	0
Trailers	0	0	0
Rods and Reels	788,691	0	0
Lines	36,336	0	0
Lures	70,419	0	4,561,224
Other Fishing Equipment	0	0	0
Camping Equipment	21,126	0	416,591,814
Boat Outfitting - Diving	0	0	0
Dive Equipment	0	0	0
Other Dive Equipment	0	0	0
Boat Outfitting - Fishing	0	0	0
Books	45,068	0	1,398,775
Capital Repairs	0	0	0
Dive Lessons	0	0	0
Memberships	33,801	0	0
Licenses	27,323	0	1,520,408
Totals	1,022,764	0	424,072,222

Recreational Diving

Annual trip and equipment expenditures associated with oil and gas structure trips by recreational divers in Alabama, Mississippi, and Louisiana are reported in Tables 4-11 to 4-13, respectively. While there were estimated dive trips near oil/gas structures in Texas (Chapter 3), no follow-up phone interviews could be completed with divers who dove near oil/gas structures in Texas. Similarly, no interviews were completed with non-coastal residents who dove near oil/gas structures in Alabama. Therefore, no results are presented for diving in Texas or for non-coastal divers in Alabama.

The results across the three states show that annual trip expenditures were generally higher for coastal residents than for non-coastal residents. This was due to the fact that coastal residents accounted for the vast majority of the total dive trips to oil and gas structures (Chapter 3) which resulted in more occasions to spend money. In general, the largest expense items for coastal residents were fuel (gasoline for the vehicle and boat) and food products. Also, expenses for diving tank air fills were a component of total expenses in each state.

For non-coastal residents in Mississippi and Louisiana, the expenses were a mixture of fuel and food product expenditures. The overall level of expenditures was low relative to other modes due to the small number of non-coastal divers who dove near oil/gas structures in these states.

Tables 4-11 to 4-13 also show that equipment expenditures by coastal residents were higher than those of non-coastal residents, but the level of equipment expenditures for divers was low relative to oil/gas structure users in other modes. All of the equipment related expenditures by non-coastal residents were made outside of the coastal counties.

Table 4-11. Annual Trip and Equipment Expenditures for Private Diving Near Oil/Gas Structures in Alabama (in $)

	Annual Expenditures		
	Coastal Resident	Non-Coastal Resident	
Expense		Near-Coast	Away-Coast

Trip Related

Expense	Coastal Resident	Near-Coast	Away-Coast
Charter/Party Fees	0	0	0
Baits	0	0	0
Tackles	15,468	0	0
Other Rentals	0	0	0
Groceries	38,669	0	0
Transportation	0	0	0
Gasoline	86,310	0	0
Fuel Costs	77,339	0	0
Clothing	0	0	0
Food Stuffs	38,669	0	0
Other Trip Expenses	10,827	0	0
Lodging Costs	0	0	0
Car Rental	0	0	0
Boat Rental	0	0	0
Launch Fees	0	0	0
Docking Fees	0	0	0
Trip Repairs	0	0	0
Dive Fees	0	0	0
Guide Fees	0	0	0
Fishing Licenses	0	0	0
Air Fees	15,468	0	0
Totals	**282,750**	**0**	**0**

Equipment Related

Expense	Coastal Resident	Near-Coast	Away-Coast
Motors	0	0	0
Auxillary Equipment	0	0	0
Boats	0	0	0
Trailers	0	0	0
Rods and Reels	0	0	0
Lines	0	0	0
Lures	0	0	0
Other Fishing Equipment	0	0	0
Camping Equipment	0	0	0
Boat Outfitting - Diving	0	0	0
Dive Equipment	0	0	0
Other Dive Equipment	0	0	0
Boat Outfitting - Fishing	0	0	0
Books	1,009	0	0
Capital Repairs	0	0	0
Dive Lessons	0	0	0
Memberships	0	0	0
Licenses	3,331	0	0
Totals	**4,340**	**0**	**0**

Table 4-12. Annual Trip and Equipment Expenditures for Private Diving Near Oil/Gas Structures in Mississippi (in $)

Expense	Coastal Resident	Non-Coastal Resident Near-Coast	Away-Coast
	Annual Expenditures		
	Coastal Resident	Non-Coastal Resident	
		Near-Coast	Away-Coast
Trip Related			
Charter/Party Fees	0	0	0
Baits	0	0	0
Tackles	95,023	0	0
Other Rentals	427,602	0	0
Groceries	213,801	0	0
Transportation	0	0	0
Gasoline	7,839	0	11,646
Fuel Costs	451,358	0	166,373
Clothing	0	0	0
Food Stuffs	95,023	0	166,373
Other Trip Expenses	23,756	0	0
Lodging Costs	0	0	0
Car Rental	0	0	0
Boat Rental	0	0	0
Launch Fees	0	0	0
Docking Fees	475,113	0	0
Trip Repairs	0	0	0
Dive Fees	0	582,307	0
Guide Fees	0	0	0
Fishing Licenses	0	0	0
Air Fees	95,023	0	0
Totals	**1,884,537**	**582,307**	**344,393**
Equipment Related			
Motors	0	0	0
Auxillary Equipment	0	0	0
Boats	0	0	0
Trailers	0	0	0
Rods and Reels	0	0	0
Lines	0	0	0
Lures	0	0	0
Other Fishing Equipment	0	0	0
Camping Equipment	0	0	0
Boat Outfitting - Diving	179,401	0	0
Dive Equipment	0	0	0
Other Dive Equipment	0	0	0
Boat Outfitting - Fishing	0	0	0
Books	0	0	0
Capital Repairs	17,940	0	0
Dive Lessons	22,425	0	41,593
Memberships	0	0	24,956
Licenses	1,794	0	5,823
Totals	**221,560**	**0**	**72,372**

Table 4-13. Annual Trip and Equipment Expenditures for Private Diving Near Oil/Gas Structures in Louisiana (in $)

Expense	Coastal Resident	Non-Coastal Resident Near-Coast	Non-Coastal Resident Away-Coast
		Annual Expenditures	
	Coastal Resident	**Non-Coastal Resident**	
		Near-Coast	**Away-Coast**

Trip Related

Expense	Coastal Resident	Near-Coast	Away-Coast
Charter/Party Fees	0	0	0
Baits	0	0	0
Tackles	640,529	0	0
Other Rentals	0	0	0
Groceries	2,135,098	41,611	0
Transportation	0	0	0
Gasoline	256,212	0	0
Fuel Costs	2,135,098	83,221	0
Clothing	0	0	0
Food Stuffs	2,135,098	0	41,611
Other Trip Expenses	0	0	0
Lodging Costs	0	288,500	0
Car Rental	0	0	0
Boat Rental	0	0	0
Launch Fees	0	0	0
Docking Fees	0	0	0
Trip Repairs	0	0	0
Dive Fees	0	0	0
Guide Fees	0	0	0
Fishing Licenses	0	0	0
Air Fees	2,135,098	0	177,538
Totals	**9,437,134**	**413,331**	**219,149**

Equipment Related

Expense	Coastal Resident	Near-Coast	Away-Coast
Motors	0	0	0
Auxillary Equipment	0	0	0
Boats	0	0	0
Trailers	0	0	0
Rods and Reels	0	0	0
Lines	0	0	0
Lures	0	0	0
Other Fishing Equipment	0	0	0
Camping Equipment	0	0	0
Boat Outfitting - Diving	0	0	0
Dive Equipment	0	0	0
Other Dive Equipment	0	0	94,842
Boat Outfitting - Fishing	0	0	0
Books	0	0	0
Capital Repairs	0	0	0
Dive Lessons	0	0	0
Memberships	190,424	0	0
Licenses	52,367	0	5,173
Totals	**242,791**	**0**	**100,015**

Economic Impacts

Individuals who participate in recreational fishing and diving near oil/gas structures purchase goods and services that are used in the pursuit of their recreational interests. These expenditures create economic activity that results in sales, employment, and income for individuals directly involved in the business. In addition, in order to sell goods and services, businesses rely on the use of inputs to produce the goods and services desired by customers. For example, charter and party boats need fuel and oil, bait, ice and a variety of other inputs to provide fishing services for their customers. As a result of the sales (output) of a charter or party boat business, other businesses make sales to charter and party boat operators. These other businesses then purchase inputs from other businesses to produce their products. This interaction between businesses leads to economic impacts that extend beyond the initial sale of a fishing trip by a charter or party boat.

Economic impact analysis provides measures of the interaction between businesses in particular states or regions within a state. In order to distinguish the sources of economic impact, three types of effects are commonly described. *Direct impacts* refer to the initial sales (output) of a business or a group of businesses contained within an industry. The direct impacts of sales by an industry cause *indirect impacts* as other businesses and industries provide goods and services. Finally, as employees earn income from the sales of businesses, the money these employees spend for goods and services for their households create additional *induced impacts* within the economy. The sum of the direct, indirect and induced impacts is the total impact of a business on an economy. These three impacts can be measured in terms of either output, income or employment. The total impact can also be expressed as a *multiplier* that indicates how much additional spending, income, or employment would result from an increase in output in a particular industry in a region. A Type I multiplier includes direct and indirect impacts while a Type II multiplier adds induced impacts to the Type I multiplier. The interested reader should consult more comprehensive references on economic impact analysis for more details on terminology, estimation methods and procedures (Miller and Blair, 1985; and Stevens and Lahr, 1988).

This section provides a description of the economic impacts of recreational fishing and diving near oil/gas structures in Alabama, Mississippi, Louisiana, and Texas. The following subsection describes the methods used. This is followed by separate subsections for each of the four types of recreational activities considered in this analysis.

Methods

Data for this analysis were from the annual trip and equipment expenditures presented earlier in Tables 4-1 to 4-13. One of the primary ingredients of an input-output model is the classification of expenditures according to an industrial sector. These sectors represent groupings of similar businesses that purchase comparable types of inputs from other businesses in order to provide final products. The extent to which each sector purchases inputs from businesses within the same region helps to determine the size of the multiplier effect associated with expenditures for final products from that sector.

Table 4-14 presents the classification of trip and equipment expenditures associated with trips to oil and gas structures according to a corresponding IMPLAN sector. These sectors are unique to the IMPLAN model and reflect the aggregation of industries under the U.S. Standard Industrial Classification (SIC) system. The one sector that is not contained within the basic IMPLAN sector classifications is the "charter/party boat" sector. This sector was created from primary data following procedures that were reported in Sutton et al (1999). Due to the type of expenditures associated with recreational uses of oil/gas structures, Table 4-14 shows that service related industries (food establishments, lodging, service stations) account for several of the sectors that are impacted by trip related expenditures. The equipment related sectors are primarily related to boat building and sporting goods.

Table 4-14. Industry Sector in IMPLAN Model and Related Expense Categories

IMPLAN	Sector	Expense
xx	Charter/Party Boat	Charter/Party Fees
357	Motors and Generators	Motors
383	Electrical Equipment, N.E.C.	Auxillary Equipment
393	Boat Building and Repairing	Boats
399	Transportation Equipment, N.E.C	Trailers
421	Sporting and Athletic Goods, N.E.C.	Baits
		Tackles
		Other Rentals
		Rods and Reels
		Lines
		Lures
		Other Fishing Equipment
		Camping Equipment
		Boat Outfitting - Diving
		Dive Equipment
		Other Dive Equipment
		Boat Outfitting - Fishing
441	Communications, Except Radio and TV	Books
450	Food Stores	Groceries
451	Automotive Dealers & Service Stations	Transportation
		Gasoline
		Fuel Costs
452	Apparel & Accessory Stores	Clothing
454	Eating & Drinking	Food Stuffs (Restaurants and Bars)
455	Miscellaneous Retail	Other Trip Expenses
463	Hotels and Lodging Places	Lodging Costs
477	Automobile Rental and Leasing	Car Rental
488	Amusement and Recreation Services, N.E.C.	Boat Rental
		Launch Fees
		Docking Fees
		Trip Repairs
		Dive Fees
		Guide Fees
		Capital Repairs
		Air Fees
		Dive Lessons
489	Membership Sports and Recreation Clubs	Memberships
523	State & Local Government - Non-Education	Fishing Licenses
		Licenses

Another important element of economic impact analysis is the definition of a "region" for analysis. For this study, the region is defined as *coastal counties* within each state as defined for the MRFSS (Chapter 2). This definition is consistent with the classification of trips to oil/gas structures by coastal and non-coastal residents discussed earlier in this chapter which was based on the MRFSS estimate of total fishing trips by mode in each Gulf state. Also, this definition is consistent with the IMPLAN modeling structure which is based on state level data or a grouping of counties (e.g. coastal counties) within a state. The IMPLAN modeling structure does not allow states to be combined to develop a multi-state analysis.

The definition of the coastal counties as the region has important implications for economic impact analysis. Expenditures by non-coastal residents who come to a coastal county region inject "new money" into the region that creates incomes and employment that would not have existed without these expenditures. This new income is the source of *induced impacts* that occur in response to employees' purchases with this new income. Expenditures by coastal residents, on the other hand, do not create induced impacts because no new income is created within the coastal region. This is because these expenditures simply represent a transfer of money from one individual to another within the region.

In the following section, economic impact estimates using the IMPLAN sectors discussed above are presented for the oil/gas structure user groups in each state and mode. The impacts are defined in terms of the direct impacts of coastal resident spending within the coastal region of each state and the multiplier impacts of non-coastal resident spending in the coastal region. Expenditures by non-coastal residents outside of the coastal region are not included in this analysis since they create no economic impacts in the coastal region and they were reported previously in Tables 4-1 to 4-13.

Impact estimates are presented for total output, value added, and employment. *Total output* measures the dollar amount of goods and services associated with expenditures in coastal counties for fishing and diving near oil/gas structures. For non-coastal resident expenditures, the total output estimate includes a Type II multiplier (direct, indirect, and induced impacts) effect caused by new money in the coastal region. *Value added* measures the payments made by businesses to workers, interest, rent, profit and indirect business taxes within the coastal region. For non-coastal resident expenditures, the value added estimate includes a Type II multiplier effect from new income that is created within the coastal region. *Employment* measures the number of jobs (in full-time equivalents (FTEs)) associated with expenditures in coastal counties for fishing and diving near oil/gas structures. The value added estimate for non-coastal resident expenditures includes a Type II multiplier effect to reflect the additional jobs created by new spending and income within the coastal region.

In the following sections, estimates for the total output, value added and employment impacts associated with coastal and non-coastal resident expenditures are presented for each mode and state. This is followed by a summary section that combines the three types of economic impacts across all modes and states within the Gulf region.

Private Boat Fishing

Tables 4-15 to 4-18 present economic impact estimates associated with private boat fishing near oil and gas structures from Alabama to Texas. These impact estimates reflect the distribution of trips between coastal and non-coastal residents and the differences in expenditures between the two groups. The economic impacts (output, value added, and employment) of coastal resident expenditures in all states are significantly greater than impacts of non-coastal residents despite the fact that non-coastal resident expenditures cause a multiplier effect in coastal counties. The differences are due to the dominance of coastal residents in this mode and the lack of equipment expenditures by non-coastal residents.

With the exception of Mississippi, coastal resident expenditures in boating equipment related sectors (boat building and repairing; motors and generators) were a significant source of total value added and employment in the region. The other sources of significant impacts across all four states were from coastal resident expenditures in the sporting and athletic goods sector (fishing tackle, etc.), the automotive dealers and service stations sector (fuel and gasoline), the food stores sector (groceries), the eating and drinking sectors (restaurants), and the amusement and recreation services sector (marina services).

On the other hand, the economic impacts of non-coastal residents who fished near oil/gas structures were concentrated in the automotive dealers and service stations sector, the hotels and lodging sectors, and food related sectors (food stores and eating and drinking sectors). There were very limited impacts in the boating equipment related sectors of the coastal counties due to the fact most equipment purchases by non-coastal residents were made outside the coastal counties (Tables 4-1 50 4-4). The largest economic impacts attributable to non-coastal resident trips to oil/gas structures occurred in Texas. This was due to the higher overall level of trip expenditures by non-coastal resident in the coastal counties of Texas (Table 4-4) than in other states.

Table 4-15. Economic Impacts of Combined Annual Trip and Equipment Expenditures for Private Boat Fishing Near Oil/Gas Structures in the Coastal Counties of Alabama

Sector	Economic Output (in $)		Value Added (in $)		Employment (in FTEs)	
	Coastal Resident	Non-Coastal Resident	Coastal Resident	Non-Coastal Resident	Coastal Resident	Non-Coastal Resident
Charter/Party Boat	0	0	0	0	0.0	0.0
Motors and Generators	4,634,214	0	0	0	0.0	0.0
Electrical Equipment, N.E.C.	0	0	0	0	0.0	0.0
Boat Building and Repairing	16,530,243	0	4,396,962	0	165.5	0.0
Transportation Equipment, N.E.C	397,218	0	61,663	0	1.9	0.0
Sporting and Athletic Goods, N.E.C.	6,348,847	401,097	3,200,850	211,218	67.1	4.6
Communications, Except Radio and TV	71,234	0	53,266	0	0.4	0.0
Food Stores	1,992,579	273,700	1,705,337	213,108	70.5	7.9
Automotive Dealers & Service Stations	4,887,906	464,312	3,722,873	330,571	95.5	8.4
Apparel & Accessory Stores	0	0	0	0	0.0	0.0
Eating & Drinking	1,345,295	0	664,183	0	39.9	0.0
Miscellaneous Retail	342,918	0	251,150	0	14.8	0.0
Hotels and Lodging Places	1,680,097	1,003,628	907,207	569,242	36.7	19.6
Automobile Rental and Leasing	0	0	0	0	0.0	0.0
Amusement and Recreation Services, N.E.C.	1,789,913	0	1,036,510	0	61.5	0.0
Membership Sports and Recreation Clubs	80,106	0	45,371	0	2.7	0.0
State & Local Government - Non-Education	401,556	0	401,556	0	12.1	0.0
Total	40,502,127	2,142,736	16,446,929	1,324,139	568.6	40.5

Table 4-16. Economic Impacts of Combined Annual Trip and Equipment Expenditures for Private Boat Fishing Near Oil/Gas Structures in the Coastal Counties of Mississippi

Sector	Economic Output (in $)		Value Added (in $)		Employment (in FTEs)	
	Coastal Resident	Non-Coastal Resident	Coastal Resident	Non-Coastal Resident	Coastal Resident	Non-Coastal Resident
Charter/Party Boat	0	0	0	0	0.0	0.0
Motors and Generators	2,294,923	0	0	0	0.0	0.0
Electrical Equipment, N.E.C.	0	0	0	0	0.0	0.0
Boat Building and Repairing	0	0	0	0	0.0	0.0
Transportation Equipment, N.E.C	0	0	0	0	0.0	0.0
Sporting and Athletic Goods, N.E.C.	4,621,990	2,173,172	2,414,656	1,164,844	54.0	26.9
Communications, Except Radio and TV	44,636	0	33,377	0	0.2	0.0
Food Stores	1,650,101	381,842	1,412,230	298,122	60.0	11.5
Automotive Dealers & Service Stations	6,378,416	870,826	4,858,118	621,394	119.3	15.5
Apparel & Accessory Stores	379,858	0	251,436	0	12.7	0.0
Eating & Drinking	1,537,663	658,370	720,262	332,487	48.9	17.4
Miscellaneous Retail	395,052	0	289,332	0	14.8	0.0
Hotels and Lodging Places	413,285	448,288	227,138	255,632	8.6	8.6
Automobile Rental and Leasing	0	0	0	0	0.0	0.0
Amusement and Recreation Services, N.E.C.	1,344,282	59,727	866,435	37,659	26.3	1.1
Membership Sports and Recreation Clubs	88,355	0	49,643	0	3.0	0.0
State & Local Government - Non-Education	911,015	0	911,015	0	31.1	0.0
Total	20,059,575	4,592,225	12,033,644	2,710,140	378.9	81.0

Table 4-17. Economic Impacts of Combined Annual Trip and Equipment Expenditures for Private Boat Fishing Near Oil/Gas Structures in the Coastal Counties of Louisiana

Sector	Economic Output (in $)		Value Added (in $)		Employment (in FTEs)	
	Coastal Resident	Non-Coastal Resident	Coastal Resident	Non-Coastal Resident	Coastal Resident	Non-Coastal Resident
Charter/Party Boat	0	0	0	0	0.0	0.0
Motors and Generators	4,553,335	0	0	0	0.0	0.0
Electrical Equipment, N.E.C.	0	0	0	0	0.0	0.0
Boat Building and Repairing	47,557,057	0	14,553,789	0	452.7	0.0
Transportation Equipment, N.E.C	1,416,593	0	124,185	0	7.2	0.0
Sporting and Athletic Goods, N.E.C.	18,580,626	1,074,944	7,705,348	502,758	271.1	15.1
Communications, Except Radio and TV	217,548	0	162,674	0	1.1	0.0
Food Stores	6,307,933	1,747,465	5,398,610	1,346,055	214.5	47.7
Automotive Dealers & Service Stations	14,864,485	2,530,610	11,321,533	1,789,749	246.1	40.4
Apparel & Accessory Stores	0	0	0	0	0.0	0.0
Eating & Drinking	5,890,429	851,581	2,933,600	450,512	172.5	20.0
Miscellaneous Retail	553,646	0	405,485	0	20.2	0.0
Hotels and Lodging Places	3,208,423	1,575,746	1,817,977	924,333	61.6	27.8
Automobile Rental and Leasing	0	0	0	0	0.0	0.0
Amusement and Recreation Services, N.E.C.	6,229,832	0	3,977,097	0	129.1	0.0
Membership Sports and Recreation Clubs	1,091,283	0	598,034	0	38.4	0.0
State & Local Government - Non-Education	1,723,523	0	1,723,521	0	57.1	0.0
Total	112,194,713	7,780,347	50,721,850	5,013,407	1,671.6	151.0

Table 4-18. Economic Impacts of Combined Annual Trip and Equipment Expenditures for Private Boat Fishing Near Oil/Gas Structures in the Coastal Counties of Texas

Sector	Economic Output (in $)		Value Added (in $)		Employment (in FTEs)	
	Coastal Resident	Non-Coastal Resident	Coastal Resident	Non-Coastal Resident	Coastal Resident	Non-Coastal Resident
Charter/Party Boat	0	0	0	0	0.0	0.0
Motors and Generators	0	0	0	0	0.0	0.0
Electrical Equipment, N.E.C.	0	0	0	0	0.0	0.0
Boat Building and Repairing	7,620,842	0	2,438,669	0	71.1	0.0
Transportation Equipment, N.E.C	0	0	0	0	0.0	0.0
Sporting and Athletic Goods, N.E.C.	16,767,311	3,300,649	8,719,002	1,821,226	165.8	35.3
Communications, Except Radio and TV	303,102	0	227,326	0	1.5	0.0
Food Stores	3,606,238	972,493	3,101,365	749,482	121.9	25.4
Automotive Dealers & Service Stations	10,189,865	2,896,409	7,744,298	2,036,946	153.6	41.5
Apparel & Accessory Stores	224,189	587,333	150,207	379,903	6.5	13.1
Eating & Drinking	2,174,632	5,371,214	1,109,062	2,904,119	61.2	115.0
Miscellaneous Retail	720,607	0	526,043	0	28.2	0.0
Hotels and Lodging Places	2,129,794	6,089,266	1,192,685	3,569,771	41.7	102.8
Automobile Rental and Leasing	0	0	0	0	0.0	0.0
Amusement and Recreation Services, N.E.C.	3,861,646	403,964	2,162,522	236,117	152.4	11.1
Membership Sports and Recreation Clubs	174,587	0	99,514	0	5.7	0.0
State & Local Government - Non-Education	488,822	0	488,822	0	13.6	0.0
Total	48,261,635	19,621,327	27,959,515	11,697,565	823.4	344.2

Charter Boat Fishing

Tables 4-19 to 4-22 present economic impact estimates associated with charter boat fishing near oil and gas structures from Alabama to Texas. These impact estimates reflect the distribution of trips between coastal and non-coastal residents and the differences in expenditures between the two groups. The economic impacts (output, value added, and employment) of coastal resident expenditures in all states, with the exception of Louisiana, are significantly less than impacts of non-coastal residents. The differences are due to the large number of non-coastal residents in this mode. The overall level of economic impact for charter boat fishing in each state was much lower than for private boat fishing due to the smaller number of trips in this mode and the limited equipment expenditures by both coastal and non-coastal residents.

The primary sources of economic impacts from coastal resident expenditures across all four states were in the charter/party boat sector, the automotive dealers and service stations sector (fuel and gasoline), the food stores sector (groceries), the eating and drinking sectors (restaurants), the sporting and athletic goods sector (fishing tackle, etc.), and the amusement and recreation services sector (marina services).

Similarly, the economic impacts of non-coastal residents who fished on charter boats near oil/gas structures were concentrated in the charter/party boat sector, the automotive dealers and service stations sector, the hotels and lodging sectors, and food related sectors (food stores and eating and drinking sectors). There were no impacts in the boating equipment related sectors of the coastal counties in any of the four states due to the lack of equipment purchases by non-coastal residents (Tables 4-5 to 4-8). The largest economic impacts attributable to non-coastal resident trips to oil/gas structures occurred in Texas and Alabama. Although the total number of charter boat trips near oil/gas structures in Texas was more than three times higher than in Alabama, the overall level of economic impacts in the two states were relatively similar. This was due to a higher overall level of trip expenditures by non-coastal residents in Alabama as compared to Texas.

Table 4-19. Economic Impacts of Combined Annual Trip and Equipment Expenditures for Charter Boat Fishing Near Oil/Gas Structures in the Coastal Counties of Alabama

Sector	Economic Output (in $)		Value Added (in $)		Employment (in FTEs)	
	Coastal Resident	Non-Coastal Resident	Coastal Resident	Non-Coastal Resident	Coastal Resident	Non-Coastal Resident
Charter/Party Boat	0	11,457,671	0	4,799,858	0.0	220.4
Motors and Generators	0	0	0	0	0.0	0.0
Electrical Equipment, N.E.C.	0	0	0	0	0.0	0.0
Boat Building and Repairing	0	0	0	0	0.0	0.0
Transportation Equipment, N.E.C	0	0	0	0	0.0	0.0
Sporting and Athletic Goods, N.E.C.	101,373	460,067	51,109	242,272	1.1	5.3
Communications, Except Radio and TV	2,482	0	1,856	0	0.0	0.0
Food Stores	14,393	661,469	12,318	515,032	0.5	19.2
Automotive Dealers & Service Stations	6,207	0	4,728	0	0.1	0.0
Apparel & Accessory Stores	0	0	0	0	0.0	0.0
Eating & Drinking	7,197	3,076,670	3,553	1,621,584	0.2	75.3
Miscellaneous Retail	0	6,208	0	4,289	0.0	0.2
Hotels and Lodging Places	0	1,053,626	0	597,600	0.0	20.5
Automobile Rental and Leasing	0	0	0	0	0.0	0.0
Amusement and Recreation Services, N.E.C.	0	0	0	0	0.0	0.0
Membership Sports and Recreation Clubs	0	0	0	0	0.0	0.0
State & Local Government - Non-Education	6,618	0	6,618	0	0.2	0.0
Total	138,270	16,715,710	80,181	7,780,635	2.1	340.9

Table 4-20. Economic Impacts of Combined Annual Trip and Equipment Expenditures for Charter Boat Fishing Near Oil/Gas Structures in the Coastal Counties of Mississippi

Sector	Economic Output (in $)		Value Added (in $)		Employment (in FTEs)	
	Coastal Resident	Non-Coastal Resident	Coastal Resident	Non-Coastal Resident	Coastal Resident	Non-Coastal Resident
Charter/Party Boat	0	272,309	0	91,882	0.0	8.4
Motors and Generators	0	0	0	0	0.0	0.0
Electrical Equipment, N.E.C.	0	0	0	0	0.0	0.0
Boat Building and Repairing	0	0	0	0	0.0	0.0
Transportation Equipment, N.E.C	0	0	0	0	0.0	0.0
Sporting and Athletic Goods, N.E.C.	378,002	0	197,479	0	4.4	0.0
Communications, Except Radio and TV	3,653	0	2,732	0	0.0	0.0
Food Stores	9,038	1,310,125	7,735	1,022,879	0.3	39.4
Automotive Dealers & Service Stations	112,970	0	86,044	0	2.1	0.0
Apparel & Accessory Stores	0	0	0	0	0.0	0.0
Eating & Drinking	310,668	332,562	145,521	167,949	9.9	8.8
Miscellaneous Retail	178,493	0	130,726	0	6.7	0.0
Hotels and Lodging Places	0	1,475,787	0	841,553	0.0	28.3
Automobile Rental and Leasing	0	0	0	0	0.0	0.0
Amusement and Recreation Services, N.E.C.	0	0	0	0	0.0	0.0
Membership Sports and Recreation Clubs	30,747	0	17,276	0	1.0	0.0
State & Local Government - Non-Education	189,528	26,794	189,528	23,066	6.5	0.7
Total	1,213,097	3,417,577	777,039	2,147,329	31.0	85.6

Table 4-21. Economic Impacts of Combined Annual Trip and Equipment Expenditures for Charter Boat Fishing Near Oil/Gas Structures in the Coastal Counties of Louisiana

Sector	Economic Output (in $)		Value Added (in $)		Employment (in FTEs)	
	Coastal Resident	Non-Coastal Resident	Coastal Resident	Non-Coastal Resident	Coastal Resident	Non-Coastal Resident
Charter/Party Boat	466,079	1,288,736	161,110	573,064	14.6	32.0
Motors and Generators	0	0	0	0	0.0	0.0
Electrical Equipment, N.E.C.	0	0	0	0	0.0	0.0
Boat Building and Repairing	0	0	0	0	0.0	0.0
Transportation Equipment, N.E.C	0	0	0	0	0.0	0.0
Sporting and Athletic Goods, N.E.C.	488,094	51,912	202,412	24,280	7.1	0.7
Communications, Except Radio and TV	4,329	0	3,237	0	0.0	0.0
Food Stores	92,888	0	79,497	0	3.2	0.0
Automotive Dealers & Service Stations	81,974	0	62,436	0	1.4	0.0
Apparel & Accessory Stores	49,234	0	32,750	0	1.6	0.0
Eating & Drinking	200,217	10,966	99,714	5,801	5.9	0.3
Miscellaneous Retail	16,739	10,942	12,260	7,515	0.6	0.3
Hotels and Lodging Places	190,370	129,243	107,869	75,814	3.7	2.3
Automobile Rental and Leasing	0	0	0	0	0.0	0.0
Amusement and Recreation Services, N.E.C.	0	0	0	0	0.0	0.0
Membership Sports and Recreation Clubs	1,896	0	1,039	0	0.1	0.0
State & Local Government - Non-Education	19,703	46,527	19,703	39,207	0.7	1.2
Total	1,611,523	1,538,326	782,026	725,680	38.7	36.7

68

Table 4-22. Economic Impacts of Combined Annual Trip and Equipment Expenditures for Charter Boat Fishing Near Oil/Gas Structures in the Coastal Counties of Texas

Sector	Economic Output (in $)		Value Added (in $)		Employment (in FTEs)	
	Coastal Resident	Non-Coastal Resident	Coastal Resident	Non-Coastal Resident	Coastal Resident	Non-Coastal Resident
Charter/Party Boat	1,759,119	12,359,333	476,076	4,968,206	44.1	248.9
Motors and Generators	0	0	0	0	0.0	0.0
Electrical Equipment, N.E.C.	0	0	0	0	0.0	0.0
Boat Building and Repairing	0	0	0	0	0.0	0.0
Transportation Equipment, N.E.C	0	0	0	0	0.0	0.0
Sporting and Athletic Goods, N.E.C.	1,039,362	0	540,468	0	10.3	0.0
Communications, Except Radio and TV	43,736	0	32,802	0	0.2	0.0
Food Stores	447,874	930,205	385,171	716,892	15.1	24.3
Automotive Dealers & Service Stations	75,923	0	57,701	0	1.1	0.0
Apparel & Accessory Stores	0	0	0	0	0.0	0.0
Eating & Drinking	248,219	2,019,519	126,592	1,091,918	7.0	43.2
Miscellaneous Retail	46,406	504,084	33,877	344,385	1.8	14.3
Hotels and Lodging Places	0	941,331	0	551,846	0.0	15.9
Automobile Rental and Leasing	0	0	0	0	0.0	0.0
Amusement and Recreation Services, N.E.C.	0	0	0	0	0.0	0.0
Membership Sports and Recreation Clubs	32,140	0	18,320	0	1.1	0.0
State & Local Government - Non-Education	69,070	266,718	69,070	224,506	1.9	5.9
Total	3,761,848	17,021,190	1,740,076	7,897,753	82.7	352.5

Party Boat Fishing

Tables 4-23 and 4-24 present economic impact estimates associated with party boat fishing near oil and gas structures in Louisiana and Texas, respectively. Because there were no party boat trips to oil and gas structures in Alabama and Mississippi, no impact estimates are provided for these states. As in the previous impact tables, the impact estimates for party boats reflect the distribution of trips between coastal and non-coastal residents and the differences in expenditures between the two groups. In Louisiana, the economic impacts (output, value added, and employment) of coastal and non-coastal resident expenditures in all states are very similar as was the number of trips taken by each group. In Texas, coastal residents impacts were significantly less than those of non-coastal residents due to the large number of non-coastal resident trips and participants in this mode. The overall level of economic impact for party boat fishing in each state was much lower than for both private and charter boat fishing due to the smaller number of trips in this mode and the lack of equipment expenditures by both coastal and non-coastal residents.

The primary sources of economic impacts from coastal resident expenditures in Louisiana and Texas were in the charter/party boat sector, the automotive dealers and service stations sector (fuel and gasoline), the food stores sector (groceries), the eating and drinking sectors (restaurants), and the sporting and athletic goods sector (fishing tackle, etc.). Similarly, the economic impacts of non-coastal residents who fished on charter boats near oil/gas structures were concentrated in the charter/party boat sector, the automotive dealers and service stations sector, the hotels and lodging sectors, and food related sectors (food stores and eating and drinking sectors). There were no impacts in the boating equipment related sectors of the coastal counties due to the lack of boating equipment purchases by non-coastal residents (Tables 4-5 to 4-8). The largest economic impacts attributable to non-coastal resident trips to oil/gas structures occurred in Texas.

Table 4-23. Economic Impacts of Combined Annual Trip and Equipment Expenditures for Party Boat Fishing Near Oil/Gas Structures in the Coastal Counties of Louisiana

Sector	Economic Output (in $)		Value Added (in $)		Employment (in FTEs)	
	Coastal Resident	Non-Coastal Resident	Coastal Resident	Non-Coastal Resident	Coastal Resident	Non-Coastal Resident
Charter/Party Boat	215,586	590,846	74,522	262,732	6.8	14.7
Motors and Generators	0	0	0	0	0.0	0.0
Electrical Equipment, N.E.C.	0	0	0	0	0.0	0.0
Boat Building and Repairing	0	0	0	0	0.0	0.0
Transportation Equipment, N.E.C	0	0	0	0	0.0	0.0
Sporting and Athletic Goods, N.E.C.	21,033	89,993	8,722	42,090	0.3	1.3
Communications, Except Radio and TV	6,135	0	4,587	0	0.0	0.0
Food Stores	70,109	0	60,003	0	2.4	0.0
Automotive Dealers & Service Stations	60,995	0	46,457	0	1.0	0.0
Apparel & Accessory Stores	0	0	0	0	0.0	0.0
Eating & Drinking	77,120	95,052	38,408	50,285	2.3	2.2
Miscellaneous Retail	13,321	0	9,756	0	0.5	0.0
Hotels and Lodging Places	127,949	25,006	72,499	14,668	2.5	0.4
Automobile Rental and Leasing	0	0	0	0	0.0	0.0
Amusement and Recreation Services, N.E.C.	0	0	0	0	0.0	0.0
Membership Sports and Recreation Clubs	0	0	0	0	0.0	0.0
State & Local Government - Non-Education	37,976	0	37,976	0	1.3	0.0
Total	630,223	800,897	352,930	369,776	17.0	18.6

Table 4-24. Economic Impacts of Combined Annual Trip and Equipment Expenditures for Party Boat Fishing Near Oil/Gas Structures in the Coastal Counties of Texas

Sector	Economic Output (in $)		Value Added (in $)		Employment (in FTEs)	
	Coastal Resident	Non-Coastal Resident	Coastal Resident	Non-Coastal Resident	Coastal Resident	Non-Coastal Resident
Charter/Party Boat	945,491	2,389,290	255,881	960,447	23.7	48.1
Motors and Generators	0	0	0	0	0.0	0.0
Electrical Equipment, N.E.C.	0	0	0	0	0.0	0.0
Boat Building and Repairing	0	0	0	0	0.0	0.0
Transportation Equipment, N.E.C	0	0	0	0	0.0	0.0
Sporting and Athletic Goods, N.E.C.	1,245,005	314,978	647,403	173,798	12.3	3.4
Communications, Except Radio and TV	45,068	0	33,801	0	0.2	0.0
Food Stores	223,932	459,556	192,581	354,171	7.6	12.0
Automotive Dealers & Service Stations	105,248	0	79,988	0	1.6	0.0
Apparel & Accessory Stores	0	0	0	0	0.0	0.0
Eating & Drinking	179,146	2,826,863	91,364	1,528,434	5.0	60.5
Miscellaneous Retail	149,288	0	108,980	0	5.9	0.0
Hotels and Lodging Places	0	0	0	0	0.0	0.0
Automobile Rental and Leasing	0	0	0	0	0.0	0.0
Amusement and Recreation Services, N.E.C.	0	0	0	0	0.0	0.0
Membership Sports and Recreation Clubs	33,801	0	19,267	0	1.1	0.0
State & Local Government - Non-Education	27,323	0	27,323	0	0.8	0.0
Total	2,954,301	5,990,688	1,456,588	3,016,851	58.2	124.0

Recreational Diving

Tables 4-25 to 4-27 present economic impact estimates associated with recreational diving near oil and gas structures from Alabama to Louisiana. With the exception of Louisiana, the impact estimates are small relative to the other modes. In all states, coastal residents dominated participation. The economic impacts (output, value added, and employment) of coastal resident expenditures in all states are significantly greater than impacts of non-coastal residents. Most of these impacts, however, were concentrated in the automotive dealers and service station sector, the sporting goods and athletic goods sector, and the food products sectors. Impacts generated by equipment expenditures by either coastal or non-coastal divers were negligible.

Table 4-25. Economic Impacts of Combined Annual Trip and Equipment Expenditures for Private Diving Near Oil/Gas Structures in the Coastal Counties of Alabama

Sector	Economic Output (in $)		Value Added (in $)		Employment (in FTEs)	
	Coastal Resident	Non-Coastal Resident	Coastal Resident	Non-Coastal Resident	Coastal Resident	Non-Coastal Resident
Charter/Party Boat	0	0	0	0	0.0	0.0
Motors and Generators	0	0	0	0	0.0	0.0
Electrical Equipment, N.E.C.	0	0	0	0	0.0	0.0
Boat Building and Repairing	0	0	0	0	0.0	0.0
Transportation Equipment, N.E.C	0	0	0	0	0.0	0.0
Sporting and Athletic Goods, N.E.C.	15,468	0	7,798	0	0.2	0.0
Communications, Except Radio and TV	1,009	0	755	0	0.0	0.0
Food Stores	38,669	0	33,095	0	1.4	0.0
Automotive Dealers & Service Stations	163,649	0	124,643	0	3.2	0.0
Apparel & Accessory Stores	0	0	0	0	0.0	0.0
Eating & Drinking	38,669	0	19,091	0	1.1	0.0
Miscellaneous Retail	10,827	0	7,930	0	0.5	0.0
Hotels and Lodging Places	0	0	0	0	0.0	0.0
Automobile Rental and Leasing	0	0	0	0	0.0	0.0
Amusement and Recreation Services, N.E.C.	0	0	0	0	0.0	0.0
Membership Sports and Recreation Clubs	0	0	0	0	0.0	0.0
State & Local Government - Non-Education	18,799	0	18,799	0	0.6	0.0
Total	287,090	0	212,111	0	6.9	0.0

74

Table 4-26. Economic Impacts of Combined Annual Trip and Equipment Expenditures for Private Diving Near Oil/Gas Structures in the Coastal Counties of Mississippi

Sector	Economic Output (in $)		Value Added (in $)		Employment (in FTEs)	
	Coastal Resident	Non-Coastal Resident	Coastal Resident	Non-Coastal Resident	Coastal Resident	Non-Coastal Resident
Charter/Party Boat	0	0	0	0	0.0	0.0
Motors and Generators	0	0	0	0	0.0	0.0
Electrical Equipment, N.E.C.	0	0	0	0	0.0	0.0
Boat Building and Repairing	0	0	0	0	0.0	0.0
Transportation Equipment, N.E.C	0	0	0	0	0.0	0.0
Sporting and Athletic Goods, N.E.C.	702,025	0	366,758	0	8.2	0.0
Communications, Except Radio and TV	0	0	0	0	0.0	0.0
Food Stores	213,801	0	182,980	0	7.8	0.0
Automotive Dealers & Service Stations	459,197	0	349,747	0	8.6	0.0
Apparel & Accessory Stores	0	0	0	0	0.0	0.0
Eating & Drinking	95,023	0	44,510	0	3.0	0.0
Miscellaneous Retail	23,756	0	17,398	0	0.9	0.0
Hotels and Lodging Places	0	0	0	0	0.0	0.0
Automobile Rental and Leasing	0	0	0	0	0.0	0.0
Amusement and Recreation Services, N.E.C.	515,478	875,447	332,243	551,991	10.1	16.1
Membership Sports and Recreation Clubs	0	0	0	0	0.0	0.0
State & Local Government - Non-Education	96,817	0	96,817	0	3.3	0.0
Total	2,106,097	875,447	1,390,454	551,991	41.9	16.1

Table 4-27. Economic Impacts of Combined Annual Trip and Equipment Expenditures for Private Diving Near Oil/Gas Structures in the Coastal Counties of Louisiana

Sector	Economic Output (in $)		Value Added (in $)		Employment (in FTEs)	
	Coastal Resident	Non-Coastal Resident	Coastal Resident	Non-Coastal Resident	Coastal Resident	Non-Coastal Resident
Charter/Party Boat	0	0	0	0	0.0	0.0
Motors and Generators	0	0	0	0	0.0	0.0
Electrical Equipment, N.E.C.	0	0	0	0	0.0	0.0
Boat Building and Repairing	0	0	0	0	0.0	0.0
Transportation Equipment, N.E.C	0	0	0	0	0.0	0.0
Sporting and Athletic Goods, N.E.C.	640,529	0	265,626	0	9.3	0.0
Communications, Except Radio and TV	0	0	0	0	0.0	0.0
Food Stores	2,135,098	64,793	1,827,312	49,909	72.6	1.8
Automotive Dealers & Service Stations	2,391,310	131,325	1,821,341	92,878	39.6	2.1
Apparel & Accessory Stores	0	0	0	0	0.0	0.0
Eating & Drinking	2,135,098	0	1,063,339	0	62.5	0.0
Miscellaneous Retail	0	0	0	0	0.0	0.0
Hotels and Lodging Places	0	491,035	0	288,041	0.0	8.7
Automobile Rental and Leasing	0	0	0	0	0.0	0.0
Amusement and Recreation Services, N.E.C.	0	0	0	0	0.0	0.0
Membership Sports and Recreation Clubs	190,424	0	104,354	0	6.7	0.0
State & Local Government - Non-Education	2,187,465	0	2,187,463	0	72.5	0.0
Total	9,679,925	687,153	7,269,436	430,829	263.3	12.5

Total Gulf Region

An overall summary of the economic impacts of recreational fishing and diving near oil/gas structures in the Gulf of Mexico is presented in Table 4-28. The summary, by state and mode, shows the aggregate impacts of both coastal and non-coastal expenditures in the coastal counties of each state. These impacts are expressed in economic output, total value added, and employment.

Private boat fishing generated the largest economic impacts across the modes in all four states. Private boat fishermen in Louisiana generated the highest overall of economic impacts followed by Texas and Alabama. Charter boat fishing generated the second largest source of economic impacts in all states except Louisiana where recreational diving was the next largest source of impacts. Party boat fishing was generally a minor source of overall impacts except in Texas.

In comparing impacts across the four states and four modes, Louisiana had the highest overall level of economic impacts due to the large private boat boating and diving components. Texas and Louisiana had the second and third highest levels of impacts, respectively.

The overall results indicate that recreational fishers and divers who took trips to oil/gas structures in the Gulf of Mexico during 1999 accounted for over $250 million in economic output in the coastal counties of the four states. This output contributed more than $135 million in income (wages and profits), rents, and indirect business taxes across the four states. In addition, more than 4,600 jobs were involved in producing the goods and services purchased by these recreational fishers and divers.

The economic impact estimates presented in this chapter can be used to inform the public as well as local, state, and federal officials about the economic activity associated with recreational fishing and diving near oil and gas platforms in the Gulf of Mexico.

Table 4-28. Total Economic Impact of Combined Annual Trip and Equipment Expenditures for Fishing and Diving Near Oil/Gas Structures in Coastal Counties by State and Mode

State	Mode	Economic Output (in $)	Value Added (in $)	Employment (in FTEs)
Alabama	private	42,644,863	17,771,068	609.1
	charter	16,853,979	7,860,816	343.0
	party	0	0	0.0
	dive	287,090	205,600	7.0
	TOTAL	59,785,933	25,837,484	959
Louisiana	private	119,975,060	55,735,257	1,822.5
	charter	3,149,849	1,507,707	75.5
	party	1,431,121	722,706	35.5
	dive	10,367,078	6,928,205	249.3
	TOTAL	134,923,108	64,893,875	2,183
Mississippi	private	24,651,800	14,743,784	459.9
	charter	4,630,674	2,924,368	116.6
	party	0	0	0.0
	dive	2,981,544	1,908,667	56.6
	TOTAL	32,264,018	19,576,820	633
Texas	private	67,882,962	39,657,080	1,167.6
	charter	20,783,038	9,637,829	435.2
	party	8,944,989	4,473,439	182.2
	dive	0	0	0.0
	TOTAL	97,610,989	53,768,348	1,785
Gulf Region	Total	324,584,048	164,076,527	5,560

Chapter 5
Private Boat Fishing Expenditures and the Incremental Effects of Oil and Gas Structures in the Gulf of Mexico

Introduction

The prior chapter focused on the level, distribution, and economic impacts of expenditures related to recreational uses of oil and gas structures in the Gulf of Mexico. The fact that these uses occur raises the question of whether the same pattern of expenditures would occur *without* oil and gas structures? To address this question, it is necessary to consider how the presence of these structures could influence recreational uses.

First, the presence of oil and gas structures may influence the decision to participate in a recreational activity such as saltwater fishing. By improving the quality of the activity, through a possible increase in catch rates, these structures may cause new participation in the activity. While this is a possibility, most research suggests that marine recreational fishing participation is determined by demographic influences such as age, gender, and race (Milon, 2000). To the extent that fishing quality does vary, it is more likely to influence species targeting and participation in particular fisheries rather than the initial decision to participate in the activity.

The presence of oil and gas structures may also influence expenditures associated with a recreational activity. Users, such as anglers, may alter their expenditures on boating and fishing related equipment to utilize structures. Or, they may change the frequency of participation in the activity. These decisions may occur for various reasons such as perceived differences in fishing quality or perceptions about other advantages offered by these structures (Milon, Holland, and Whitmarsh, 2000). Both of these effects would be reflected in the expenditures of oil/gas structure users and can be evaluated by comparing the expenditures of users and nonusers.

A framework to evaluate expenditure decisions can be developed from economic theory. Beginning with the basic proposition that individuals choose goods and services that provide the most satisfaction or, in mathematical terms, individuals maximize

$$U = F(x_1 , ..., x_n)$$

subject to a budget constraint

$$\Sigma \, p_i x_i = y$$

where U represents utility or satisfaction, x_i represents the ith good or service, p_i represents the price of the ith good or service, and y represents income. A basic Engel function can be described as

$$E_{kj} = a + by_k$$

where E represents the annual expenditures by the kth individual for the jth commodity or commodity group and a,b quantify the relationship between income and expenditures (Deaton and Muellbauer, 1986).

Extending this framework to recreational fishing and the use of oil/gas structures, the expenditure function can be expressed as

$$E_{kj} = a + by_k + \Sigma cs_k + dr_k$$

where s represents demographic and socioeconomic variables for each angler, r indicates whether the angler used an oil and gas structure during the prior year, and c,d provide additional information about the quantitative relationship between expenditures and the characteristics of the angler. This relationship indicates that income along with other factors influence the preferences of recreational anglers. In addition, the coefficient d provides information about the *incremental* effect of oil and gas structure use on angler expenditures while accounting for other factors such as age, income and gender that may also influence expenditures.

This expenditure function can be estimated using data from the survey of private boat anglers described previously in Chapter 2. Unlike the data analysis provided in Chapter 3 that was based only on users of oil and gas structures, this analysis includes both users and nonusers. The expenditure function can be estimated using standard statistical procedures such as ordinary least squares (OLS) if it is assumed that the expenditure data are normally distributed and/or there is no selectivity by individuals that may bias the estimation. If the data are not normally distributed, then an alternative estimation procedure is necessary to correct the problem. Since all the expenditure data were collected from anglers who participated in the activity, there are no 0 or negative expenditures. Also, infrequent participants, who may have low expenditures, may be underrepresented in the field and/or telephone survey results. This suggests that the data may be "censored" which would indicate that the coefficient estimates from OLS are inconsistent. A censored regression procedure (such as the Tobit model) should be used instead of OLS to correct the inconsistency (Greene, 2000).

If there is also some self-selectivity in the choice of whether to use oil/gas structures, then both OLS and a censored regression model will not account for the selectivity bias. Therefore the OLS and Tobit estimators will be inefficient. The selectivity may occur because certain types of individuals (e.g. fishing club members, residents of certain states, or anglers who target particular species) may be more likely to choose to fish near oil/gas structures. These same individuals may also be more likely to spend more for larger boats and more equipment because they derive satisfaction from these goods. These differences between individuals are not fully captured in the estimated coefficients of the OLS model or the Tobit. To evaluate the possible effects of selectivity, the basic expenditure function must be estimated using a statistical procedure that accounts for these effects and yields both efficient and consistent coefficient estimates (Maddala, 1983).

In the following section, results are presented from estimating the basic expenditure function using the sample data for private boat anglers and three alternative estimation procedures: OLS, a Tobit model, and a Selection model with a Tobit correction. The Tobit procedure utilized maximum likelihood estimation whereas the selection model procedure utilized full information maximum likelihood to account for the correlation between the site choice and expenditure decisions. The estimation results were generated with LIMDEP, a statistical software package designed to perform limited dependent variable estimation procedures (Greene, 1998). The sample data for private boat anglers were weighted to account for the differences between the proportion of oil/gas structure users and nonusers in the follow-up telephone survey as compared to the field survey (Chapter 2). The weights were calculated as:

> ((population proportion that fished near oil/gas structures on interview date in state i) ÷ (sample proportion that fished near oil/gas structures on interview date in state i)).

Predicted mean values and 95% confidence intervals are provided from each of these estimation procedures.

Statistical Results

Table 5-1 presents descriptive statistics for the variables used in the expenditure function for users and nonusers of oil/gas structures. All of the variables were constructed from data collected during the follow-up telephone survey. The dependent variable, *Expenditures*, was calculated by summing daily trip costs for trips during the prior 12 months plus annual expenditures for fishing and boating equipment. These trip costs include trips to both oil/gas structures and other non-structure sites. Annual expenditures were calculated by multiplying the daily trip costs times the reported number of days fishing at oil/gas structures and/or other sites during the past 12 months. Current period equipment expenditures are also included because these may be directly influenced by the decision whether to use an oil/gas structure during the survey year.

The *Capital Stock* variable includes fishing and equipment expenditures that were made in years prior to the survey year. Prior equipment expenditures may influence current period trip and equipment expenditures because they represent past decisions about the type of equipment infrastructure needed to fish at certain sites. For example, the purchase of a larger boat in a prior period in order to fish at offshore oil/gas structures may lead to increased fuel expenses in the current period. This relationship, however, can only be considered for current year expenditures because there is no information to determine whether anglers fished near oil/gas structures in prior years.

Income is total household income for the respondent since this measure indicates the full budget constraint facing the recreational angler. Household income data were collected as part of the telephone survey in interval categories. These categorical variables were included in the analysis rather than converting the categories to specific dollar amounts that could bias the data. The categories were: 1 = $15,000 or less, 2 = $15,001 to $25,000, 3 = $25,001 to $35,000, 4 = $35,001 to 45,000, 5= $45,001 to $60,000, 6 = $60,001 to $75,000, 7 = $75,001 to $100,000, 8 = $100,001 to $125,000, 9 = $125,001 to $150,000, 10 = $150,001 to $175,000, and 11 = $175,001 or greater. If a respondent did not disclose their household income in the survey, the mean value for the respondent's state and coastal resident status was substituted.

Louisiana, Mississippi, and Texas Resident indicator variables were included to account for differences in angler's preferences across states. These variables take a value of 1 if the angler resides in that state or a 0 if they do not. Alabama residents are included as a base for comparison and do not have a separate indicator to avoid multicollinearity.

Coastal Resident is a 0,1 variable to indicate whether the angler resided in a coastal county (using the MRFSS definition of coastal counties). *Gender* is a 0,1 variable with a 1 indicating the angler was a female. *Memberships* is also a 0,1 variable to indicate whether the angler belonged to a fishing club. *Boat Length 1 and Boat Length 2* are also 0,1 variables designed to identify whether an angler owns a boat and to distinguish small from large boats. *Boat Length 1* has a value of 1 if the boat an angler owns is less than 20 feet and *Boat Length 2* has a value of 1 if the boat is greater than 20 feet. Anglers who do not own boats are the base.

Finally, the variable *Visit Rigs* is a 0,1 variable with a value of 1 if the angler fished near oil/gas structures (a user) during the past 12 months and 0 if they did not fish near structures (a nonuser) in the past 12 months.

Descriptive statistics for each of these variables in Table 5-1 show some of the differences between users and nonusers of oil/gas structures. Average annual expenditures by users ($5,306.18) were more than double those of nonusers ($2,071.21). There was considerable variation in both groups, however, as the standard deviation was approximately 2 times larger than the mean for both groups. Similarly, the mean of capital stock for users was double that of nonusers and both groups had standard deviations that were nearly twice as large as the means. The user group had slightly higher proportions of the group from coastal counties and they were more likely to be members of fishing clubs. Also, users were more likely to own a boat than nonusers and, if they owned a boat, the boat was more likely to be greater than 20 feet in length. Note also that the proportion of the sample who fished near oil/gas structures *in the past 12 months* (.63) was considerably higher that the proportion of the field sample who fished near oil/gas structures *on the day of the field interview* (.21)(Chapter 3). This suggests that many in the user group vary their site choice over a year from fishing near rigs to fishing at other non-rig sites depending on weather, target species, or other factors.

Table 5-1. Sample Mean and Standard Deviations for Expenditure Model Variables

Variable	Non-Users (n=154)	Users (n=426)	Total Sample
Annual Trip and Equipment Expenditures ($)	2,071.21 (4756.69)*	5,306.18 (10459.31)	4,111.30 (8927.83)
Capital Stock ($)	5,701.16 (10318.52)	11,610.40 (19516.09)	9,427.75 (16950.9)
Income ($)	5.34 (1.79)	5.63 (2.25)	5.52 (2.09)
Louisana Resident (1=yes, 0=no)	0.47 (0.5)	0.31 (0.46)	0.37 (0.48)
Mississippi Resident (1=yes, 0=no)	0.13 (0.33)	0.10 (0.29)	0.11 (0.31)
Texas Resident (1=yes, 0=no)	0.23 (0.42)	0.24 (0.42)	0.23 (0.42)
Coastal Resident (1=yes, 0=no)	0.84 (0.36)	0.89 (0.31)	0.87 (0.33)
Gender (1=female, 0=male)	0.12 (0.32)	0.08 (0.27)	0.10 (0.29)
Memberships (1=yes, 0=no)	0.11 (0.31)	0.18 (0.38)	0.16 (0.36)
Own a Boat < 20ft (1=yes, 0=no)	0.38 (0.48)	0.33 (0.47)	0.35 (0.47)
Own a Boat > 20ft (1=yes, 0=no)	0.17 (0.38)	0.38 (0.48)	0.30 (0.45)
Visit Rigs (1=yes, 0=no)	0.00 (0)	1.00 (0)	0.63 (0.48)

*Standard deviations shown in parentheses.

Statistical results for the annual fishing trip and equipment expenditure function are presented in Table 5-2. The first column of coefficient estimates is the OLS estimation of the expenditure function. Several of the variables were statistically significant at the .05 level. Capital stock, Mississippi and Texas residents, fishing club members, and anglers who fished near oil/gas structures all had a positive relationship with annual expenditures. On the other hand, household income, gender, and coastal residency status were not statistically significant explanatory variables. The variables Boat Length 1,2 were dropped from the final estimation due to collinearity with the capital stock variable. The overall goodness of fit measure, adjusted R^2, indicated that 28 percent of the variation in annual expenditures was explained by the variables. This statistic suggests there was considerable variation in annual expenditures that may be attributable to other factors.

The coefficient estimate for the Visit Rigs variable in the OLS model provides one measure of the magnitude of the incremental effect of fishing near oil/gas structures on expenditures. For the sample as a whole, the average angler who fished near oil/gas structures spent $2,256.82 more per year than anglers who did not fish near these structures. This incremental effect indicates that the annual trip and equipment expenditures of users were significantly higher. It is important to note, however, that the coefficient only established an *association* between expenditures and fishing near oil/gas structures. It does not determine causation. Whether these same anglers would have reduced their level of expenditures in the absence of oil/gas structures cannot be determined with certainty. Moreover, this coefficient alone does not account for the effects of selectivity in the choice of fishing sites that will also influence the difference between anglers who fish near oil/gas structures and those who do not.

The additional statistical results in the second, third and fourth columns of Table 5-2 for the Tobit and Selection models indicate the effects of censoring and selectivity on the estimated coefficients. In the Tobit model, the coefficient estimates are the same as in the OLS model but the standard errors (reported in parentheses) have been corrected to remove the inconsistency introduced by the censored, nonnormal distribution of the expenditure data. Note that the change in the standard errors was relatively small and none of the significance levels for the coefficients changed as a result of the standard error correction. On the other hand, the dispersion parameter, Sigma, was positive and relatively large (7,515.94) indicating that the correction for nonnormality in the expenditure data distribution would yield significantly different predicted values for users and non-users. The log-likelihood ratio statistics at the bottom of Table 5-2 indicate that the model coefficients were significantly different from 0 at the .05 level.

The Selection model was estimated in two stages. The results in Table 5-2 present the first stage probit equation that was used to account for the probability of an angler choosing to participate in fishing near an oil/gas structure during the prior 12 months. The probit results were then used in a second stage estimation of the expenditure function using a Tobit model. Note that the probit model results replace the 0,1 Visit Rigs variable in the expenditure model.

The probit model results indicate that several factors influenced the probability of fishing near oil/gas structures. The capital stock, coastal resident, and membership variables were all statistically significant (at the .05 level or higher) and positively related to participation. On the other hand, the variables for Louisiana, Mississippi, and Texas residents were significant and negative indicating that anglers from these states were less likely to fish near oil/gas structures than anglers from Alabama. Also, female anglers were less likely to fish near oil/gas structures. The second stage Tobit model coefficient estimates indicate that capital stock, Mississippi and Texas residents were all statistically significant and positively related to annual expenditures. These results are comparable to the OLS model results. But, the dispersion parameter, Sigma, was once again relatively large (8834.87) and the correlation parameter, Rho, was statistically significant. The latter result indicates that self-selectivity did occur and predicted values from the selectivity model would be more reliable indicators of the differences in expenditures between users and non-users of oil and gas structures.

Table 5-2. Parameter Estimates for Alternative Models of Annual Trip and Equipment Expenditures

Variables	OLS	Tobit	Selection Probit	Selection Tobit
Constant	105.15 (1366.27)	105.15 (1354.44)	0.26 (0.22)	4,112.44 (2997.83)
Capital Stock ($)	0.21 (0.01)*	0.21 (0.01)*	1.86E-05 (0)*	0.19 (0.02)*
Income ($)	-127.68 (156)	-127.68 (154.65)	0.03 (0.02)	-236.68 (227.37)
Louisana Resident (1=yes, 0=no	932.04 (809.25)	932.04 (802.24)	-0.77 (0.13)*	1,987.11 (1857.04)
Mississippi Resident (1=yes, 0=r	7,399.56 (1140.29)*	7,399.56 (1130.42)*	-0.77 (0.2)*	13,812.50 (1570.45)*
Texas Resident (1=yes, 0=no)	2,196.20 (917.37)*	2,196.20 (909.43)*	-0.52 (0.15)*	3,966.38 (1817.54)*
Coastal Resident (1=yes, 0=no)	-664.38 (963.01)	-664.38 (954.67)	0.30 (0.15)*	-808.69 (1641.12)
Gender (1=female, 0=male)	-1,271.15 (1073.06)	-1,271.15 (1063.77)	-0.36 (0.16)*	NA
Memberships (1=yes, 0=no)	2,241.60 (900.96)*	2,241.60 (893.16)*	0.33 (0.14)*	NA
Visit Rigs (1=yes, 0=no)	2,256.82 (687.1)*	2,256.82 (681.15)*	NA	NA
Sigma	NA	7,515.94 (220.67)*	NA	8,834.87 (448.5)*
Rho	NA	NA	NA	-0.39 (0.17)*
Adjusted R^2	0.28	NA	NA	NA
Likelihood Ratio Statistic	198.68*	198.68*	20.54*	151.95*

*Significant at the 0.05 level.
NA = not applicable.

Predicted values for annual fishing trip and equipment expenditures from the OLS, Tobit, and Selection models are presented in Table 5-3. The predicted values were calculated for user and non-user groups by state and the Gulf region along with 95% confidence intervals for the regional estimates. For comparison with the predicted values, actual expenditures for these groups are reported for the weighted sample.

The results in Table 5-3 show that the single stage Tobit model produced the highest overall expenditure estimates and these predicted values were significantly larger than actual expenditures. On the other hand, the OLS model yielded the largest differences in predicted expenditures between user and non-users. For the Gulf region, the OLS estimated difference between users and non-users was $3,603 with an average of $4,619 for both groups. For the actual sample, the difference was $3,232 with an average of $4,451 for both groups. Note that the OLS model produced the largest differences between user and non-user expenditures in each state. And, the OLS model produced negative expenditure estimates for non-users in Alabama due to the fact that the OLS model did not account for the censored, nonnormal distribution of the expenditure data.

The Selection model yielded the smallest differences in predicted expenditures between users and non-users with a difference of $1,532 for the Gulf region. Also, the 95% confidence interval estimates for the Selection model results were tighter reflecting the fact that the standard error from the Selection model was smaller than the standard errors from the OLS and Tobit models. The differences in predicted expenditures between users and non-users in each state varied from a high of $5,446 in Mississippi to a low of $719 in Texas. The variation of these differences indicates that the factors determining angler expenditures in each state were relatively unique. In light of the fact that the Selection model accounted for both self-selectivity and nonnormality in the expenditure data, the Selection model predicted values were considered to be the best estimate of the effect of oil and gas structures on angler expenditures in the Gulf region.

Table 5-3. Sample Mean and Predicted Values from the Alternative Models of Annual Trip and Equipment Expenditures (In $)

Results		Sample and Predicted Means					95% Confidence	
		Alabama	Mississippi	Louisiana	Texas	Region	Lower	Upper
Sample								
	Non-Users	1,249	1,235	2,066	3,118	2,071	1,185	2,957
	Users	3,195	18,975	3,227	5,514	5,306	4,386	6,226
	Average	2,789	11,203	2,676	4,633	4,111		
OLS								
	Non-Users	-504	7,172	1,061	3,036	1,973	1,455	2,490
	Users	3,692	13,734	4,332	6,200	5,576	5,081	6,071
	Average	3,035	11,889	3,201	5,363	4,619		
Tobit								
	Non-Users	2,807	7,888	3,653	5,029	4,327	3,962	4,692
	Users	5,459	13,971	5,853	7,328	6,946	6,515	7,378
	Average	5,044	12,261	5,092	6,719	6,251		
Selection								
	Non-Users	2,045	7,436	1,973	4,262	3,159	2,721	3,597
	Users	3,658	12,882	2,825	4,981	4,691	4,198	5,183
	Average	3,405	11,350	2,531	4,791	4,284		

Summary

Many factors influence the expenditure decisions of recreational anglers. The presence of oil/gas structures may encourage anglers to alter their expenditures in boating and fishing related equipment to utilize these structures or they may change the number of trips they take. These decisions may occur for various reasons such as perceived differences in fishing quality or perceptions about other advantages offered by these structures. To estimate the *incremental* effect of oil/gas structures on angler expenditures in the Gulf of Mexico region, it is necessary to statistically account for the variety of factors that may influence these decisions. Also, it is important to recognize that statistical procedures can only establish an *association* between expenditures and fishing near oil/gas structures; they can not determine causation.

A methodology was presented that provided estimates of differences in the expected expenditures between users and non-users of oil and gas structures. The econometric estimation procedure addressed the problems of nonnormality in the sample expenditure data and the potential for self-selectivity in the choice of whether to fish near oil/gas structures. Self-selectivity is particularly important because some individuals may be more likely to choose to fish near oil/gas structures. These same individuals may also be more likely to spend more for larger boats and more equipment or to take more trips because they derive satisfaction from these expenditures.

The sample data indicated that the difference in annual trip and equipment expenditures between users and nonusers of oil and gas structures was $3,232 per angler across the Gulf region. After correcting for nonnormality in the distribution of expenditures and self-selection in the choice of fishing sites, predicted values from a Selection model indicated that the difference in expenditures between the two groups was much smaller. The predicted average expenditures for users were $4,691 with a 95% confidence interval of $4,198 to $5,183. For non-users, predicted average expenditures were $3,159 with a 95% confidence interval of $2,721 to $3,597. The resulting difference of $1,532 per angler is the most reliable estimate of the difference in annual expenditures between users and non-users of oil and gas structures across the Gulf of Mexico region. However, there was considerable variation in the predicted expenditures of users and non-users across the Gulf states. This variation indicated that the factors determining angler expenditures in each state were relatively unique. Therefore, it would not be advisable to summarize the incremental effect of oil/gas structures on angler expenditures in the Gulf of Mexico region in a single dollar figure.

Chapter 6
Results of Interviews with Charter Boat,
Party Boat, and Dive Shop Operators

Introduction

The results provided in the previous chapters are based upon data obtained directly from recreational participants. Other important groups include the for hire fishing industry and operators of dive shops that organize trips to Gulf locations. In order to include opinions from these important groups, independent surveys of for hire boat operators and dive shop operators were conducted. Results of interviews with these groups are provided in this chapter of the report.

Results of For Hire Industry Survey

As noted in Chapter 2, a total of 62 completed interviews were obtained with charter boat and party boat operators. One of these, during the course of the interview, indicated that he had not taken any charter trips during the previous 12 months and was therefore excluded from the analysis. Another captain refused early in the survey and his data could not be used. A total of 60 completed records was used in the analysis.

The distribution of respondents by state is shown in Table 6-1. Only 2 interviews were obtained with Texas for hire boat operators. This is the result of the fact that the charter boat list provided by the Gulf States Marine Fisheries Commission did not include Texas boats and QuanTech met with limited success in locating names and phone numbers of operators through directory and internet searches.

Table 6-1. Distribution of For Hire Interviews by State

State	Number	Percent
Alabama	27	45.0
Mississippi	5	8.3
Louisiana	26	43.3
Texas	2	3.4
Total	**60**	**100.0**

Responding captains were asked to indicate the number of charter boat and party boat trips they had taken during the past 12 months. The results are shown in Table 6-2. A wide range of responses was observed, with one fourth of the captains taking 25 trips a year or fewer. The mean trips reported was 83.2 annually. Table 6-2 also indicates that 46 of the 60 captains (76.6 percent) reported that one or more of these trips was taken to within 300 feet of an oil or gas structure. The mean trips annually near oil or gas structures was 30.7.

Table 6-2. Distribution of Captains by Number of Trips Taken in Past 12 Months

Number of Trips	All Trips		Trips to Oil/Gas Structures	
	Number	Percent	Number	Percent
1 – 25	15	25.0	9	19.6
26 – 50	8	13.3	7	15.2
51 – 75	7	11.7	7	15.2
76 – 100	10	16.7	9	19.6
101 – 125	5	8.3	3	6.5
126 – 150	8	13.3	6	13.0
150+	6	10.0	5	10.9
Don't Know	1	1.7		
Total	**60**	**100.0**	**46**	**100.0**

Responding captains were also asked if they considered fishing near oil and gas structures to be better, the same, or worse than at other locations. As shown in Table 6-3, the vast majority (86.7 percent) indicated that they considered fishing near oil and gas structures to be better than at other locations. Even among those captains who did not taken any fishing trips to an oil or gas structure, half of them (50.0 percent) said that fishing near oil and gas structures was better.

Table 6-3. Assessment of Fishing Quality Near Oil/Gas Structures

	No Fishing Near Rigs		Did Fish Near Rigs		Total	
	Number	Percent	Number	Percent	Number	Percent
Better	7	50.0	45	97.8	52	86.7
Same	3	21.4	0		3	5.0
Worse	1	7.1	0		1	1.7
Don't Know	3	21.5	1	2.2	4	6.6
Total	**14**	**100.0**	**46**	**100.0**	**60**	**100.0**

Those who fished near oil and gas structures were asked to indicate the species primarily targeted during those trips. Table 6-4 shows the results. The most frequently targeted species were Spotted Seatrout, King Mackerel, Red Snapper, and Red Drum.

Table 6-4. Species Targeted on Trips Near Oil/Gas Structures

Species	Number Targeting Species 1	Number Targeting Species 2	Number Targeting Species 3	Number Targeting Species 4
Amberjack	1	1	2	
Black Drum		2	2	2
Bluefish		1	3	1
Cobia	2	6	1	1
Flounder		2	1	
Grouper		3	5	1
King Mackerel	15	3	1	1
Marlin	1	1	2	
Red Drum	5	10		
Red Snapper	10	7		
Sheepshead			1	
Spotted Seatrout	16	2		
Triggerfish		1	2	1
Tuna	3	4	1	
Wahoo		2	1	

Respondents were asked to indicate how important they though the presence of oil and gas structures was to the for hire fishing industry in the Gulf of Mexico. As shown in Table 6-5, the presence of such structures was considered to be very important by 70 percent of the respondents. Only 5.0 percent indicated oil and gas structures were not too important and none of the respondents said they were not at all important.

Table 6-5. Importance of Oil/Gas Structure to the For Hire Fishing Industry

	Number	Percent
Very Important	42	70.0
Somewhat Important	11	18.3
Not Too Important	3	5.0
Not at All Important	0	0.0
Don't Know	4	6.7
Total	**60**	**100.0**

In fact, most respondents indicated that the For Hire Fishing industry would be hurt economically by the removal of oil and gas structures. As shown in Table 6-6, 83.3 percent of the respondents said the industry would be hurt by the removal of these oil and gas structures.

Table 6-6. Perceived Effect on For Hire Industry of Removal of Oil and Gas Structures

	Number	Percent
Helped by Removal	4	6.7
Hurt by Removal	50	83.3
Don't Know	6	10.0
Total	**60**	**100.0**

Finally, respondents were specifically asked if oil and gas structures should be left in place after they are no longer used to extract oil. As shown in Table 6-7, 85.0 percent responded positively.

Table 6-7. Responses to Question About Leaving Oil and Gas Structures in the Gulf in Place

	Number	Percent
Yes, Leave	51	85.0
No, Remove	4	6.7
Don't Know	5	8.3
Total	**60**	**100.0**

The results of the survey of boat operators in the for hire fishing industry indicated that oil and gas structures are frequently used as fishing locations. Most boat captains considered the fishing near these structures to be better than at other locations. The vast majority thinks the structures should be left in place after they are no longer used to extract oil or gas and believe the fishing industry would be economically harmed by their removal.

Results of Dive Shop Survey

As noted in Chapter 2, a total of 13 completed interviews were obtained with dive shop owners and managers. Of the 13 dive shops contacted, 11 (84.6 percent) reported that they provide guide boat services to divers in the Gulf of Mexico. Table 6-8 shows the numbers organizing guide boat trips and the number organizing trips specifically to oil and gas structures or artificial reefs created from oil and gas structures.

Table 6-8. Distribution of Dive Shops by Number of Gulf Dive Trips Organized in Past 12 Months

Number of Trips	Total Trips		Trips to Oil/Gas Structures	
	Number	Percent	Number	Percent
None	1	9.1	2	18.2
1 – 25	5	45.4	6	54.5
26 – 50	2	18.2	3	27.3
51 – 75	0	0.0	0	0.0
76 – 100	1	9.1	0	0.0
101+	2	18.2	0	0.0
Total	**11**	**100.0**	**11**	**100.0**

The mean number of all dive trips to the Gulf organized by the responding shops was 41.5 for a total of 456 trips. The mean number of such trips on which an oil or gas structure was visited was 13.1 for a total of 144 trips. This means that oil or gas structures were visited on 31.6 percent of all Gulf dive trips organized by these respondents. The average group size was 18 persons per trip.

Respondents were asked to indicate how important they thought the presence of oil and gas structures was to the diving industry in the Gulf of Mexico. As shown in Table 6-9, the presence of such structures was considered to be very important by 84.6 percent of the respondents. Only 15.4 percent indicated oil and gas structures were not too important or not at all important.

Table 6-9. Importance of Oil/Gas Structure to the For Hire Fishing Industry

	Number	Percent
Very Important	11	84.6
Somewhat Important	1	7.7
Not Too Important	1	7.7
Not at All Important	0	0.0
Total	**13**	**100.0**

In fact, most respondents indicated that the diving industry would be hurt economically by the removal of oil and gas structures. As shown in Table 6-10, 100.0 percent of the respondents said the industry would be hurt by the removal of these oil and gas structures.

Table 6-10. Perceived Effect on For Hire Industry of Removal of Oil and Gas Structures

	Number	Percent
Helped by Removal	0	0.0
Hurt by Removal	13	100.0
Total	**13**	**100.0**

Finally, respondents were specifically asked if oil and gas structures should be left in place after they are no longer used to extract oil. As shown in Table 6-11, 100.0 percent responded positively.

Table 6-11. Responses to Question About Leaving Oil and Gas Structures in the Gulf in Place

	Number	Percent
Yes, Leave	13	100.0
No, Remove	0	0.0
Total	**13**	**100.0**

Summary

These surveys of charter and party boat operators and dive shop managers obtained results that were consistent with the findings of the base surveys of participants described in Chapters 3 through 5. Participation in activities near oil and gas structures in the Gulf of Mexico was in the range of about one third. However, these respondent strongly expressed the opinions that the availability of such structures for recreational activities was important to their industry. The vast majority felt their industries would be economically hurt by the removal of oil and gas structures and expressed the view that these structures should be left in place after they were no longer used for oil or gas extraction.

Chapter 7
Summary and Conclusions

The results of the surveys of recreational fishermen and divers strongly indicated that the availability of oil and gas structures as well as artificial reefs created from such structures is extremely important to the coastal counties of the Gulf states. Of the 4.5 million recreational fishing trips estimated in the Gulf states from Alabama through Texas in 1999, 21.9 percent of them were within 300 feet of an oil or gas structure. Of the 83,780 estimated diving trips, 93.6 percent were within 300 feet of such a structure.

The results also indicated that multiple structures were generally visited during these recreational trips. On average, more than two structures were visited per trip, with the total annual structure-visits estimated at 2.2 million annually.

The economic activity associated with these visits was substantial. According to the analyses performed, there were $172.9 million in direct expenditures during 1999 associated with recreational visits to oil and gas structures in the Gulf states plus another $640.0 million in annual equipment-related expenditures. The total economic output in coastal associated with recreational fishing and diving near oil and gas structures in the Gulf was $324.6 million, including $164.1 million in the value added component and employment estimated at 5,560 full time equivalents.

An analysis of the incremental value of oil and gas structures for recreational activities indicated that the typical angler who visited such structures spent more than those who did not. The most reliable estimate is that anglers who visited oil and gas structures spent an additional $1,532 annually.

In summary, it can be concluded as a result of this study that there is substantial recreational activity associated with the presence of oil and gas structures in the Gulf of Mexico from Alabama through Texas and these activities have a substantial economic impact. Several issues are raised by these findings:

- Because the presence of oil and gas structures is important to recreational fishing and diving in the Gulf, consideration should be given to assuring the continued availability of at least some of these structures across the range of the Gulf Coast area, even after they are no longer used for oil or gas extraction.

- Decisions on structure removal must take into account the effects on recreational activities and the economic value they represent. It is uncertain how fishermen and divers would respond to the removal of oil and gas structures that are targets of frequent visits. If participants simply went to other locations, then the impact would be minimal. The decision to fish and dive at other places, however, may be a complex one involving such factors as distance from shore, size of structure, number of other participants at the location (i.e., crowdedness), and availability of acceptable alternatives (both at other structures and at nonstructure locations). It is possible that structure removal would result in reduced demand with a corresponding negative economic impact.

- Fishing and diving occur at oil and gas structures in large part because of the availability of marine life near such structures. While beyond the scope of the present study and not included in this report, preliminary indications from the surveys indicated that fishing success, particularly for preferred species, near oil and gas structures was at least equal to and in many cases greater than at other locations. There is, therefore, the question of the effect on marine life of the removal of structures that have been in place for decades. It is likely that any loss of marine life, or at least a reduction in its density such that fishing or diving is no longer rewarding, would have a negative impact on recreational fishing and diving coupled with the loss of economic value associated with those activities.

- The process by which fishermen and divers select the specific oil and gas structures to visit is not understood. Both the incremental value which was established in this research and the fact that fishermen and divers visit multiple structures on each trip suggest that there is a decision process which underlies the selection of particular structures for recreational activities. If a decision about removal of a specific structure is being considered, it would be extremely useful to have in hand a set of variables which are known to be associated with structure recreational usage. These might include such elements as ease of access, distance from shore, distance from boat launch sites, water depth, size and configuration of structure, history of "success" at the site, perceptions of safety, availability of recreational alternatives, and site popularity. Without an understanding of the variables that affect participants' decisions to use a particular site, decisions on structure removal cannot fully take into account the needs of recreational fishermen and divers.

- It is important that government and private interests develop and utilize decision-making processes for structure removal that include consideration of the needs of recreational fishermen and divers. Fishing and diving interests across the Gulf should be kept informed about the processes of structure removal and given opportunity to participate in such decisions. There is considerable potential for local opposition to removal of popular fishing and diving sites, especially if there are no alternatives available.

- Additional research may be required to answer questions raised by the current study:

    □ How many oil and gas structures can be removed in a particular area without resulting in a decline in the number of recreational fishing and diving trips being taken?

    □ Which of the existing structures, if any, are most frequently visited by fishermen and divers for their recreational activities?

    □ What are the characteristics of the most preferred structures?

    □ In the event of selective removal of oil and gas structures, how will the behavior of fishermen and divers change? Will they shift to other available structures, to nonstructure locations, or withdraw from the activity?

References

American Fisheries Society. 1990. Creel and Angler Surveys in Fisheries Management. International Symposium and Workshop on Creel and Angler Surveys in Fisheries Management. The American Fisheries Society, Houston, Texas. 528 pp.

Bockstael, N.E., A.R. Graefe, I.E. Strand, and D.B. Rockland. 1985. Economic Analysis of Artificial Reefs: An Assessment of Issues and Methods. Artificial Reef Development Center, Sport Fishing Institute, Washington, D.C. 94 pp.

Dauterive, L. 2000. Rigs-to-Reefs Policy, Progress, and Perspective. U.S. Department of the Interior, Minerals Management Service, Gulf of Mexico OCS Region, New Orleans, LA. OCS Report MMS 2000-073. 8 pp.

Deaton, A. and J. Meullbauer. 1986. Economic and Consumer Behavior. Cambridge: Cambridge University Press. 450 pp.

Ditton, R.B., and J. Auyong. 1984. Fishing Offshore Platforms Central Gulf of Mexico—An Analysis of Recreational and Commercial Fishing Use at 164 Major Offshore Petroleum Structures. U.S. Department of the Interior, Minerals Management Service, Gulf of Mexico OCS Region, New Orleans, LA. OCS Monograph MMS 84-0006. 158 pp.

Driessen, P.K. 1989. Offshore Oil Platforms: Mini-Ecosystems. In: Reggio, V.C., Jr. Petroleum Structures as Artificial Reefs: A Compendium. Fourth International Conference on Artificial Habitats for Fishers, Rigs-to-Reefs Special Session, Miami, FL, November 4, 1987. U.S. Department of the Interior, Minerals Management Service, Gulf of Mexico OCS Region, New Orleans, LA. OCS Study MMS 89-0021. 176 pp.

Gordon, W.R., Jr. 1993. Travel Characteristics of Marine Anglers Using Oil and Gas Platforms in the Central Gulf of Mexico. Marine Fisheries Review 55(1):25–31.

Greene, W.H. 2000. Econometric Analysis. New Jersey: Prentice Hall. 1004 pp.

Maddala, G.S. 1983. Limited-Dependent and Qualitative Variables in Econometrics. Cambridge: Cambridge University Press.

Milon, J.W. 1991. Social and Economic Evaluation of Artificial Aquatic Habitats. In: Seaman, W. and L.M. Sprague (eds). Artificial Habitats for Marine and Freshwater Fisheries. San Diego, CA: Academic Press. Pp. 237-270.

Milon, J.W. 2000. Current and Future Participation in Marine Recreational Fishing in the Southeast U.S. Region. NOAA Technical Memorandum, National Marine Fisheries Service, Washington, D.C.

Milon, J.W., S.M. Holland, and D.J. Whitmarsh. 2000. Social and Economic Evaluation Methods. In: Seaman, W. and L.M. Sprague (eds.). Artificial Habitats for Marine and Freshwater Fisheries. San Diego, CA: Academic Press. Pp. 165-194.

Miller, R.E. and P.D. Blair. 1985. Input-Output Analysis: Foundation and Extensions. New Jersey: Prentice Hall.

National Marine Fisheries Service. 1992. Marine Recreational Fishery Statistics Survey, Atlantic and Gulf Coasts, 1990 – 1991. Current Fisheries Statistics Number 9204. U.S. Department of Commerce, National Oceanic and Atmospheric Administration, Silver Spring, MD. 273 pp.

National Marine Fisheries Service. 2000. Internet site at http://remora.ssp.nmfs.gov/.

Pollock, K.H., C.M. Jones, and T.L. Brown. 1994. Angler Survey Methods and the Applications in Fisheries Management. Bethesda, Maryland: American Fisheries Society. 362 pp.

Roberts, K.J., M.E. Thompson, and P.W. Pawlyk. 1985. Contingent Valuation of Recreational Diving at Petroleum Rigs, Gulf of Mexico. Transactions of the American Fisheries Society. 114:214-219.

Stevens, B.H. and M.L. Lahr. 1988. Regional Economic Multipliers: Definition, Measurement, and Application. Economic Development Quarterly. 2:88-96.

Sutton, S.G., R.B. Ditton, J.R. Stoll, and J.W. Milon. 1999. A Cross-sectional Study and Longitudinal Perspective on the Social and Economic Characteristics of the Charter and Party Boat Fishing Industry of Alabama, Mississippi, Louisiana, and Texas. Report to the National Marine Fisheries Service under MARFIN Grant No. NA77FF0551. Human Dimension of Recreational Fisheries Research Laboratory Report No. HD-612.

Witzig, J.F. 1986. Rig Fishing in the Gulf of Mexico—1984 Marine Recreational Fishing Survey Results. In: Proceedings, Sixth Annual Gulf of Mexico Information Transfer Meeting. OCS Study MMS 86-0073. U.S. Department of the Interior, Minerals Management Service, Gulf of Mexico OCS Region, New Orleans, LA. Pp. 103-105.

Appendix A: Field Questionnaires
Private Boat Questionnaire
Charter Boat Questionnaire
Party Boat Questionnaire
Diver Questionnaire

1. INTERVIEWER CODE
2. YEAR/MONTH/DAY
3. INTERCEPT NO
4. TIME OF INTERVIEW

5. STATE CODE
6. COUNTY CODE
7. SITE CODE

8. Was most of your fishing effort today in...
   1. The Gulf
   2. A Sound
   3. A river
   A bay *(See List)*
   5. Other *(Specify)* _____

9. What type of gear was primarily used?

01	Hook and Line	07	Trap
02	Dip Net, A-frame	08	Spear
03	Cast Net	09	Hand
04	Gill Net	10	Other *(Specify)* _____
05	Seine	98	Don't Know/Unknown
06	Trawl	99	Refused

10. To the nearest half-hour, how many hours have you spent fishing today? That is, how many hours have you actually spent with your gear in the water?

11. Were you fishing for any particular kinds of fish today?
    (If "Yes") What species were you targeting?

12. Not counting today, within the past 12 months, that is since *(insert current month)* of last year, how many days have you gone saltwater sport fishing from a private boat launched in this state?
    998   Don't Know
    999   Refused

13. Not counting today, within the past 2 months, how many days?
    98   Don't Know
    99   Refused

14. What is the ZIP code of your residence?
    99997   Foreign Country
    99998   Don't Know
    99999   Refused

15. How many years old were you on your last birthday?
    998   Don't Know
    998   Refused

16. How many fish did you catch which are not available for me to look at?
    (RECORD TOTAL NUMBER OF UNAVAILABLE FISH BY SPECIES ON CHART)
    May I see the fish that you kept?
    (RECORD TOTAL NUMBER OF AVAILABLE FISH BY SPECIES ON CHART)

17. Was any of your private/rental boat fishing today within 300 feet of an oil or gas rig or within 300 feet of an artificial reef created from an oil or gas rig?
    1   Yes   *(CONTINUE)*
    2   No   *(GO TO QUESTION 23)*
    3   Don't know / Refused   *(TERMINATE)*

18. How many different oil or gas rigs or artificial reefs created from rigs did you fish within 300 feet of today?
    98   Don't Know / Not Sure
    99   Refused

Interviewer Note: For each rig or reef, obtain the information requested in Questions 19 through 22

19. Can you tell me the name of the first/next oil or gas rig or the reef created from a rig at which you fished today?
    1   Yes *(RECORD NAME AND THEN SKIP TO Q.22)*
    2   No *(CONTINUE TO Q.20)*

20. Can you give me the GPS coordinates (Lat./Long.) or LORAN readings for that particular rig or the reef created from a rig?
    1   Yes *(RECORD GPS COORDINATES OR LORAN READING AND THEN SKIP TO Q.22)*
    2   No *(CONTINUE TO Q.21)*

21. Here is a map which shows most of the locations at which people in our area fish. Could you indicate the location of the oil or gas rig or artificial reef?
    1   Yes *(RECORD LORAN READING FROM LOCATION INDICATED BY RESPONDENT AND THEN SKIP TO Q.22)*
    2   No *(CONTINUE)*

22. Of the (insert number of hours from Q.10) total hours you spent today with your gear in the water, how many hours did you spend fishing within 300 feet of this rig/reef?

23. As part of our study, we are trying to learn how important oil and gas rigs and reefs created from these rigs are to people who fish and dive in the Gulf. May we call you for a telephone follow-up interview to obtain more detailed information about these sites and the costs involved in getting there?
    1. Yes   *(RECORD NAME AND PHONE NUMBER)*

    2. No   *(THANK RESPONDENT)*

1. INTERVIEWER CODE ☐☐☐☐

5. STATE CODE ☐☐

6. COUNTY CODE ☐☐

2. YEAR/MONTH/DAY ⑨⑨☐☐☐

7. SITE CODE ☐☐

3. INTERCEPT NO. ☐☐

4. TIME OF INTERVIEW ☐☐☐☐ *(Use 24 Hour Clock)*

8. ☐   Where fished   9. ☐☐ Gear   10 ☐☐ • ☐ Hours

11. 1ˢᵗ Target _____ ☐☐☐☐☐☐☐   No Particular Species ☐

2ⁿᵈ Target _____ ☐☐☐☐☐☐☐

12. ☐☐☐ 12 Months   13. ☐☐ 2 Months   14. ☐☐☐☐☐ Zip   15. ☐☐☐ Age

16.

SPECIES - ACCEPTED COMMON NAME	SPECIES CODE	# OF FISH AVAILABLE	# OF FISH UNAVAILABLE
1. _____			
2. _____			
3. _____			
4. _____			
5. _____			
6. _____			

17. ☐   Oil/gas rig   18. ☐☐   Number of rigs

Rig/Reef Visited	Name (Q.19)	GPS (Q.20)		LORAN (Q.20 or Q.21)	Hours Fished (Q.22)
1		LAT. ☐☐☐☐☐☐		☐☐☐☐☐	☐☐ • ☐
		LONG. ☐☐☐☐☐☐		☐☐☐☐☐	
2		LAT. ☐☐☐☐☐☐		☐☐☐☐☐	☐☐ • ☐
		LONG. ☐☐☐☐☐☐		☐☐☐☐☐	
3		LAT. ☐☐☐☐☐☐		☐☐☐☐☐	☐☐ • ☐
		LONG. ☐☐☐☐☐☐		☐☐☐☐☐	
4		LAT. ☐☐☐☐☐☐		☐☐☐☐☐	☐☐ • ☐
		LONG. ☐☐☐☐☐☐		☐☐☐☐☐	
5		LAT. ☐☐☐☐☐☐		☐☐☐☐☐	☐☐ • ☐
		LONG. ☐☐☐☐☐☐		☐☐☐☐☐	

23. Name: _____   Telephone: (☐☐☐) ☐☐☐ — ☐☐☐☐

Circle one: Home   Office

1. INTERVIEWER CODE
2. YEAR/MONTH/DAY
3. INTERCEPT NO
4. TIME OF INTERVIEW

5. STATE CODE
6. COUNTY CODE
7. SITE CODE

8. Was most of your fishing effort today in...
   1. The Gulf
   2. A Sound
   3. A river
   A bay *(See List)*
   5. Other *(Specify)* _____

9. What type of gear was primarily used?

01	Hook and Line	07	Trap
02	Dip Net, A-frame	08	Spear
03	Cast Net	09	Hand
04	Gill Net	10	Other *(Specify)* _____
05	Seine	98	Don't Know/Unknown
06	Trawl	99	Refused

10. To the nearest half-hour, how many hours have you spent fishing today? That is, how many hours have you actually spent with your gear in the water?

11. Were you fishing for any particular kinds of fish today?
    (If "Yes") What species were you targeting?

12. Not counting today, within the past 12 months, that is since *(insert current month)* of last year, how many days have you gone saltwater sport fishing from a charter boat launched in this state?
998	Don't Know
999	Refused

13. Not counting today, within the past 2 months, how many days?
98	Don't Know
99	Refused

14. What is the ZIP code of your residence?
99997	Foreign Country
99998	Don't Know
99999	Refused

15. How many years old were you on your last birthday?
998	Don't Know
998	Refused

16. How many fish did you catch which are not available for me to look at?
    (RECORD TOTAL NUMBER OF UNAVAILABLE FISH BY SPECIES ON CHART)
    May I see the fish that you kept?
    (RECORD TOTAL NUMBER OF AVAILABLE FISH BY SPECIES ON CHART)

> Obtain the following detailed information about specific oil and gas rigs and reefs from rigs by interviewing the captain or a knowledgeable crewmember. Record the information separately on each member of the fishing party who is interviewed.

17. Was any of your charter boat fishing today within 300 feet of an oil or gas rig or within 300 feet of an artificial reef created from an oil or gas rig?
1	Yes	*(CONTINUE)*
2	No	*(GO TO QUESTION 23)*
3	Don't know / Refused	*(TERMINATE)*

18. How many different oil or gas rigs or artificial reefs created from rigs did you fish within 300 feet of today?
98	Don't Know / Not Sure
99	Refused

Interviewer Note: For each rig or reef, obtain the information requested in Questions 19 through 22.

19. Can you tell me the name of the first/next oil or gas rig or the reef created from a rig at which you fished today?
1	Yes	*(RECORD NAME AND THEN SKIP TO Q.22)*
2	No	*(CONTINUE TO Q.20)*

20. Can you give me the GPS coordinates (Lat./Long.) or LORAN readings for that particular rig or the reef created from a rig?
1	Yes	*(RECORD GPS COORDINATES OR LORAN READING AND THEN SKIP TO Q.22)*
2	No	*(CONTINUE TO Q.21)*

21. Here is a map which shows most of the locations at which people in our area fish. Could you indicate the location of the oil or gas rig or artificial reef?
1	Yes	*(RECORD LORAN READING FROM LOCATION INDICATED BY RESPONDENT AND THEN SKIP TO Q.22)*
2	No	*(CONTINUE)*

22. Of the (insert number of hours from Q.10) total hours you spent today with your gear in the water, how many hours did you spend fishing within 300 feet of this rig/reef?

23. As part of our study, we are trying to learn how important oil and gas rigs and reefs created from these rigs are to people who fish and dive in the Gulf. May we call you for a telephone follow-up interview to obtain more detailed information about these sites and the costs involved in getting there?
    1. Yes *(RECORD NAME AND PHONE NUMBER)*
    2. No *(THANK RESPONDENT)*

1. INTERVIEWER CODE

2. YEAR/MONTH/DAY 9 9

3. INTERCEPT NO.

4. TIME OF INTERVIEW   *(Use 24 Hour Clock)*

5. STATE CODE

6. COUNTY CODE

7. SITE CODE

8.   Where fished   9.   Gear   10   •   Hours

11. 1ˢᵗ Target _____

    No Particular Species

     2ⁿᵈ Target _____

12.   12 Months   13.   2 Months   14.   Zip   15.   Age

16.

SPECIES - ACCEPTED COMMON NAME	SPECIES CODE	# OF FISH AVAILABLE	# OF FISH UNAVAILABLE
1. _____			
2. _____			
3. _____			
4. _____			
5. _____			
6. _____			

17.   Oil/gas rig   18.   Number of rigs

Rig/Reef Visited	Name (Q.19)	GPS (Q.20)		LORAN (Q.20 or Q.21)	Hours Fished (Q.22)
1		LAT.			
		LONG.			
2		LAT.			
		LONG.			
3		LAT.			
		LONG.			
4		LAT.			
		LONG.			
5		LAT.			
		LONG.			

23. Name: _____   Telephone: (_____) _____ — _____

Circle one: Home   Office

1. INTERVIEWER CODE
2. YEAR/MONTH/DAY
3. INTERCEPT NO
4. TIME OF INTERVIEW

5. STATE CODE
6. COUNTY CODE
7. SITE CODE

8. Was most of your fishing effort today in...
   1. The Gulf
   2. A Sound
   3. A river
      A bay *(See List)*
   5. Other *(Specify)* _____

9. What type of gear was primarily used?

01	Hook and Line	07	Trap
02	Dip Net, A-frame	08	Spear
03	Cast Net	09	Hand
04	Gill Net	10	Other (Specify) _____
05	Seine	98	Don't Know/Unknown
06	Trawl	99	Refused

10. To the nearest half-hour, how many hours have you spent fishing today? That is, how many hours have you actually spent with your gear in the water?

11. Were you fishing for any particular kinds of fish today?
    (If "Yes") What species were you targeting?

12. Not counting today, within the past 12 months, that is since *(insert current month)* of last year, how many days have you gone saltwater sport fishing from a party boat launched in this state?
    998   Don't Know
    999   Refused

13. Not counting today, within the past 2 months, how many days?
    98   Don't Know
    99   Refused

14. What is the ZIP code of your residence?
    99997   Foreign Country
    99998   Don't Know
    99999   Refused

15. How many years old were you on your last birthday?
    998   Don't Know
    998   Refused

16. How many fish did you catch which are not available for me to look at?
    (RECORD TOTAL NUMBER OF UNAVAILABLE FISH BY SPECIES ON CHART)
    May I see the fish that you kept?
    (RECORD TOTAL NUMBER OF AVAILABLE FISH BY SPECIES ON CHART)

Obtain the following detailed information about specific oil and gas rigs and reefs from rigs by interviewing the captain or a knowledgeable crewmember. Record the information separately on each member of the fishing party who is interviewed.

17. Was any of your party boat fishing today within 300 feet of an oil or gas rig or within 300 feet of an artificial reef created from an oil or gas rig?
    1   Yes   *(CONTINUE)*
    2   No   *(GO TO QUESTION 23)*
    3   Don't know / Refused   *(TERMINATE)*

18. How many different oil or gas rigs or artificial reefs created from rigs did you fish within 300 feet of today?
    98   Don't Know / Not Sure
    99   Refused

Interviewer Note: For each rig or reef, obtain the information requested in Questions 19 through 22.

19. Can you tell me the name of the first/next oil or gas rig or the reef created from a rig at which you fished today?
    1   Yes   *(RECORD NAME AND THEN SKIP TO Q.22)*
    2   No   *(CONTINUE TO Q.20)*

20. Can you give me the GPS coordinates (Lat./Long.) or LORAN readings for that particular rig or the reef created from a rig?
    1   Yes   *(RECORD GPS COORDINATES OR LORAN READING AND THEN SKIP TO Q.22)*
    2   No   *(CONTINUE TO Q.21)*

21. Here is a map which shows most of the locations at which people in our area fish. Could you indicate the location of the oil or gas rig or artificial reef?
    1   Yes   *(RECORD LORAN READING FROM LOCATION INDICATED BY RESPONDENT AND THEN SKIP TO Q.22)*
    2   No   *(CONTINUE)*

22. Of the (insert number of hours from Q.10) total hours you spent today with your gear in the water, how many hours did you spend fishing within 300 feet of this rig/reef?

23. As part of our study, we are trying to learn how important oil and gas rigs and reefs created from these rigs are to people who fish and dive in the Gulf. May we call you for a telephone follow-up interview to obtain more detailed information about these sites and the costs involved in getting there?
    1. Yes   *(RECORD NAME AND PHONE NUMBER)*

1. INTERVIEWER CODE   □ □ □ □   5.   STATE CODE   □ □

6.   COUNTY CODE   □ □

2. YEAR/MONTH/DAY   [9] [9] □ □ □ □   7.   SITE CODE   □ □ □

3. INTERCEPT NO.   □ □

4. TIME OF INTERVIEW   □ □ □ □   *(Use 24 Hour Clock)*

---

8. □   Where fished   9. □ □   Gear   10 □ □ • □   Hours

11. 1ˢᵗ Target _____   □ □ □ □ □ □ □ □   No Particular Species □

     2ⁿᵈ Target _____   □ □ □ □ □ □ □ □

12. □ □   12 Months   13. □ □   2 Months   14. □ □ □ □ □   Zip   15. □ □   Age

---

16.

SPECIES - ACCEPTED COMMON NAME	SPECIES CODE	# OF FISH AVAILABLE	# OF FISH UNAVAILABLE
1. _____			
2. _____			
3. _____			
4. _____			
5. _____			
6. _____			

17. □   Oil/gas rig   18. □ □   Number of rigs

Rig/Reef Visited	Name (Q.19)	GPS (Q.20)		LORAN (Q.20 or Q.21)	Hours Fished (Q.22)
1		LAT.			□ □ • □
		LONG.			
2		LAT.			□ □ • □
		LONG.			
3		LAT.			□ □ • □
		LONG.			
4		LAT.			□ □ • □
		LONG.			
5		LAT.			□ □ • □
		LONG.			

23.   Name:_____   Telephone: (□ □ □) □ □ □ — □ □ □ □

Circle one: Home   Office

1. INTERVIEWER CODE	5. STATE CODE
2. YEAR/MONTH/DAY	6. COUNTY CODE
3. INTERCEPT NO	7. SITE CODE
4. TIME OF INTERVIEW	

8. Was any of your diving today within 300 feet of an oil or gas rig or within 300 feet of an artificial reef created from an oil or gas rig?

    1   Yes   *(CONTINUE)*

    2   No   *(GO TO QUESTION 23)*

    3   Don't know / Refused   *(TERMINATE)*

9. How many different oil or gas rigs or artificial reefs created from rigs did you dive within 300 feet of today?

    98   Don't Know / Not Sure

    99   Refused

> **Interviewer Note:** For each rig or reef, obtain the information requested in Questions 10 through 14.

10. Can you tell me the name of the first/next oil or gas rig or the reef created from a rig at which you dove today?

    1   Yes   *(RECORD NAME AND THEN SKIP TO Q.13)*

    2   No   *(CONTINUE TO Q.11)*

11. Can you give me the GPS coordinates (Lat./Long.) or LORAN readings for that particular rig or the reef created from a rig?

    1   Yes   *(RECORD GPS COORDINATES OR LORAN READING AND THEN SKIP TO Q.13)*

    2   No   *(CONTINUE TO Q.12)*

12. Here is a map that shows most of the locations at which people in our area fish. Could you indicate the location of the oil or gas rig or artificial reef?

    1   Yes   *(RECORD LORAN READING FROM LOCATION INDICATED BY RESPONDENT AND THEN SKIP TO Q.13)*

    2   No   *(CONTINUE)*

13. Of the (insert number of hours from Q.10) total hours you spent today diving, how many hours did you spend within 300 feet of this rig/reef?

14. As part of our study, we are trying to learn how important oil and gas rigs and reefs created from these rigs are to people who fish and dive in the Gulf. May we call you for a telephone follow-up interview to obtain more detailed information about these sites and the costs involved in getting there?

    1.   Yes   *(RECORD NAME AND PHONE NUMBER)*

    2.   No   *(THANK RESPONDENT)*

1. INTERVIEWER CODE [   ][   ][   ]

2. YEAR/MONTH/DAY [9][9][   ][   ][   ]

3. INTERCEPT NO. [   ][   ]

4. TIME OF INTERVIEW [   ][   ][   ] *(Use 24 Hour Clock)*

5. STATE CODE [   ][   ]

6. COUNTY CODE [   ][   ]

7. SITE CODE [   ][   ][   ]

8. [   ] Oil/gas rig   9. [   ][   ] Number of rigs

Rig/Reef Visited	Name (Q.10)	GPS (Q.11)		LORAN (Q.11 or Q.12)	Hours Fished (Q.13)
1		LAT. [ ][ ][ ][ ][ ][ ]		[ ][ ][ ][ ][ ]	[ ][ ].[ ]
		LONG. [ ][ ][ ][ ][ ][ ]		[ ][ ][ ][ ][ ]	
2		LAT. [ ][ ][ ][ ][ ][ ]		[ ][ ][ ][ ][ ]	[ ][ ].[ ]
		LONG. [ ][ ][ ][ ][ ][ ]		[ ][ ][ ][ ][ ]	
3		LAT. [ ][ ][ ][ ][ ][ ]		[ ][ ][ ][ ][ ]	[ ][ ].[ ]
		LONG. [ ][ ][ ][ ][ ][ ]		[ ][ ][ ][ ][ ]	
4		LAT. [ ][ ][ ][ ][ ][ ]		[ ][ ][ ][ ][ ]	[ ][ ].[ ]
		LONG. [ ][ ][ ][ ][ ][ ]		[ ][ ][ ][ ][ ]	
5		LAT. [ ][ ][ ][ ][ ][ ]		[ ][ ][ ][ ][ ]	[ ][ ].[ ]
		LONG. [ ][ ][ ][ ][ ][ ]		[ ][ ][ ][ ][ ]	

14. Name:_____   Telephone: ([   ][   ][   ]) [   ][   ][   ] — [   ][   ][   ][   ]

Circle one: Home   Office

Appendix B: Telephone Questionnaires
 Private Boat Follow-up Questionnaire
 Charter Boat Follow-up Questionnaire
 Party Boat Follow-up Questionnaire
 Diver Follow-up Questionnaire

Private Boat Followup Telephone Survey

[ORIGNUM]   Telephone number

[NAME]   Name of respondent

[ID]   ID number

[STATE]   State of field interview

[TRIPDATE]   Date of field interview

[MODE_FX]   Mode of fishing

[UNIQUE]   Unique ID code linking to field interview

[MARKET]   Mode of fishing

[INTDATE]   Date of telephone interview

[RESI]   1 = Coastal resident; 2 = noncoastal

[CTY]   Location of residence for noncoastal respondents

[ANG_TYP]   1 = hook and line

Hello, this is _____ calling from QuanTech in Rosslyn, Virginia. You recently spoke with one of our field staff members during your day of fishing in _____[STATE] on _____[TRIPDATE].

We are calling now with a follow-up to that survey to collect more detailed information that could not be collected in the field. As our interviewer who spoke with you in the field mentioned, we are evaluating the importance of oil and gas rigs in the Gulf of Mexico to recreational fishermen. One of the things I will be asking you about is how much it costs you to go fishing in the Gulf. This study is being conducted in accordance with the privacy act of 1974 and your answers will be kept completely confidential.

[ONE]

1.   When our interviewer spoke with you on [INSERT TRIP DATE] you said that, not counting the day on which you were interviewed, you had been saltwater sport finfishing _____ [NUMBER OF DAYS] in _____[NAME OF STATE] within the past 12 months. On how many of those days did you fish from a privately owned or rental boat within 300 feet of an oil or gas rig or within 300 feet of an artificial reef created from an oil or gas rig?

DON'T KNOW = 998
REFUSED   = 999

[TWO]

2.   When our interviewer spoke with you on TRIP DATE] you said that, not counting the day on which you were interviewed, you had been saltwater sport finfishing _____[NUMBER OF DAYS] in [NAME OF STATE] within the past 2 months. On how many of those days did you fish from a privately owned or rental boat within 300 feet of an oil or gas rig or within 300 feet of an artificial reef created from an oil or gas rig?

DON'T KNOW = 998
REFUSED   = 999

[THREE]

3.   On the trip of _____[TRIP DATE] did you do any diving within 300 feet of an oil or gas platform or within 300 feet of an artificial reef created from an oil or gas rig?

    YES   1
    NO   2
    DK   8
    REF   9

[FOUR]

4.   Was the fishing you did on [TRIPDATE] part of a longer trip in which you spent at least one night away from your primary residence?

    YES   1
    NO   2 (skip to q.15A)
    DK   8 (skip to q.15A)
    REF   9 (skip to q.15A)

[FIVE]

5.   How many nights were you away from your residence on this trip?

DON'T KNOW = 98
REFUSED   = 99

B2

[SIX]

6. On how many days of that trip did you fish?

DON'T KNOW = 98
REFUSED = 99

[SEVEN]

7. Did you travel to the place where you stayed overnight by privately owned car, plane, train, or other means?

PRIVATELY OWNED CAR 1 *(skip to q.11)*
TRAIN 2
BUS 3
AIRPLANE 4
OTHER 5 (SPECIFY: _____ **[SEVENOT]**_____)
DK 8
REF 9

[EIGHT]

8 What did you personally pay for your transportation?

DON'T kNOW = 9998
REFUSED = 9999

[NINE]

9. Did you personally pay for use of a rental car on the trip?

YES 1
NO 2 (skip to q.11)
DK 8 (skip to q.11)
REF 9 (skip to q.11)

[TEN]

10. What did you personally pay for the rental car?

DON'T KNOW = 9998
REFUSED = 9999

[ELEVEN]

11. Since you stayed at least one evening overnight, I need some information about your lodging. Did you stay overnight on a boat, in a hotel or motel, at a campground, with family or friends, in a second residence which you own or rent permanently, or in some other type of lodging?

        ON A BOAT   1 (go to q.16)
        HOTEL/MOTEL   2
        CAMPGROUND   3
        FAMILY/FRIENDS   4
        SECONDARY RESIDENCE 5
        OTHER   6 (specify:____[ELEVENOT]_____)
        DK   8
        REF   9

[TWELVE]

12.   In what city or town was that lodging located?

        NAME OF CITY OR TOWN_____

[THIRTEEN]

13. How much did you personally pay per night for the lodging associated with this fishing trip?

        | | | | |

        DON'T KNOW = 9998
        REFUSED   = 9999

[FOURTEEN]

14. Approximately how many miles did you travel <u>one-way</u> from your residence to the place where you stayed overnight on that trip?

        | | | | |

        DON'T KNOW = 9998
        REFUSED   = 9999

[FIFTEEN]

15. Approximately how many miles did you travel from where you stayed overnight on that trip to the boat launch site?

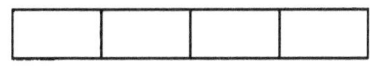

DON'T KNOW = 9998
REFUSED = 9999

(Skip to Q.16)

[FIFTEENA]

15A. Approximately how many miles did you travel from your home to the boat launch site?

DON'T KNOW = 9998
REFUSED = 9999

[SIXTEEN]

16. Did you personally spend any money associated with your fishing trip on the day in which we interviewed you in the field? You might not have paid anything personally, for example, if someone else in your party made the payments on your behalf. Did you personally spend any money on your fishing that day?

YES   1
NO   2 *(go to q.20)*
DK   8 *(go to q.20)*
REF   9 *(go to q.20)*

[SEVTN_1 through NINTN_15]

17. I'm going to ask you a series of questions about your own personal expenditures on the day of the fishing trip in which we interviewed you in the field. As I read the following list, please remember that I'm only interested in items for which you personally paid. On the fishing trip on [TRIP DATE] did you personally spend any money

	SEVTN_ DID YOU SPEND MONEY ON? Yes = 1 No = 2 DK = 8 REF = 9	EIGTN_ IF YES 18. Thinking about your own personal expenditures [USING RESPONSE FROM ITEM 17], how much would you estimate you spent on that day of fishing?	NINTN_ IF YES 19. Of that amount, approximately how much of it would you say was spent within **15 miles** of the boat launch site?
1. In restaurants or bars for food and drink?	SEVTN_1	EIGTN_1	NINTN_1
2. In grocery or convenience stores for food, drinks, or ice?	SEVTN_2	EIGTN_2	NINTN_2
3. At a service station or marina for fuel?	SEVTN_3	EIGTN_3	NINTN_3
4. At a boat dock or marina for boat rental?	SEVTN_4	EIGTN_4	NINTN_4
5. At a boat ramp, dock, or marina for boat launch fees?	SEVTN_5	EIGTN_5	NINTN_5
6. At a dock or marina for docking fees?	SEVTN_6	EIGTN_6	NINTN_6
7. For boat repairs or towing?	SEVTN_7	EIGTN_7	NINTN_7
8. For bait?	SEVTN_8	EIGTN_8	NINTN_8
9. For fishing licenses?	SEVTN_9	EIGTN_9	NINTN_9
10. For fishing tackle which you used that day?	SEVTN_10	EIGTN_10	NINTN_10
11. For the rental of any equipment other than a boat?	SEVTN_11	EIGTN_11	NINTN_11
12. For any special clothing which you wore on the day of the trip?	SEVTN_12	EIGTN_12	NINTN_12

	SEVTN_ DID YOU SPEND MONEY ON? Yes = 1 No = 2 DK = 8 REF = 9	EIGTN_ IF YES 18. Thinking about your own personal expenditures [USING RESPONSE FROM ITEM 17], how much would you estimate you spent on that day of fishing?	NINTN_ IF YES 19. Of that amount, approximately how much of it would you say was spent within **15 miles** of the boat launch site?
13. For sundries such as suntan lotions or bug repellent which you used on the trip?	SEVTN_13	EIGTN_13	NINTN_13
14. For film or souvenirs?	SEVTN_14	EIGTN_14	NINTN_14
15. For the services of a fishing guide who accompanied you on your trip?	SEVTN_15	EIGTN_15	NINTN_15

[TWENTY]

20. Do you own a boat that you use primarily for saltwater sport fishing?

      YES   1
      NO   2 *(skip to q.60)*
      DK   8 *(skip to q.60)*
      REEF   9 *(skip to q.60)*

[TWENONE]

21. Did you purchase the boat within the past 12 months?

      YES   1 *(skip to q.23)*
      NO   2
      DK   8 *(skip to q.23)*
      REF   9 *(skip to q.23)*

[TWENTWO]

22.   How many years have you owned this boat?

```
┌──────┬──────┐
│      │      │
└──────┴──────┘
```

DON'T KNOW = 98
REFUSED   = 99

[TWENTHREE]

23.   Was it new or used when you bought it?

NEW   1
USED   2
DK   8
REF   9

[TWENFOUR]

24.   What is the approximate length of the boat in feet?

LESS THAN 10 FEET 1
10 TO 14 FEET   2
15 TO 19 FEET   3
20 TO 24 FEET   4
25 TO 29 FEET   5
30 TO 39 FEET   6
40 FEET OR MORE   7
DK   8
REF   9

[TWENFIV]

25.   Is the boat equipped with an inboard motor?

YES   1
NO   2 *(skip to q.27)*
DK   8 *(skip to q.27)*
REF   9 *(skip to q.27)*

B8

[TWENSIX]

26.   What is the horsepower of the motor?

        0 - 50 HP   1
        51 - 100 HP   2
        101 - 150 HP   3
        151 - 200 HP   4
        Over 200 HP   5
        DK   8
        REF   9

[TWENSEV]

27.   What was the total price you personally paid for the boat, exclusive of trailer, outboard
        motor, or equipment?

        DON'T KNOW = 99998
        REFUSED   = 99999

28.   What was the state and county, or parish, in which you purchased the boat?

        STATE: _____[TWEIGHT]_____

        COUNTY/PARISH: _____[TWEIGHTB]_____

[TWENNIN]

29.   Is the boat equipped with an outboard motor?

        YES   1
        NO   2 *(skip to q.36)*
        DK   8 *(skip to q.36)*
        REF   9 *(skip to q.36)*

[THIRTY]

30.   Did you purchase an outboard motor for a boat within the past 12 months?

        YES   1 *(skip to q.32)*
        NO   2
        DK   8 *(skip to q.32)*
        REF   9 *(skip to q.32)*

[THIRONE]

31. How many years have you owned the outboard motor?

DON'T KNOW = 98
REFUSED   = 99

[THIRTWO]

32. Was it new or used when you bought it?

NEW   1
USED   2
DK   8
REF   9

[THIRTHRE]

33. What is the total horsepower of the motors?

0 - 50 HP   1
51 - 100 HP   2
101 - 150 HP   3
151 - 200 HP   4
Over 200 HP   5
DK   8
REF   9

[THIRFOUR]

34. What was the total price you personally paid for the outboard motor?

DON'T KNOW = 9998
REFUSED   = 9999

35. What was the state and county or parish in which you purchased the outboard motor?

STATE: _____ [THIRFIVE]_____

COUNTY/PARISH: _____ [THIRFVEB]_____

[THIRSIX]

36. Do you own a trailer that you use with this boat?

YES   1
NO   2 *(skip to q.42)*
DK   8 *(skip to q.42)*
REF   9 *(skip to q.42)*

[THIRSEV]

37   Did you purchase the trailer for the boat within the past 12 months?

YES   1 (go to q.40)
NO   2
DK   8 (go to q.40)
REF   9 (go to q.40)

[THIEIGHT]

38. How many years have you owned the trailer?

DON'T KNOW = 98
REFUSED   = 99

[FORTY]

40. What was the total price you personally paid for the trailer?

DON'T KNOW = 9998
REFUSED   = 9999

41. What was the state and county or parish in which you purchased the trailer?

STATE: _____ [FORTYONE] _____

COUNTY/PARISH: _____ [FORTYONB] _____

[FORTYTW]

42. Is the boat equipped with any additional equipment other than fishing related equipment? Additional equipment would include electronics such as LORAN or GPS, safety gear, or similar accessories.

YES	1
NO	2 (skip to q.48)
DK	8 (skip to q.48)
REF	9 (skip to q.48)

[FORTHRE]

43 Did you purchase any of this additional equipment for a boat within the past 12 months other than fishing related equipment?

YES	1 (skip to q.45)
NO	2
DK	8 (skip to q.45)
REF	9 (skip to q.45)

[FORTFOUR]

44. How many years have you owned this additional equipment?

```
┌──────┬──────┐
│      │      │
└──────┴──────┘
```

DON'T KNOW = 98
REFUSED   = 99

[FORTFIV]

45. Was it new or used?

NEW	1
USED	2
DK	8
REF	9

[FORTYSIX]

46. What was the total price you personally paid for the additional equipment?

```
┌──────┬──────┬──────┬──────┬──────┐
│      │      │      │      │      │
└──────┴──────┴──────┴──────┴──────┘
```

DON'T KNOW = 9998
REFUSED   = 9999

47. What was the state and county, or parish in which you purchased the majority of that equipment?

STATE: _____[FORTSEVE]_____

COUNTY/PARISH: _____[FORTSEVB]_____

[FORTEIG]

48. Is the boat equipped with special rigging for fishing? This would include such things as outriggers, downriggers, fighting chairs, and the like.

YES   1
NO   2 *(skip to q.54)*
DK   8 *(skip to q.54)*
REF   9 *(skip to q.54)*

[FORTNIN]

49. Did you purchase any equipment to outfit the boat for fishing within the past 12 months? Please include such things as outriggers, downriggers, fighting chairs, and the like.

YES   1 *(go to q.51)*
NO   2
DK   8 *(go to q.51)*
REEF   9 *(go to q.51)*

[FIFTY]

50. How many years have you owned the special rigging for fishing?

DON'T KNOW = 98
REFUSED   = 99

[FIFTYONE]

51. Was it new or used when you bought it?

NEW   1
USED   2
DK   8
REF   9

[FIFTYTWO]

52. What was the total price you personally paid for equipment to outfit the boat for fishing?

DON'T KNOW = 9998
REFUSED = 9999

53. What was the state and county, or parish in which you purchased the majority of this equipment?

STATE: _____[FIFTHREE]_____

COUNTY/PARISH: _____[FIFTHREB]_____

[FIFTFOU]

54. Did you personally pay for any repairs to your boat, motor, trailer, or equipment during the past 12 months?

YES   1
NO   2 *(go to q.57)*
DK   8 *(go to q.57)*
REF   9 *(go to q.57)*

[FIFTFIVE]

55. What was the total estimated amount you personally paid for these repairs?

DON'T KNOW = 9998
REFUSED = 9999

56. What was the town, county, or parish in which you had the majority of these repairs done?

STATE: _____[FFTYSIX]_____

COUNTY/PARISH: _____[FFTYSIXB]_____

[FIFTSEV]

57   Did you purchase any rods and reels for use in saltwater sport fishing within the past 12
      months?

      YES   1
      NO   2 *(go to q.60)*
      DK   8 *(go to q.60)*
      REF   9 *(go to q.60)*

[FIFTEIGT]

58.   What was the total estimated price you personally paid for the rods and reels?

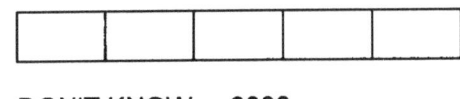

      DON'T KNOW = 9998
      REFUSED   = 9999

59.   What was the town, county, or parish in which you purchased the rods and reels?

      STATE: _____[FIFTNNE]_____

      COUNTY/PARISH: _____[FIFTNNEB]_____

[SIXTY]

60.   Did you purchase any fishing line for use in saltwater sport fishing within the past 12
      months?

      YES   1
      NO   2 *(go to q.63)*
      DK   8 *(go to q.63)*
      REF   9 *(go to q.63)*
      Yes

[SIXTYONE]

61.   What was the total estimated price you personally paid for the fishing line?

      DON'T KNOW = 9998
      REFUSED   = 9999

62.   What was the town, county, or parish in which you purchased the fishing line?

STATE: _____ [SIXTYTW] _____

COUNTY/PARISH: _____ [SIXTYTWB] _____

[SIXTHRE]

63.   Did you purchase any lures and other artificial bait for use in saltwater sport fishing within the past 12 months?

YES   1
NO   2 *(go to q.66)*
DK   8 *(go to q.66)*
REF   9 *(go to q.66)*

[SIXTFOUR]

64.   What was the total estimated price you personally paid for the lures and other artificial bait?

DON'T KNOW = 9998
REFUSED   = 9999

65.   What was the town, county, or parish in which you purchased the lures and other artificial bait?

STATE: _____ [SIXTFIV] _____

COUNTY/PARISH: _____ [SIXTFIVB] _____

[SIXTYSI]

66.   Can you think of any other fishing related equipment that you might have purchased within the past 12 months that I have not mentioned?

YES   1
NO   2 (go to q.70)
DK   8 (go to q.70)
REF   9 (go to q.70)

[SIXTSEVN]

67.   What did you purchase?

_____

[SIXTEIGT]

68.   What was the total estimated price you personally paid for that equipment?

DON'T KNOW = 9998
REFUSED   = 9999

69.   What was the town, county, or parish in which you purchased the majority of that equipment?

STATE: _____[SIXTNNE]_____

COUNTY/PARISH: _____[SIXTNNEB]_____

[SEVENTY]

70.   Have you purchased any fishing magazines or books within the past 12 months?

YES   1
NO   2 (go to q.72)
DK   8 (go to q.72)
REF   9 (go to q.72)

[SEVENONE]

71.   What was the total estimated price you personally paid for those magazines or books?

DON'T KNOW = 9998
REFUSED   = 9999

[SEVENTW]

72.   Have you paid for any memberships in fishing clubs or organizations within the past 12 months?

YES   1
NO   2 (go to q.74)
DK   8 (go to q.74)
REF   9 (go to q.74)

[SEVNTHRE]

73. What was the total estimated price you personally paid for those memberships?

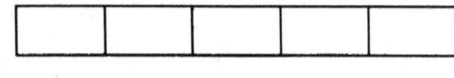

DON'T KNOW = 9998
REFUSED   = 9999

[SEVNFOU]

74. Have you purchased any camping equipment within the past 12 months that you use when you go fishing?

YES	1
NO	2 *(go to q.76)*
DK	8 *(go to q.76)*
REF	9 *(go to q.76)*

[SEVNFIVE]

75. What was the total estimated price you personally paid for that equipment?

DON'T KNOW = 9998
REFUSED   = 9999

[SEVENSI]

76. Have you personally paid for any saltwater fishing licenses within the past 12 months?

YES	1
NO	2 *(go to q.78)*
DK	8 *(go to q.78)*
REF	9 (go to q.78)

[SEVNSEVN]

77. What was the total estimated cost of those licenses?

DON'T KNOW = 9998
REFUSED   = 9999

Those are all the questions I have specifically about your fishing. I have just a few background questions about you and your hoousehold and then we'll be done.

[SEVNEIGT]

78.   In what year were you born?

[IF RESPONDENT IS RELUCTANT, ENTER '99' AND GO TO Q79, OTHERWISE, RECORD INFORMATION AND GO TO Q80; DON'T KNOW=98]

19 _____

IF REFUSES, ASK Q79; OTHERWISE, GO TO Q80

[SEVNNINE]

79.   Okay, please tell me in which of the following age groups do you belong:

1   16 to 25
2   26 to 35
3   36 to 45
4   46 to 55
5   56 to 64
6   65 and over

8   Don't Know
9   Refused

[EIGHTY]

80.   How many years have you been saltwater sport finfishing in [STATE OF INTERCEPT]?

DON'T KNOW = 98
REFUSED   = 99

[EIGTONE]

81.   Are you, yourself, employed? This includes self-employment.

1   Yes/self-employed
2   No/unemployed (GOTO Q83)

8   Don't Know (GOTO Q90)
9   Refused (GOTO Q90)

[EIGTTWO]

82.   Are you employed part-time or full-time?

        1   Part-time
        2   Full-time
        3   Variable/seasonal

        8   Don't Know
        9   Refused

[GO TO Q84]

[EIGTHRE]

83.   Which of the following reasons best explains your unemployed status:

        1   Looking for employment
        2   Retired (GO TO Q90)
        3   Full-time homemaker (GO TO Q90)
        4   Student (GO TO Q90)

        5   Other (specify) (GO TO Q90)
        8   Don't Know (GO TO Q90)
        9   Refused (GO TO Q90)

[EIGTFOUR]

84.   How many hours <u>a week</u> do you usually work?

        [998=DONT KNOW, 999=REFUSED]

        _____ number of hours

[EIGTFIVE]

85.   Did you give up any wages or salary by taking the trip when you were interviewed on site?

        YES   1
        NO   2 *(go to q.87)*
        DK   8 *(go to q.87)*
        REF   9 *(go to q.87)*

B20

[EIGTSIX]

86. How much in wages or salary did you give up to take that trip?

DON'T KNOW = 998
REFUSED   = 999

[EIGTSEVN]

87. Are you paid an hourly wage, or an annual salary or income?

    1   Hourly wage (GOTO Q88)
    2   Annual salary/income (GOTO Q89)

    8   Don't Know (GOTO Q90)
    9   Refused (GOTO Q90)

[EIGTSEVN]

88. What is your hourly wage?

		C		

DON'T KNOW = 99.98
REFUSED   = 99.99

[EIGTNINE]

89. What is your <u>personal</u> current salary or income?

    01   Less than $15,000
    02   15,001 to 25,000
    03   25,001 to 35,000
    04   35,001 to 45,000
    05   45,001 to 60,000
    06   60,001 to 75,000
    07   75,001 to 100,000
    10   100,001 to 125,000
    11   125,001 to 150,000
    12   150,001 to 175,000
    13   Greater than 175,000

    99998 Don't Know
    99999 Refused

[NINETY]

90. I'm going to read a list of income categories. We would like to know your <u>total annual</u> <u>household</u> income, before taxes? Stop me when I get to the income category that best describes your household.

 01   Less than $15,000
 02   15,001 to 25,000
 03   25,001 to 35,000
 04   35,001 to 45,000
 05   45,001 to 60,000
 06   60,001 to 75,000
 07   75,001 to 100,000
 10   100,001 to 125,000
 11   125,001 to 150,000
 12   150,001 to 175,000
 13   Greater than 175,000

 98   Don't Know
 99   Refused

[NINTONE]

91. WITHOUT ASKING, RECORD GENDER OF RESPONDENT.

 Male   1
 Female   2
 Can't Tell   8

Charter Boat Followup Telephone Survey

[CITY]

[COASTAL]

[FISH2]

[FISH12]

[ID_NO_]

[MONTH]

Hello, this is _____ calling from QuanTech in Rosslyn, Virginia. You recently spoke with one of our field staff members during your day of fishing in _____[STATE] on _____[TRIPDATE].

We are calling now with a follow-up to that survey to collect more detailed information that could not be collected in the field. As our interviewer who spoke with you in the field mentioned, we are evaluating the importance of oil and gas rigs in the Gulf of Mexico to recreational fishermen. One of the things I will be asking you about is how much it costs you to go fishing in the Gulf. This study is being conducted in accordance with the privacy act of 1974 and your answers will be kept completely confidential.

[Q1]

1. When our interviewer spoke with you on _____[INSERT TRIP DATE] you said that, not counting the day on which you were interviewed, you had been saltwater sport finfishing _____ [NUMBER OF DAYS] in _____[NAME OF STATE] within the past **12 months**. On how many of those days did you fish from a privately owned or rental boat within **300 feet** of an oil or gas rig or within **300 feet** of an artificial reef created from an oil or gas rig?

DON'T KNOW = 998
REFUSED = 999

[Q2]

2.   When our interviewer spoke with you on _____[TRIP DATE] you said that, not counting the day on which you were interviewed, you had been saltwater sport finfishing _____[NUMBER OF DAYS] in _____[NAME OF STATE] within the past **2 months**. On how many of those days did you fish from a privately owned or rental boat within 300 feet of an oil or gas rig or within **300 feet** of an artificial reef created from an oil or gas rig?

DON'T KNOW = 98
REFUSED   = 99

[Q3]

3.   On the trip of _____[TRIP DATE] did you do any diving within 300 feet of an oil or gas platform or within 300 feet of an artificial reef created from an oil or gas rig?

YES   1
NO   2
DK   8
REF   9

[Q4]

4.   Was the fishing you did on [TRIPDATE] part of a longer trip in which you spent at least one night away from your primary residence?

YES   1 (go to q.5)
NO   2 (skip to q.15A)
DK   8 (skip to q.15A)
REF   9 (skip to q.15A)

[Q5]

5.   How many nights were you away from your residence on this trip?

DON'T KNOW = 98
REFUSED   = 99

6.   On how many days of that trip did you fish?

[|]

DON'T KNOW = 98
REFUSED   = 99

7.   Did you travel to the place where you stayed overnight by privately owned car, plane, train, or other means?

PRIVATELY OWNED CAR   1 *(skip to q.11)*
TRAIN   2
BUS   3
AIRPLANE   4
OTHER   5 (SPECIFY: _____)
DK   8
REF   9

8   What did you personally pay for your transportation?

[| | |]

DON'T KNOW = 9998
REFUSED   = 9999

9.   Did you personally pay for use of a rental car on the trip?

YES   1
NO   2 (skip to q.11)
DK   8 (skip to q.11)
REF   9 (skip to q.11)

[Q10]

10.   What did you personally pay for the rental car?

DON'T KNOW = 9998
REFUSED   = 9999

[Q11]

11.   Since you stayed at least one evening overnight, I need some information about your lodging. Did you stay overnight on a boat, in a hotel or motel, at a campground, with family or friends, in a second residence which you own or rent permanently, or in some other type of lodging?

ON A BOAT   1 *(go to q.16)*
HOTEL/MOTEL   2
CAMPGROUND   3
FAMILY/FRIENDS   4
SECONDARY RESIDENCE 5
OTHER   6 specify:_____**[Q110TH]**_____)
DK   8
REF   9

[Q12]

12.   In what city or town was that lodging located?

NAME OF CITY OR
TOWN_____

[Q13]

13.   How much did you personally pay per night for the lodging associated with this fishing trip?

DON'T KNOW = 9998
REFUSED   = 9999

[Q14]

14.   Approximately how many miles did you travel <u>one-way</u> from your residence to the place where you stayed overnight on that trip?

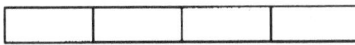

DON'T KNOW = 9998
REFUSED   = 9999

[Q15]

15.   Approximately how many miles did you travel from where you stayed overnight on that trip to the boat launch site?

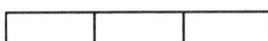

DON'T KNOW = 998
REFUSED   = 999

(Skip to Q.16)

[Q15A]

15A. Approximately how many miles did you travel from your home to the boat launch site?

DON'T KNOW = 9998
REFUSED   = 9999

[Q16]

16.   Did you personally spend any money associated with your fishing trip on the day in which we interviewed you in the field? You might not have paid anything personally, for example, if someone else in your party made the payments on your behalf. Did **you personally** spend any money on your fishing that day?

YES   1
NO   2 *(go to q.57)*
DK   8 *(go to q.57)*
REF   9 *(go to q.57)*

[Q17]

17.   I'm going to ask you a series of questions about your own personal expenditures on the day of the fishing trip in which we interviewed you in the field. As I read the following list, please remember that I'm only interested in items for which you personally paid. On the fishing trip on [TRIP DATE] did you personally spend any money

	17. DID YOU SPEND MONEY ON? Yes = 1 No = 2 DK = 8 REF = 9	IF YES 18. Thinking about your own personal expenditures [USING RESPONSE FROM ITEM 17], how much would you estimate you spent on that day of fishing?	IF YES 19. Of that amount, approximately how much of it would you say was spent within **15 miles** of the boat launch site?
A. In restaurants or bars for food and drink?			
B. In grocery or convenience stores for food, drinks, or ice?			
I. For bait?			
J. For fishing licenses?			
K. For fishing tackle which you used that day?			
L. For the rental of any equipment other than a boat?			
N. For any special clothing which you wore on the day of the trip?			
O. For sundries such as suntan lotions or bug repellent which you used on the trip?			
P. For film?			
Q. For souvenirs?			
R. For head boat or charter boat fees?			

[Q57]

57   Did you purchase any rods and reels for use in saltwater sport fishing within the past 12 months?

    YES   1
    NO   2 *(go to q.60)*
    DK   8 *(go to q.60)*
    REF   9 *(go to q.60)*

[Q58]

58.   What was the total estimated price you personally paid for the rods and reels?

    DON'T KNOW = 998
    REFUSED   = 999

59.   What was the state and county or parish in which you purchased the rods and reels?

    STATE: _____[Q59ST]_____

    COUNTY/PARISH: _____[Q59COUN]_____

[Q60]

60.   Did you purchase any fishing line for use in saltwater sport fishing within the past 12 months?

    YES   1
    NO   2 *(go to q.63)*
    DK   8 *(go to q.63)*
    REF   9 *(go to q.63)*

[Q61]

61.   What was the total estimated price you personally paid for the fishing line?

    DON'T kNOW = 998
    REFUSED   = 999

62. What was the state and county or parish in which you purchased the fishing line?

STATE: _____[Q62ST]_____

COUNTY/PARISH: _____[Q62COUN]_____

[Q63]

63. Did you purchase any lures and other artificial bait for use in saltwater sport fishing within the past 12 months?

YES   1
NO   2 *(go to q.66)*
DK   8 *(go to q.66)*
REF   9 *(go to q.66)*

[Q64]

64. What was the total estimated price you personally paid for the lures and other artificial bait?

DON'T kNOW = 998
REFUSED   = 999

65. What was the state and county or parish in which you purchased the lures and other artificial bait?

STATE: _____[Q65ST]_____

COUNTY/PARISH: _____[Q65COUN]_____

[Q66]

66. Can you think of any other fishing related equipment that you might have purchased within the past 12 months that I have not mentioned?

YES   1
NO   2 (go to q.70)
DK   8 (go to q.70)
REF   9 (go to q.70)

[Q67]

67. What did you purchase?

_____

[Q68]

68. What was the total estimated price you personally paid for that equipment?

DON'T kNOW = 9998
REFUSED   = 9999

69. What was the state and county or parish in which you purchased the majority of that equipment?

STATE: _____[Q69ST]_____

COUNTY/PARISH: _____[Q69COUN]_____

[Q70]

70. Have you purchased any fishing magazines or books within the past 12 months?

YES   1
NO   2 (go to q.72)
DK   8 (go to q.72)
REF   9 (go to q.72)

[Q71]

71. What was the total estimated price you personally paid for those magazines or books?

DON'T kNOW = 9998
REFUSED   = 9999

[Q72]

72. Have you paid for any memberships in fishing clubs or organizations within the past 12 months?

YES   1
NO   2 *(go to q.74)*
DK   8 *(go to q.74)*
REF   9 *(go to q.74)*

[Q73]

73.   What was the total estimated price you personally paid for those memberships?

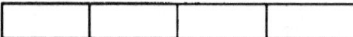

DON'T kNOW = 9998
REFUSED   = 9999

[Q74]

74.   Have you purchased any camping equipment within the past 12 months that you use when you go fishing?

YES   1
NO   2 *(go to q.76)*
DK   8 *(go to q.76)*
REF   9 *(go to q.76)*

[Q75]

75.   What was the total estimated price you personally paid for that equipment?

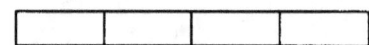

DON'T kNOW = 9998
REFUSED   = 9999

[Q76]

76.   Have you personally paid for any saltwater fishing licenses within the past 12 months?

YES   1
NO   2 *(go to q.78)*
DK   8 *(go to q.78)*
REF   9 (go to q.78)

[Q77]

77.   What was the total estimated cost of those licenses?

DON'T kNOW = 9998
REFUSED   = 9999

Those are all the questions I have specifically about your fishing. I have just a few background questions about you and your hoousehold and then we'll be done.

[Q78]

78.   In what year were you born?

       [IF RESPONDENT IS RELUCTANT, ENTER '99' AND GO TO Q79,
       OTHERWISE, RECORD INFORMATION AND GO TO Q80; DON'T KNOW=98]

       19 _____

                                        (IF REFUSES, ASK Q79;
                                        OTHERWISE, GO TO Q80)

[Q79]

79.   Okay, please tell me in which of the following age groups do you belong:

       1   16 to 25
       2   26 to 35
       3   36 to 45
       4   46 to 55
       5   56 to 64
       6   65 and over

       8   Don't know
       9   Refused

[Q80]

80.   How many years have you been saltwater sport finfishing in [STATE OF INTERCEPT]?

DON'T KNOW = 98
REFUSED   = 99

[Q81]

81.　Are <u>you</u>, yourself, employed? This includes self-employment.

　　1　　Yes/self-employed
　　2　　No/unemployed (GOTO Q83)

　　8　　Don't know (GOTO Q90)
　　9　　Refused (GOTO Q90)

[Q82]

82.　Are you employed part-time or full-time?

　　1　　Part-time
　　2　　Full-time
　　3　　Variable/seasonal

　　8　　Don't know
　　9　　Refused

(Go to Q.84)

[Q83]

83.　Which of the following reasons best explains your unemployed status:

　　1　　Looking for employment
　　2　　Retired
　　3　　Full-time homemaker
　　4　　Student

　　5　　Other (specify)
　　8　　Don't know
　　9　　Refused

(Go to Q.90)

[Q84]

84.　How many hours <u>a week</u> do you usually work?

　　[998=DONT KNOW, 999=REFUSED]

　　_____ number of hours

[Q85]

85.   Did you give up any wages or salary by taking the trip when you were
        interviewed on site?

        YES   1
        NO   2 *(go to q.87)*
        DK   8 *(go to q.87)*
        REF   9 (go to q.87)

[Q86]

86.   How much in wages or salary did you give up to take that trip?

        DON'T KNOW = 998
        REFUSED   = 999

[Q87]

87.   Are you paid an hourly wage, or an annual salary or income?

        1   Hourly wage (GOTO Q88)
        2   Annual salary/income (GOTO Q89)

        8   Don't know (GOTO Q90)
        9   Refused (GOTO Q90)

[Q88]

88.   What is your hourly wage?

        DON'T KNOW = 99.98
        REFUSED   = 99.99

[Q89]

89.   What is your <u>personal</u> current salary or income?

        01   Less than $15,000
        02   15,001 to 25,000
        03   25,001 to 35,000
        04   35,001 to 45,000
        05   45,001 to 60,000
        06   60,001 to 75,000
        07   75,001 to 100,000
        10   100,001 to 125,000
        11   125,001 to 150,000
        12   150,001 to 175,000
        13   Greater than 175,000

        98   Don't know
        99   Refused

[Q90]

90.   I'm going to read a list of income categories. We would like to know your <u>total annual household</u> income, before taxes? Stop me when I get to the income category that best describes your household.

        01   Less than $15,000
        02   15,001 to 25,000
        03   25,001 to 35,000
        04   35,001 to 45,000
        05   45,001 to 60,000
        06   60,001 to 75,000
        07   75,001 to 100,000
        10   100,001 to 125,000
        11   125,001 to 150,000
        12   150,001 to 175,000
        13   Greater than 175,000

        98   Don't know
        99   Refused

[Q91]

91.   WITHOUT ASKING, RECORD GENDER OF RESPONDENT.

        Male   1
        Female   2
        Can't Tell   8

Party Boat Followup Telephone Survey

[ID_NO]   ID number

[YEAR]   1999

[MONTH]   Month of fishing trip

[TRIPDATE]   Date of field interview

[STATETRP]   State of fishing trip

[FISH12]   Number of fishing trips reported in previous 12 months

[FISH2]   Number of fishing trips reported in previous 2 months

[SC1]   Screener to verify respondent was interviewed in the field

[STATERES]   Respondent's state of residence

[COASTAL]

Do you live in a coastal county?

        Yes   1
        No   2 (GO TO Q1)

[CITY]

What city do you reside in?

Hello, this is _____ calling from QuanTech in Rosslyn, Virginia. You recently spoke with one of our field staff members during your day of fishing in [STATE] on [TRIPDATE].

We are calling now with a follow-up to that survey to collect more detailed information that could not be collected in the field. As our interviewer who spoke with you in the field mentioned, we are evaluating the importance of oil and gas rigs in the Gulf of Mexico to recreational divers and fishermen. This study is being conducted in accordance with the privacy act of 1974. You are not required to answer any question than you consider to be an invasion of your privacy.

[Q4]

4.   Was the diving you did on [TRIPDATE] part of a longer trip in which you spent at least one night away from your primary residence?

      Yes   1
      No   2 (GO TO Q15A)
      Don't Know   8 (GO TO Q15A)
      Refused   9 (GO TO Q15A)

[Q5]

5.   How many nights were you away from your residence on this trip?

      Don't Know   98
      Refused   99

[Q6]

6.   On how many days of that trip did you fish?

      Don't Know   98
      Refused   99

[Q7]

7.   Did you travel to the place where you stayed overnight by privately owned car, plane, train, or other means?

      Privately owned car   1 (GO TO Q11)
      Train   2
      Bus   3
      Airplane   4
      Other (specify)   5 (_____)
      Don't Know   8
      Refused   9

[Q8]

8.   What did you personally pay for your transportation?

      Don't Know   9998
      Refused   9999

B38

[Q9]

9.   Did you personally pay for use of a rental car on the trip?

      Yes   1
      No   2 (GO TO Q11)
      Don't Know   8 (GO TO Q11)
      Refused   9 (GO TO Q11)

[Q10]

10.   What did you personally pay for the rental car?

      Don't Know   9998
      Refused   9999

[Q11]

11.   Since you stayed at least one evening overnight, I need some information about your lodging. Did you stay overnight on a boat, in a hotel or motel, at a campground, with family or friends, in a second residence which you own or rent permanently, or in some other type of lodging?

      On a boat   1 (GO TO Q16)
      Hotel/Motel   2
      Campground   3
      Family/Friends   4
      Secondary residence 5
      Other (specify)   6 (_____[Q11OTH]_____)
      Don't Know   8
      Refused   9

[Q12]

12.   In what city or town was that lodging located?

[Q13]

13.   How much did you personally pay per night for the lodging associated with this fishing trip?

      Don't Know   9998
      Refused   9999

B39

[Q14]

14.   Approximately how many miles did you travel <u>one-way</u> from your residence to the place where you stayed overnight on that trip?

        Don't Know   9998
        Refused   9999

[Q15]

15.   Approximately how many miles did you travel from where you stayed overnight on that trip to the boat launch site?

        Don't Know   998
        Refused   999

(Skip to Q.16)

[Q15A]

15A.   Approximately how many miles did you travel from your home to the boat launch site?

        Don't Know   9998
        Refused   9999

[Q16]

16.   Did you personally spend any money associated with your fishing trip on the day in which we interviewed you in the field? You might not have paid anything personally, for example, if someone else in your party made the payments on your behalf. Did you personally spend any money on your fishing that day?

        Yes   1
        No   2 (GO TO Q57)
        Don't Know   8 (GO TO Q57)
        Refused   9 (GO TO Q57)

I'm going to ask you a series of questions about your own personal expenditures on the day of the fishing trip in which we interviewed you in the field. As I read the following list, please remember that I'm only interested in items for which you personally paid. On the fishing trip on [TRIP DATE] did you personally spend any money

	DID YOU SPEND MONEY ON? Yes = 1 No = 2 DK = 8 REF = 9	IF YES 18. Thinking about your own personal expenditures [USING RESPONSE FROM ITEM 17], how much would you estimate you spent on that day of fishing?	IF YES 19. Of that amount, approximately how much of it would you say was spent within 15 miles of the boat launch site?
A. In restaurants or bars for food and drink?	Q17A	Q18A	Q19A
B. In grocery or convenience stores for food, drinks, or ice?	Q17B	Q18B	Q19B
C. At a service station or marina for fule?	Q17C	Q18C	Q19C
D. At a boat dock or marina for boat rental?	Q17D	Q18D	Q19D
E. At a boat ramp, dock, or marina for boat launch fees?	Q7E	Q18E	Q19E
F. At a dock or marina for docking fees?	Q17F	Q18F	Q19F
G. For boat repairs?	Q17G	Q18G	Q19G
H. For boat towing?	Q17H	Q18H	Q19H
J. For diving trip fees?	Q17J	Q18J	Q19J
K. For fishing tackle or diving equipment which you used that day?	Q17K	Q18K	Q19K
L. For the rental of any diving equipment other than a boat?	Q17L	Q18L	Q19L
M. For the services of a guide who accompanied you on your trip?	Q17M	Q18M	Q19M

	DID YOU SPEND MONEY ON? Yes = 1 No = 2 DK = 8 REF = 9	IF YES 18.Thinking about your own personal expenditures [USING RESPONSE FROM ITEM 17], how much would you estimate you spent on that day of fishing?	IF YES 19.Of that amount, approximately how much of it would you say was spent within **15 miles** of the boat launch site?
N. For any special clothing which you wore on the day of the trip?	Q17N	Q18N	Q19N
O. For sundries such as suntan lotions or bug repellent which you used on the trip?	Q17O	Q18O	Q19O
P. For film?	Q17P	Q18P	Q19P
Q. For souvenirs?	Q17Q	Q18Q	Q19Q
S. For air fills fees?	Q17S	Q18S	Q19S

[Q57]

57   Did you purchase any rods and reels for use in saltwater sport fishing within the past 12 months?

Yes   1
No   2 (GO TO Q60)
Don't Know   8 (GO TO Q60)
Refused   9 (GO TO Q60)

[Q58]

58.   What was the total estimated price you personally paid for the rods and reels?

Don't Know   = 9998
Refused   = 9999

59.   What was the sate and county or parish in which you purchased the rods and reels?

State: _____[Q59ST]_____

County: _____[Q59COUN]_____

[Q60]

60.   Did you purchase any fishing line for use in saltwater sport fishing within the past 12 months?

Yes   1
No   2 (GO TO Q63)
Don't Know   8 (GO TO Q63)
Refused   9 (GO TO Q63)

[Q61]

61.   What was the total estimated price you personally paid for the fishing line?

Don't Know   = 9998
Refused   = 9999

62.   What was the state and county or parish in which you purchased the fishing line?

State: _____[Q62ST]_____

County: _____[Q62COUN]_____

[Q63]

63.   Did you purchase any lures and other artificial bait for use in saltwater sport fishing within the past 12 months?

Yes   1
No   2 (GO TO Q66)
Don't Know 8 (GO TO Q66)
Refused   9 (GO TO Q66)

[Q64]

64.   What was the total estimated price you personally paid for the lures and other artificial bait?

Don't Know = 9998
Refused   = 9999

65.   What was the state and county or parish in which you purchased the lures and other artificial bait?

State: _____[Q65ST]_____

County: _____[Q65COUN]_____

[Q66]

66.   Can you think of any other fishing related equipment that you might have purchased within the past 12 months that I have not mentioned?

Yes   1
No   2 (GO TO Q70)
Don't Know 8 (GO TO Q70)
Refused   9 (GO TO Q70)

[Q67]

67.   What did you purchase?

[Q68]

68.   What was the total estimated price you personally paid for that equipment?

Don't Know = 9998
Refused   = 9999

69. What was the state and county or parish in which you purchased the majority of that equipment?

State: _____[Q69ST]_____

County: _____[Q69COUN]_____

[Q70]

70. Have you purchased any fishing magazines or books within the past 12 months?

Yes   1
No   2 (GO TO Q72)
Don't Know   8 (GO TO Q72)
Refused   9 (GO TO Q72)

[Q71]

71. What was the total estimated price you personally paid for those magazines or books?

Don't Know   = 9998
Refused   = 9999

[Q72]

72. Have you paid for any memberships in fishing clubs or organizations within the past 12 months?

Yes   1
No   2 (GO TO Q74)
Don't Know   8 (GO TO Q74)
Refused   9 (GO TO Q74)

[Q73]

73. What was the total estimated price you personally paid for those memberships?

Don't Know   = 9998
Refused   = 9999

[Q74]

74.   Have you purchased any camping equipment within the past 12 months that you use when you go fishing?

       Yes   1
       No   2 (GO TO Q76)
       Don't Know   8 (GO TO Q76)
       Refused   9 (GO TO Q76)

[Q75]

75.   What was the total estimated price you personally paid for that equipment?

       Don't Know   = 9998
       Refused   = 9999

[Q76]

76.   Have you personally paid for any saltwater fishing licenses within the past 12 months?

       Yes   1
       No   2 (GO TO Q78)
       Don't Know   8 (GO TO Q78)
       Refused   9 (GO TO Q78)

[Q77]

77.   What was the total estimated cost of those licenses?

       Don't Know   = 9998
       Refused   = 9999

Those are all the questions I have specifically about your fishing. I have just a few background questions about you and your holds and then we'll be done.

[Q78]

78.   In what year were you born?

       [IF RESPONDENT IS RELUCTANT, ENTER '99' AND GO TO Q79, OTHERWISE, RECORD INFORMATION AND GO TO Q80; DON'T KNOW=98]

       19 ___year 0-83___

[Q79]

79.   Okay, please tell me in which of the following age <u>groups</u> do you belong:

        16 to 25   1
        26 to 35   2
        36 to 45   3
        46 to 55   4
        56 to 64   5
        65 and over   6

        Don't know   8
        Refused   9

[Q80]

80.   How many years have you been saltwater sport finfishing in [STATE OF INTERCEPT]?

        Don't Know   = 98
        Refused   = 99

[Q81]

81.   Are <u>you</u>, yourself, employed? This includes self-employment.

        Yes/self-employed   1
        No/unemployed   2 (GOTO Q83)
        Don't know   8 (GOTO Q90)
        Refused   9 (GOTO Q90)

[Q82]

82.   Are you employed part-time or full-time?

        Part-time   1
        Full-time   2
        Variable/seasonal   3
        Don't know   8
        Refused   9

(GO TO Q84)

[Q83]

83.   Which of the following reasons best explains your unemployed status:

Looking for employment   1
Retired   2
Full-time homemaker   3
Student   4
Other (specify)   5
Don't know   8
Refused   9

[Q84]

84.   How many hours <u>a week</u> do you usually work?

998=DONT KNOW
999=REFUSED

[Q85]

85.   Did you give up any wages or salary by taking the trip on [TRIPDATE] when you were interviewed on site?

Yes   1
No   2 (GOTO Q87)
Don't know/remember8 (GOTO Q87)
Refused   9 (GOTO Q87)

[Q86]

86.   How much in wages or salary did you give up to take that trip?

998=DONT KNOW/REMEMBER
999=REFUSED

[Q87]

87.   Are you paid an hourly wage, or an annual salary or income?

Hourly wage   1(GOTO Q88)
Annual salary/income 2 (GOTO Q89)
Don't know   8 (GOTO Q90)
Refused   9 (GOTO Q90)

[Q88]

88.   What is your hourly wage?

        999.98=DONT KNOW
        999.99=REFUSED

[Q89]

89.   What is your <u>personal</u> current salary or income?

        01   Less than $15,000
        02   15,001 to 25,000
        03   25,001 to 35,000
        04   35,001 to 45,000
        05   45,001 to 60,000
        06   60,001 to 75,000
        07   75,001 to 100,000
        10   100,001 to 125,000
        11   125,001 to 150,000
        12   150,001 to 175,000
        13   Greater than 175,000

        98   Don't know
        99   Refused

[Q90]

90.   I'm going to read a list of income categories. We would like to know your <u>total annual</u>
        <u>household</u> income, before taxes? Stop me when I get to the income category that best
        describes your household.

        01   Less than $15,000
        02   15,001 to 25,000
        03   25,001 to 35,000
        04   35,001 to 45,000
        05   45,001 to 60,000
        06   60,001 to 75,000
        07   75,001 to 100,000
        10   100,001 to 125,000
        11   125,001 to 150,000
        12   150,001 to 175,000
        13   Greater than 175,000

        98   Don't know
        99   Refused

[Q91]

91.   WITHOUT ASKING, RECORD GENDER OF RESPONDENT.

MALE   1
FEMALE   2

DON'T KNOW   8

Diver Followup Telephone Survey

[ID_NO_]   ID number

[YEAR]   1999

[MONTH]   Month of fishing trip

[TRIPDATE]   Date of field interview

[STATETRP]   State of fishing trip

[FISH12]   Number of fishing trips reported in previous 12 months

[FISH2]   Number of fishing trips reported in previous 2 months

[SC1]   Screener to verify respondent was interviewed in the field

[STATERES]   Respondent's state of residence

[COASTAL]

Do you live in a coastal county?

      Yes   1
      No   2 (GO TO Q1)

[CITY]

What city do you reside in?

Hello, this is _____ calling from QuanTech in Rosslyn, Virginia. You recently spoke with one of our field staff members during your day of fishing in [STATE] on [TRIPDATE].

We are calling now with a follow-up to that survey to collect more detailed information that could not be collected in the field. As our interviewer who spoke with you in the field mentioned, we are evaluating the importance of oil and gas rigs in the Gulf of Mexico to recreational divers and fishermen. This study is being conducted in accordance with the privacy act of 1974. You are not required to answer any question than you consider to be an invasion of your privacy.

[Q4]

4.   Was the diving you did on [TRIPDATE] part of a longer trip in which you spent at least one night away from your primary residence?

       Yes   1
       No   2 (GO TO Q15A)
       Don't Know   8 (GO TO Q15A)
       Refused   9 (GO TO Q15A)

[Q5]

5.   How many nights were you away from your residence on this trip?

       Don't Know   98
       Refused   99

[Q6]

6.   On how many days of that trip did you fish?

       Don't Know   98
       Refused   99

[Q7]

7.   Did you travel to the place where you stayed overnight by privately owned car, plane, train, or other means?

       Privately owned car   1 (GO TO Q11)
       Train   2
       Bus   3
       Airplane   4
       Other (specify)   5 (_____)
       Don't Know   8
       Refused   9

[Q8]

8.   What did you personally pay for your transportation?

       Don't Know   9998
       Refused   9999

[Q9]

9.   Did you personally pay for use of a rental car on the trip?

      Yes   1
      No   2 (GO TO Q11)
      Don't Know   8 (GO TO Q11)
      Refused   9 (GO TO Q11)

[Q10]

10.   What did you personally pay for the rental car?

      Don't Know   9998
      Refused   9999

[Q11]

11.   Since you stayed at least one evening overnight, I need some information about your lodging. Did you stay overnight on a boat, in a hotel or motel, at a campground, with family or friends, in a second residence which you own or rent permanently, or in some other type of lodging?

      On a boat   1 (GO TO Q16)
      Hotel/Motel   2
      Campground   3
      Family/Friends   4
      Secondary residence 5
      Other (specify)   6 (_____[Q11OTH]_____)
      Don't Know   8
      Refused   9

[Q12]

12.   In what city or town was that lodging located?

[Q13]

13.   How much did you personally pay per night for the lodging associated with this fishing trip?

      Don't Know   9998
      Refused   9999

B53

[Q13A]

13A. Approximately how many miles is it one way from your residence to the lodging associated with this diving trip?

Don't Know 9998
Refused 9999

[Q14]

14. Approximately how long did it take you to travel <u>one-way</u> from your residence to the place where you stayed overnight on that trip?

Don't Know 9998
Refused 9999

[Q15]

15. Approximately how long did it take you to travel from where you stayed overnight on that trip to the boat launch site?

Don't Know 998
Refused 999

(Skip to Q.16)

[Q15A]

15A. Approximately how many miles did you travel from your home to the boat launch site?

Don't Know 9998
Refused 9999

[Q16]

16. Did you personally spend any money associated with your fishing trip on the day in which we interviewed you in the field? You might not have paid anything personally, for example, if someone else in your party made the payments on your behalf. Did you personally spend any money on your fishing that day?

Yes 1
No 2 (GO TO Q57)
Don't Know 8 (GO TO Q57)
Refused 9 (GO TO Q57)

I'm going to ask you a series of questions about your own personal expenditures on the day of the fishing trip in which we interviewed you in the field. As I read the following list, please remember that I'm only interested in items for which you personally paid. On the fishing trip on

B54

[TRIP DATE] did you personally spend any money

	DID YOU SPEND MONEY ON? Yes = 1 No = 2 DK = 8 REF = 9	IF YES 18.Thinking about your own personal expenditures [USING RESPONSE FROM ITEM 17], how much would you estimate you spent on that day of fishing?	IF YES 19.Of that amount, approximately how much of it would you say was spent within **15 miles** of the boat launch site?
A. In restaurants or bars for food and drink?	Q17A	Q18A	Q19A
B. In grocery or convenience stores for food, drinks, or ice?	Q17B	Q18B	Q19B
C. At a service station or marina for fule?	Q17C	Q18C	Q19C
D. At a boat dock or marina for boat rental?	Q17D	Q18D	Q19D
E. At a boat ramp, dock, or marina for boat launch fees?	Q7E	Q18E	Q19E
F. At a dock or marina for docking fees?	Q17F	Q18F	Q19F
G. For boat repairs?	Q17G	Q18G	Q19G
H. For boat towing?	Q17H	Q18H	Q19H
J. For diving trip fees?	Q17J	Q18J	Q19J
K. For fishing tackle or diving equipment which you used that day?	Q17K	Q18K	Q19K
L. For the rental of any diving equipment other than a boat?	Q17L	Q18L	Q19L

	DID YOU SPEND MONEY ON? Yes = 1 No = 2 DK = 8 REF = 9	IF YES 18.Thinking about your own personal expenditures [USING RESPONSE FROM ITEM 17], how much would you estimate you spent on that day of fishing?	IF YES 19.Of that amount, approximately how much of it would you say was spent within **15 miles** of the boat launch site?
M. For the services of a guide who accompanied you on your trip?	**Q17M**	**Q18M**	**Q19M**
N. For any special clothing which you wore on the day of the trip?	**Q17N**	**Q18N**	**Q19N**
O. For sundries such as suntan lotions or bug repellent which you used on the trip?	**Q17O**	**Q18O**	**Q19O**
P. For film?	**Q17P**	**Q18P**	**Q19P**
Q. For souvenirs?	**Q17Q**	**Q18Q**	**Q19Q**
S. For air fills fees?	**Q17S**	**Q18S**	**Q19S**

[Q20]

20. Do you own a boat that you use primarily for saltwater sport fishing?

       YES   1
       NO   2 *(skip to q.57A)*
       DK   8 *(skip to q.57A)*
       REEF   9 *(skip to q.57A)*

[Q21]

21. Did you purchase the boat within the past 12 months?

       YES   1 *(skip to q.23)*
       NO   2
       DK   8 *(skip to q.23)*
       REF   9 *(skip to q.23)*

[Q22]

22.   How many years have you owned this boat?

```
┌─────────┬─────────┐
│         │         │
└─────────┴─────────┘
```

DON'T kNOW = 98
REFUSED   = 99

[Q23]

23.   Was it new or used when you bought it?

NEW   1
USED   2
DK   8
REF   9

[Q24]

24.   What is the approximate length of the boat in feet?

LESS THAN 10 FEET1
10 TO 14 FEET   2
15 TO 19 FEET   3
20 TO 24 FEET   4
25 TO 29 FEET   5
30 TO 39 FEET   6
40 FEET OR MORE 7
DK   8
REF   9

[Q25]

25.   Is the boat equipped with an inboard motor?

YES   1
NO   2 *(skip to q.27)*
DK   8 *(skip to q.27)*
REF   9 *(skip to q.27)*

[Q26]

26.   What is the horsepower of the motor?

        0 - 50 HP   1
        51 - 100 HP   2
        101 - 150 HP   3
        151 - 200 HP   4
        Over 200 HP   5
        DK   8
        REF   9

[Q27]

27.   What was the total price you personally paid for the boat, exclusive of trailer, outboard motor, or equipment?

        DON'T kNOW = 99998
        REFUSED   = 99999

28.   What was the state and county, or parish, in which you purchased the boat?

        STATE: _____ [Q28A] _____

        COUNTY/PARISH: _____ [Q28B] _____

[Q29]

29.   Is the boat equipped with an outboard motor?

        YES   1
        NO   2 *(skip to q.36)*
        DK   8 *(skip to q.36)*
        REF   9 *(skip to q.36)*

[Q30]

30.   Did you purchase an outboard motor for a boat within the past 12 months?

        YES   1 *(skip to q.32)*
        NO   2
        DK   8 *(skip to q.32)*
        REF   9 *(skip to q.32)*

[Q31]

31.   How many years have you owned the outboard motor?

DON'T kNOW = 98
REFUSED   = 99

[Q32]

32.   Was it new or used when you bought it?

NEW   1
USED   2
DK   8
REF   9

[Q33]

33.   What is the total horsepower of the motors?

0 - 50 HP   1
51 - 100 HP   2
101 - 150 HP   3
151 - 200 HP   4
Over 200 HP   5
DK   8
REF   9

[Q34]

34.   What was the total price you personally paid for the outboard motor?

DON'T kNOW = 9998
REFUSED   = 9999

35.   What was the state and county or parish in which you purchased the outboard motor?

STATE: _____[Q35A]_____

COUNTY/PARISH: _____[Q35B]_____

[Q36]

36. Do you own a trailer that you use with this boat?

YES	1
NO	2 (*skip to q.42*)
DK	8 (*skip to q.42*)
REF	9 (*skip to q.42*)

[Q37]

37. Did you purchase the trailer for the boat within the past 12 months?

YES	1 (go to q.40)
NO	2
DK	8 (go to q.40)
REF	9 (go to q.40)

[Q38]

38. How many years have you owned the trailer?

DON'T kNOW = 98
REFUSED = 99

[Q39]

39. Was it new or used when you bought it?

New	1
Used	2
Don't Know	8
Refused	9

[Q40]

40. What was the total price you personally paid for the trailer?

DON'T kNOW = 9998
REFUSED = 9999

41. What was the state and county or parish in which you purchased the trailer?

STATE: _____[Q41A]_____

COUNTY/PARISH: _____[Q41B]_____

[Q42]

42. Is the boat equipped with any additional equipment other than fishing related equipment? Additional equipment would include electronics such as LORAN or GPS, safety gear, or similar accessories.

YES   1
NO   2 (skip to q.48)
DK   8 (skip to q.48)
REF   9 (skip to q.48)

[Q43]

43 Did you purchase any of this additional equipment for a boat within the past 12 months other than fishing related equipment?

YES   1 (skip to q.45)
NO   2
DK   8 (skip to q.45)
REF   9 (skip to q.45)

[Q44]

44. How many years have you owned this additional equipment?

DON'T kNOW = 98
REFUSED   = 99

[Q45]

45. Was it new or used?

NEW   1
USED   2
DK   8
REF   9

[Q46]

46.   What was the total price you personally paid for the additional equipment?

DON'T kNOW = 9998
REFUSED   = 9999

47.   What was the state and county, or parish in which you purchased the majority of that equipment?

STATE: _____[Q47A]_____

COUNTY/PARISH: _____[Q47B]_____

[Q48]

48.   Is the boat equipped with special equipment for diving?

YES   1
NO   2 *(skip to q.54)*
DK   8 *(skip to q.54)*
REF   9 *(skip to q.54)*

[Q49]

49.   Did you purchase any equipment to outfit the boat for diving within the past 12 months?

YES   1 *(go to q.51)*
NO   2
DK   8 *(go to q.51)*
REEF   9 *(go to q.51)*

[Q50]

50.   How many years have you owned the special equipment for diving?

DON'T kNOW = 98
REFUSED   = 99

[Q51]

51.   Was it new or used when you bought it?

        NEW   1
        USED   2
        DK   8
        REF   9

[Q52]

52.   What was the total price you personally paid for equipment to outfit the boat for diving?

        DON'T kNOW = 9998
        REFUSED   = 9999

53.   What was the state and county, or parish in which you purchased the majority of this equipment?

        STATE: _____[Q53A]_____

        COUNTY/PARISH: _____[Q53B]_____

[Q54]

54.   Did you personally pay for any repairs to your boat, motor, trailer, or equipment during the past 12 months?

        YES   1
        NO   2 *(go to q.57A)*
        DK   8 *(go to q.57A)*
        REF   9 *(go to q.57A)*

[Q55]

55.   What was the total estimated amount you personally paid for these repairs?

        DON'T kNOW = 9998
        REFUSED   = 9999

56. What was the town, county, or parish in which you had the majority of these repairs done?

STATE: _____[Q56A]_____

COUNTY/PARISH: _____[Q56B]_____

[Q57A]

57A. Did you purchase any diving equipment such as tanks and backpacks, masks, fins, wet suits, trip computers, and the like within the past 12 months

Yes   1
No   2 (GO TO Q60)
Don't Know   8 (GO TO Q60)
Refused   9 (GO TO Q60)

[Q58A]

58. What was the total estimated price you personally paid for the diving equipment?

Don't Know   = 9998
Refused   = 9999

59A. What was the sate and county or parish in which you purchased the diving equipment?

State: _____[Q59A1]_____

County: _____[Q59A2]_____

[Q60A]

60A. Did you pay for any dive lessons within the past 12 months?

Yes   1
No   2 (GO TO Q63)
Don't Know   8 (GO TO Q63)
Refused   9 (GO TO Q63)

[Q61A]

61A. What was the total estimated price you personally paid for the diving lessons?

Don't Know   = 9998
Refused   = 9999

62A. What was the state and county or parish in which you took the dive lessons?

State: _____[Q62A1]_____

County: _____[Q62A2]_____

[Q66A]

66A. Can you think of any other dive related expenses that you might have incurred within the past 12 months that I have not mentioned?

Yes   1
No   2 (GO TO Q70)
Don't Know 8 (GO TO Q70)
Refused   9 (GO TO Q70)

[Q67A]

67A. What was the expense?

[Q68A]

68A. What was the total estimated price you personally paid?

Don't Know = 9998
Refused   = 9999

69. What was the state and county or parish in which you purchased the majority of that equipment?

State: _____[Q69A1]_____

County: _____[Q69A2]_____

[Q70A]

70A. Have you purchased any diving magazines or books within the past 12 months?

Yes   1
No   2 (GO TO Q72)
Don't Know 8 (GO TO Q72)
Refused   9 (GO TO Q72)

[Q71A]

71A.   What was the total estimated price you personally paid for those magazines or books?

Don't Know   = 9998
Refused   = 9999

[Q72A]

72A.   Have you paid for any memberships in diving clubs or organizations within the past 12 months?

Yes   1
No   2 (GO TO Q74)
Don't Know   8 (GO TO Q74)
Refused   9 (GO TO Q74)

[Q73A]

73A.   What was the total estimated price you personally paid for those memberships?

Don't Know   = 9998
Refused   = 9999

[Q74]

74.   Have you purchased any camping equipment within the past 12 months that you use when you go diving?

Yes   1
No   2 (GO TO Q76)
Don't Know   8 (GO TO Q76)
Refused   9 (GO TO Q76)

[Q75]

75.   What was the total estimated price you personally paid for that equipment?

Don't Know   = 9998
Refused   = 9999

[Q76]

76.   Have you personally paid for any saltwater fishing licenses within the past 12 months?

Yes   1
No   2 (GO TO Q78)
Don't Know   8 (GO TO Q78)
Refused   9 (GO TO Q78)

[Q77]

77.   What was the total estimated cost of those licenses?

Don't Know   = 9998
Refused   = 9999

Those are all the questions I have specifically about your fishing. I have just a few background questions about you and your holds and then we'll be done.

[Q78]

78.   In what year were you born?

[IF RESPONDENT IS RELUCTANT, ENTER '99' AND GO TO Q79, OTHERWISE, RECORD INFORMATION AND GO TO Q80; DON'T KNOW=98]

19 ___year 0-83___

[Q79]

79.   Okay, please tell me in which of the following age groups do you belong:

16 to 25   1
26 to 35   2
36 to 45   3
46 to 55   4
56 to 64   5
65 and over   6

Don't know   8
Refused   9

[Q80]

80.   How many years have you been diving in [STATE OF INTERCEPT]?

Don't Know   = 98
Refused   = 99

[Q81]

81.   Are <u>you</u>, yourself, employed? This includes self-employment.

Yes/self-employed	1
No/unemployed	2 (GOTO Q83)
Don't know	8 (GOTO Q90)
Refused	9 (GOTO Q90)

[Q82]

82.   Are you employed part-time or full-time?

Part-time	1
Full-time	2
Variable/seasonal	3
Don't know	8
Refused	9

(GO TO Q84)

[Q83]

83.   Which of the following reasons best explains your unemployed status:

Looking for employment	1
Retired	2
Full-time homemaker	3
Student	4
Other (specify)	5
Don't know	8
Refused	9

[Q84]

84.   How many hours <u>a week</u> do you usually work?

998=DONT KNOW
999=REFUSED

[Q85]

85.   Did you give up any wages or salary by taking the trip on [TRIPDATE] when you were interviewed on site?

Yes	1
No	2 (GOTO Q87)
Don't know/remember	8 (GOTO Q87)
Refused	9 (GOTO Q87)

B68

[Q86]

86.   How much in wages or salary did you give up to take that trip?

        998=DONT KNOW/REMEMBER
        999=REFUSED

[Q87]

87.   Are you paid an hourly wage, or an annual salary or income?

        Hourly wage   1(GOTO Q88)
        Annual salary/income 2 (GOTO Q89)
        Don't know   8 (GOTO Q90)
        Refused   9 (GOTO Q90)

[Q88]

88.   What is your hourly wage?

        999.98=DONT KNOW
        999.99=REFUSED

[Q89]

89.   What is your <u>personal</u> current salary or income?

        01   Less than $15,000
        02   15,001 to 25,000
        03   25,001 to 35,000
        04   35,001 to 45,000
        05   45,001 to 60,000
        06   60,001 to 75,000
        07   75,001 to 100,000
        10   100,001 to 125,000
        11   125,001 to 150,000
        12   150,001 to 175,000
        13   Greater than 175,000

        98   Don't know
        99   Refused

[Q90]

90.   I'm going to read a list of income categories. We would like to know your <u>total annual household</u> income, before taxes? Stop me when I get to the income category that best describes your household.

    01   Less than $15,000
    02   15,001 to 25,000
    03   25,001 to 35,000
    04   35,001 to 45,000
    05   45,001 to 60,000
    06   60,001 to 75,000
    07   75,001 to 100,000
    10   100,001 to 125,000
    11   125,001 to 150,000
    12   150,001 to 175,000
    13   Greater than 175,000

    98   Don't know
    99   Refused

[Q91]

91.   WITHOUT ASKING, RECORD GENDER OF RESPONDENT.

    MALE   1
    FEMALE   2

    DON'T KNOW   8

Appendix C: Operator Questionnaires
    Charter Boat Operator Questionnaire
    Party Boat Operator Questionnaire
    Diver Operator Questionnaire

1999 MMS Charter Boat Captain Telephone Survey

[IDNUM]

[NAME]

[STATE]

[BOATNAME]

[AREACODE]

[FONNUM]

Hello, this is _____ calling from QuanTech in Rosslyn, Virginia. We are conducting a survey of charter boat operators in the Gulf of Mexico on behalf of the Minerals Management Service of the U.S. Department of the Interior. The purpose of the survey is to better understand the importance to the charter boat industry of oil and gas rigs as well as artificial reefs created from oil and gas rigs.

Your name was provided to us as a charter boat captain in the state of (NAME OF STATE). All information you give will be kept completely confidential and your participation is voluntary. Your answers will be combined with those of other captains to help Minerals Management Service make decisions about the future of Gulf-based oil and gas rigs.

[Q1]

1.   Is the boat you operate considered to be a charter boat, a head boat, or do you function primarily as a guide service?

        Charter boat   1
        Head Boat   2----GO TO HEAD BOAT QUESTIONNAIRE
        Guide Service   3----GO TO GUIDE SERVICE QUESTIONNAIRE
        Don't Know   8----THANK AND TERMINATE
        Refused   9----THANK AND TERMINATE

[Q2]

2.   In what state did you primarily operat as a charter boat captain during the past 12 months?

   AL
   MS
   LA
   TX

   Other----THANK AND TERMINATE

[Q3]

3.   Have you taken out one or more charter boat trips as a captain during the past season?

   No   1----TERMINATE
   Yes   2

[Q4]

4.   How many total charter boat trips would you estimate you went on as captain within the past 12 months?

   (Record number)

   Don't Know = 998
   Refused = 999

[Q5]

5.   How many of those would you estimate to be half day trips?

   (Record number)

   Don't Know = 998
   Refused = 999

[Q6]

6.   How many of those would you estimate to be three quarter day trips?

   (Record number)

   Don't Know = 998
   Refused = 999

[Q7]

7.   How many of those would you estimate to be full day trips?

(Record number)

Don't Know = 998
Refused = 999

[Q8]

8.   What is the name of the charter boat you primarily took out as captain during the past season?

[Q9]

9.   What is the name of the dock or marina where you typically pick up your passengers for a trip for that boat?

[Q10]

10.   In what country or parish is that dock or marina locations?

	a. Half Day Trips	b. Three-quarter Day Trips	c. Full Day Trips
11. Of the (number of trips from q3a) half day/three quarter day/full day trips, on how many did you fish within 300 feet of an oil or gas rig or within 300 feet of an artificial reef created from an oil or gas rig? **[Q11A – C]**			
12. Could you give me the names of the rigs or reefs at which you fished on these trips? **[Q12A – C]**			
13. Could you give me the locations of the rigs or reefs at which you fished on these half day/three quarter/full day trips? For location I can record either GPS readings, LORAN readings, or latitude and longitude. **[Q13A – C]**			
14. About how many miles from shore would you estimate that rig or reef to be? **[Q14A – C]**			
15. What is the normal per person adult fee charged for a half day/three quarter/ full day trip on the weekend this time of year? **[Q15A – C]**			
16. What is the normal per person adult fee charged for a half day/three quarter/ full day trip on a weekday this time of year? **[Q16A – C]**			

[Q17]

17.   In your experience as a charter boat captain, would you say that the fishing near an oil or gas rig is usually better than fishing at other locations, about the same as fishing at other locations, or worse than fishing at other locations?

Better   1
Same   2
Worse   3

Don't Know 4

Refused   5

[Q18]

18.   Are there particular species that your patrons usually target when you fish near an oil or gas platform or a reef created from an oil or gas platform?

Yes   1
No   2----GO TO Q20

[Q19A - D]

19.   Which species?

(Record species)

[Q20]

20.   How important would you say the presence of oil and gas rigs or artificial reefs created from oil and gas rigs are to the Gulf of Mexico charter boat industry? Would you say it was very important, somewhat important, not too important, or not at all important?

Very Important   1
Somewhat Important   2
Not Too Important   3
Not at All Important   4

Don't Know   8
Refused   9

[Q21]

21.   Do you think the charter boat industry would be helped or hurt economically by the removal of oil and gas rigs from the Gulf?

Helped   1
Hurt   2

Don't Know   8
Refused   9

[Q22]

22.　Do you think the Government should leave rigs in place after they are no longer used to extract oil or gas because of their benefit to the fishing industry?

Yes　　　　　1
No　　　　　2

Don't Know　8
Refused　　　9

[Q23]

23.　How many years have you been working as a charter boat captain?

[Q24]

24.　Is operating a charter boat your only source of earned income or do you do other work as well?

Only source of income　　　1
Do other work　　　　　　　2

Don't Know　　　　　　　　8
Refused　　　　　　　　　　9

1999 MMS Party Boat Captain Telephone Survey

[IDNUM]

[NAME]

[STATE]

[BOATNAME]

[AREACODE]

[FONNUM]

Hello, this is _____ calling from QuanTech in Rosslyn, Virginia. We are conducting a survey of charter boat operators in the Gulf of Mexico on behalf of the Minerals Management Service of the U.S. Department of the Interior. The purpose of the survey is to better understand the importance to the head boat industry of oil and gas rigs as well as artificial reefs created from oil and gas rigs.

You name was provided to us as a party boat captain in the state of (NAME OF STATE). All information you give will be kept completely confidential and your participation is voluntary. Your answers will be combined with those of other captains to help Minerals Management Service make decisions about the future of Gulf-based oil and gas rigs.

[Q1]

1.   Is the boat you operate considered to be a charter boat, a head boat, or do you function primarily as a guide service?

Charter boat	1----GO TO CHARTER BOAT QUESTIONNAIRE
Head Boat	2
Guide Service	3----GO TO GUIDE SERVICE QUESTIONNAIRE
Don't Know	8----THANK AND TERMINATE
Refused	9----THANK AND TERMINATE

[Q2]

2.   In what state did you primarily operat as a party boat captain during the past 12 months?

AL
MS
LA
TX

Other----THANK AND TERMINATE

[Q3]

3.   Have you taken out one or more party boat trips as a captain during the past season?

No   1----TERMINATE
Yes   2

[Q4]

4.   How many total charter boat trips would you estimate you went on as captain within the past 12 months?

(Record number)

Don't Know = 998
Refused = 999

[Q5]

5.   How many of those would you estimate to be half day trips?

(Record number)

Don't Know = 998
Refused = 999

[Q6]

6.   How many of those would you estimate to be three quarter day trips?

(Record number)

Don't Know = 998
Refused = 999

[Q7]

7.   How many of those would you estimate to be full day trips?

(Record number)

Don't Know = 998
Refused = 999

[Q8]

8.   What is the name of the head boat you primarily took out as captain during the past season?

[Q9]

9.   What is the name of the dock or marina where you typically pick up your passengers for a trip for that boat?

[Q10]

10.   In what country or parish is that dock or marina locationed?

	a. Half Day Trips	b. Three-quarter Day Trips	c. Full Day Trips
11. Of the (number of trips from q3a) half day/three quarter day/full day trips, on how many did you fish within 300 feet of an oil or gas rig or within 300 feet of an artificial reef created from an oil or gas rig? **[Q11A – C]**			
12. Could you give me the names of the rigs or reefs at which you fished on these trips? **[Q12A – C]**			
13. Could you give me the locations of the rigs or reefs at which you fished on these half day/three quarter/full day trips? For location I can record either GPS readings, LORAN readings, or latitude and longitude. **[Q13A – C]**			
14. About how many miles from shore would you estimate that rig or reef to be? **[Q14A – C]**			
15. What is the normal per person adult fee charged for a half day/three quarter/ full day trip on the weekend this time of year? **[Q15A – C]**			
16. What is the normal per person adult fee charged for a half day/three quarter/ full day trip on a weekday this time of year? **[Q16A – C]**			

[Q17]

17.   In your experience as a party boat captain, would you say that the fishing near an oil or gas rig is usually better than fishing at other locations, about the same as fishing at other locations, or worse than fishing at other locations?

    Better   1
    Same   2
    Worse   3

    Don't Know 4

Refused   5

[Q18]

18.   Are there particular species that your patrons usually target when you fish near an oil or gas platform or a reef created from an oil or gas platform?

Yes   1
No   2----GO TO Q20

[Q19A - D]

19.   Which species?

(Record species)

[Q20]

20.   How important would you say the presence of oil and gas rigs or artificial reefs created from oil and gas rigs are to the Gulf of Mexico party boat industry? Would you say it was very important, somewhat important, not too important, or not at all important?

Very Important   1
Somewhat Important   2
Not Too Important   3
Not at All Important   4

Don't Know   8
Refused   9

[Q21]

21.   Do you think the party boat industry would be helped or hurt economically by the removal of oil and gas rigs from the Gulf?

Helped   1
Hurt   2

Don't Know   8
Refused   9

[Q22]

22. Do you think the Government should leave rigs in place after they are no longer used to extract oil or gas because of their benefit to the fishing industry?

Yes	1
No	2
Don't Know	8
Refused	9

[Q23]

23. How many years have you been working as a party boat captain?

[Q24]

24. Is operating a party boat your only source of earned income or do you do other work as well?

Only source of income	1
Do other work	2
Don't Know	8
Refused	9

1999 MMS Dive Shop Survey

[IDNUM]

[NAME]

[AREACODE]

[PHONE]

[STATE]

Hello, this is _____ calling from QuanTech in Rosslyn, Virginia. We are conducting a survey of dive shops and guide services in the Gulf of Mexico on behalf of the Minerals Management Service of the U.S. Department of the Interior. The purpose of the survey is to better understand the importance to the recreational diving industry of oil and gas rigs as well as artificial reefs created from oil and gas rigs.

All information you give will be kept completely confidential and your participation is voluntary. Your answers will be combined with those of other dive shop and guide service operators to help Minerals Management Service make decisions about the future of Gulf-based oil and gas rigs.

[Q1]

1.   First I need to verify what type of business you are. Do you sell or rent diving related equipment?

       Yes   1
       No   2

[Q2]

2.   Do you provide guide boat services to divers in the Gulf?

       Yes   1
       No   2

[Q3]

3.   Do you offer diving lessons?

       Yes   1
       No   2

[IF NO TO Q.1 AND Q.2 AND Q.3, TERMINATE INTERVIEW]

5.   In what city and state are you located?

      [CITY]

      [STATE]

[IF YES TO Q2, CONTINUE WITH Q6; OTHERWISE, GO TO Q10]

[Q6]

6.   During the 1999 dive season, approximately how many recreational dive trips into Gulf waters would you estimate your firm has organized for your patrons?

[Q7]

7.   How many of those trips involved diving within 300 feet of an oil or gas platform or within 300 feet of an artificial reef created from an oil or gas platform?

[Q8]

8.   Approximately how many divers would you take on a typical recreational dive trip into Gulf waters?

[IF ONE OR MORE TRIPS ORGANIZED IN 1999 TO AN OIL/GAS RIG, CONTINUE WITH Q9; OTHERWISE, SKIP TO Q.10]

[Q9]

9.   Could you list for me the specific oil or gas rigs or reefs created from rigs at which you typically take divers? I can record either the name of the rig, its GPS coordinates, or LORAN readings for the site.

      [Record Name/Location]

[Q9A]

9A.   What launch site do you typically use when you take patrons to that dive
         location?

[Q9B]

9B.   What is the approximate distance from the launch site to that oil or gas rig or
         reef?

[Q10]

10.   In your experience in the recreational dive industry, would you say that the diving
         near an oil or gas rig is usually better than diving at other Gulf locations, about
         the same as diving at other locations, or worse than diving at other locations?

         Better   1
         Same   2
         Worse   3

         Don't Know   8
         Don't Know   9

[Q11]

11.   How important would you say the presence of oil and gas rigs or artificial reefs
         created from oil and gas rigs are to the Gulf of Mexico dive industry? Would you
         say it was very important, somewhat important, not too important, or not at all
         important?

         Very Important   1
         Somewhat Important   2
         Not Too Important   3
         Not at All Important   4

         Don't Know   8
         Refused   9

[Q12]

12. Do you think the dive industry would be helped or hurt economically by the removal of oil and gas rigs from the Gulf?

Helped   1
Hurt   2

[Q13]

13. Do you think the Government should leave rigs in place after they are no longer used to extract oil or gas because of their benefit to the dive industry?

Yes   1
No   2

[Q14]

14. How many years have you been working in the dive business?

[Q15]

15. Is operating a dive related business your only source of earned income or do you do other work as well?

Only source of income   1
Do other work   2

[Q16]

16. On average, what is the diving fee per individual per trip?

Appendix D: Field Procedures

Field Procedures for MMS Study
Of Economic Impact of Fishing and Diving
Near Gulf Oil and Gas Rigs

Background

There are more than 5,000 oil and gas rigs located in the Gulf of Mexico. Research in recent years has indicated that these rigs, over time, create their own ecosystems and attract a variety of fish. As a result, many fishermen and divers use these these rigs. In fact, there is an effort in Gulf states to convert permenantly many rigs to artificial reefs under a "rigs to reefs" program.

Under MMS rules, a company which has leased an offshore area and built a rig is required to remove the rig at the end of its useful life. However, the fact that many of these rigs have become important to fishing and diving may affect decisions MMS makes about the future of these rigs. The current study is being conducted during 1999 to determine the extent to which these rigs are used for fishing and diving and to measure their economic impact.

Method and Design

The following table provides detailed information on the design of the project. There are two methods of data collection which will be employed--a field interview and a telephone interview. The field interview will be used to obtain information from private boat fishermen (6,513), charter boat fishermen (1,331), party boat fishermen (400), and divers (200). Because of the distribution of rigs in the Gulf, we are only conducting the study in the states of Alabama, Mississippi, Louisiana, and Texas.

We have developed questionnaires for each of these groups. Each questionnaire consists of three parts:

- An introduction;
- A questionnaire;
- An answer sheet; and
- Maps.

Copies of these materials for the private boat fishermen (PR mode) are included in the Appendix. Other materials will be provided directly to field interviewers as they become available. The maps are especially important because we need to find out from fishermen and divers exactly which rigs were used for their activities. This may be the most difficult part of the field work. The number of field interviews shown in the following table have been distributed by state and month to create a quota that must be obtained by our field interviewers. Each interviewer will be advised as to the number of interviews we need in each state, month, and type of fishing or diving.

Summary of Data Collection Sample Plan

	MMS Field Interviews	Followup Telephone	Non-Followup Telephone
Private Boat Fishermen	6,513	3,255	-
Charter Boat Fishermen	1,331	920	-
Party Boat Fishermen	400	280	-
Charter Boat Operators	-	-	200
Party Boat Operators			50
Divers	200	200	
Dive Shop/Guide Services			50

Sampling Methods

The basic sample design for the field surveys involves the development of a listing of fishing locations within each state with some measure of the level of fishing activity at each location. We then randomly sample each site with busier sites sampled more frequently. Some sites are then designated for weekend interviewing and some sites designated for weekday interviewing. We will then ask each interviewer to visit the sampled site some time during the month, either weekend or weekday as specified, to obtain interviews.

Each interviewer will be provided with a copy of a listing of fishing sites in each state. On a day when an interviewer goes to the assigned site, but there are not enough fishermen interview productively, other nearby sites may be visited in order to obtain the required interviews. There are no specific rules regarding the selection of alternate sites for this survey. If it is necessary to visit an alternate, that site should be nearby and should be productive.

Interviewers will record on the Assignment Summary Form the name and identification numbers of each site visited.

Field Activities

Each interviewer will be contacted by QuanTech and given the names of the sites at which interviews are to be obtained during each month. The interviewer should monitor weather and fishing conditions to determine the best days to interview. On a day in which interviews can be obtained, the interviewer should visit the assigned site and, if necessary, any alternate sites, in order to obtain the required quota of interviews.

Interviewers should have available for interviewing the following materials:

- A copy of the **screener** form which introduces the interview;
- A copy of the **questionnaire** in a plastic sleeve;
- Multiple copies of the **coding sheets** to be completed for each fishermen or diver;
- An **Assignment Summary Form**;
- **Maps** that show locations and names of rigs;
- **Brochures** to give to respondents explaining the survey;
- A **coding manual** which lists all species codes for fish;
- A **field guide** for use in fish identification;
- **Name tags**; and
- A **site list**.

Interviewing Procedures

Interviewers should arrive at sites in order to interview during peak hours as anglers and divers return from their trips. **Shore fishermen are excluded from this survey**. Each person in the boat should be approached for an interview even if they live in the same household. One coding form should be completed for each person interviewed.

There is **no time limit** on how long an interviewer can remain on site as long as productivity levels are high. As noted previously, during this project it is important that we average **three interviews per hour** during the 12 months of data collection. This should not be difficult since the average interview can be completed in five minutes or less.

Interviewers should approach every available boat fisherman, hand them one of the brochures, and introduce the survey using the screening introduction. He should then read the questions on the questionnaire and record the answers on the coding sheet. Those respondents who indicated that they fished near and oil or gas platform should be shown the maps and asked to indicate the name or location of the map.

All questions should be **read as written** to assure consistency in responses.

Please note that we **do not interview persons five or younger**.

A key part of the interview for those who have been fishing within 300 feet or an oil or gas platform or and artificial reef created from an oil or gas platform will be the **identification of the specific rig at which respondents were fishing**. Interviewers are provided with a series of maps which show most of the rigs with their names. Interviewers should show these maps to those who fished near a rig in order to obtain either (1) the name of the rig or (2) the LORAN readings for the rig or (3) a GPS reading for the rig.

While QuanTech has no formal dress code, each interviewer is expected to be presentable for work in public. Tee shirts containing some design or logo are acceptable. Shorts are acceptable. Shoes or sandals are required. Bathing suits may not be worn. Interviewers may not fish while they are on site.

Followup Interview

It is **very important that we obtain telephone numbers** so we can recontact respondents to obtain information on costs and spending for each trip. If respondents seem unwilling to provide a name and phone number for telephone follow-up, please remind them that:

- All information will be kept **strictly confidential**;
- They can specify either a **home or business number** for a followup call;
- The evaluation of the importance of rigs for fishing and diving **cannot be met unless a large number of people participate in the followup**;
- The followup call can take as little as **five minutes** for some people and will average less than **15 minutes** for most people.

A common problem in the past has been the **failure to obtain the area code**, especially if the area code is different from those fishermen from local areas. Please be careful to properly obtain a good phone number with area code and mark it as either home or office.

Fish Codes

Each coding form should include both the accepted common name of the fish caught (whether kept or returned to the water) and the 10-digit species code. Species codes are to be found in the separately bound coding manual which has been provided to each interviewer. This list of codes is organized by **family**. An interviewer who knows the name of a species but is uncertain as to the family should look up the species in the index of the Peterson's field guide. This will provide the family name for the species.

Sending in Forms

It is vital that we recontact each respondent within two or three days of the field interview while they can still recall accurately information about their trip. In order to accomplish this, each interviewer is being provided with access to a **fax machine** and is **expected to fax in all completed forms each evening**. The QuanTech corporate fax number is **(703) 312-5104**. You should then retain all original copies of forms so we can call you if we have any questions about a particular answer. Each month you will be asked to mail completed forms to QuanTech.

Conflicts with Other Surveys

In Alabama, Mississippi, and Louisiana we may have instances where a QuanTech interviewer is assigned to the same site as a state interviewer working on the MRFSS. In that case, we have advised the Gulf States Marine Fisheries Commission that we would interview at alternate sites. You may ask the interviewer how long they intend to work for the day and return at a later time, if that is possible.

In Texas, we may be interviewing at the same sites as state personnel working on their sport fishing survey. The state has advised us that they are willing to work cooperatively at the same sites.

Any conflict problems that occur **must be brought to QuanTech's attention immediately**. Please call the office whenever a conflict occurs.

Administration

Interviewers working directly for QuanTech will continue to be paid twice monthly. We will writ checks on the 15th and last day of each month for work invoiced to us by the 10th and 25th. Please call the office with any questions about pay.

Appendix E: Interviewing Sites

Alabama Site Listing

COUNTY	SITE NUMBER	SITE NAME
3	0001	FAIRHOPE PUBLIC PIER
3	0005	COTTON BAYOU BOAT RAMPS
3	0010	GULF STATE PARK PIER
3	0012	ALABAMA POINT
3	0019	BAYWATCH MARINA
3	0027	GULF SHORES BEACHES
3	0056	ORANGE BEACH MARINA
3	0068	SPORTSMAN MARINA
3	0073	BOGGY POINT PUBLIC BOAT RAMPS
3	0075	WEEKS BAY PUBLIC BOAT RAMP
3	0091	FT MORGAN MARINA
3	0109	PERDIDO PASS MARINA
3	0115	FT MORGAN PUBLIC PIER
3	0116	ZEKE'S LANDING
3	0118	POOR MAN'S FISHING PIER
3	0119	MEAHER STATE PARK
3	0121	BEAR POINT MARINA
3	0123	PUBLIC PIER AT END OF GROUNDS LANE
3	0140	PUBLIC BOAT RAMP
3	0142	MULLET POINT PARK
3	1227	EARL GRIFFITHS
3	1228	TRENT MARINA
3	1229	OUTCAST MARINA
3	1230	ROY WALKER MARINA
3	1231	HUDSON MARINA
3	1232	BOBBY WALKER MARINA
97	0028	DAUPHIN ISLAND BAY PIER & RAMPS
97	0036	DAUPHIN ISLAND PUBLIC BOAT RAMPS
97	0037	FOWL RIVER MARINA
97	0040	DAUPHIN ISLAND MARINA
97	0041	DAUPHIN ISLAND GULF PIER
97	0043	BEACHCOMBER MARINA
97	0112	JEMISONS SEAFOOD MARKET
97	0114	CEDAR POINT FISHING PIER
97	0117	DAUPHIN ISLAND BAIT AND TACKLE
97	0124	THEODORE INDUST. CANAL- DAYTIME ONLY
97	0125	HOPPES FISHING CAMP
97	0126	MCNALLY PARK LAUNCH
97	0132	WHARF HOUSE FISHING PIER

Mississippi Site Listing

COUNTY	SITE NUMBER	SITE NAME
45	0053	BAY ST. LOUIS BRIDGE
45	0055	LA FRANCE'S FISHING CAMP
45	0064	BAYOU CADDY LAUNCHING RAMP
45	0065	BORDAGE'S FISHING CAMP
45	0066	BAY ST LOUIS FISHING PIER
45	0070	CEDAR POINT BOAT LAUNCH
45	0071	BAYOU LA CROIX MARINA
45	0076	WASHINGTON ST BEACH PARK
45	0081	PLEASURE ST
45	0082	8 MILE WATERFRONT, S BEACH BLVD
45	0100	WAVELAND MUN PIER
45	0105	PEARLINGTON PUBLIC BOAT RAMP
47	0035	OLD HIGHWAY 90 FISHING BRIDGE
47	0047	PASS CHRISTIAN MUNICIPAL HARBOR
47	0048	GULFPORT SMALL CRAFT HARBOR
47	0049	BILOXI SMALL CRAFT HARBOR
47	0051	LONG BEACH HARBOR
47	0052	BROADWATER BEACH MARINA
47	0084	GULF MARINE STATE PARK
47	0087	OLD POPPS FERRY CSWAY
47	0088	KUHN ST BOAT RAMP & PIER
47	0092	KREMER MARINE
47	0095	D'IBERVILLE RAMP
47	0096	LITTLE JOE'S FISH CAMP
47	0103	POINT CADET MARINA
47	0107	URIE PIER
47	0108	MOSES PIER
47	0113	GRAND CASINO CATWALK
47	0120	COMMUNITY HOUSE PIER
47	0122	JAMES HILL PARK AND FISHING PIER
47	0275	COURTHOUSE PIER
47	0276	COLISEUM PIER
47	0277	OLD BACK BAY BRIDGE
59	0032	MARY WALKER MARINA
59	0033	OCEAN SPRINGS HARBOR & FISHING PIER
59	0058	HWY 90 BOAT LAUNCH-PASCAGOULA
59	0059	WEST BEACH LAUNCH
59	0073	RIVER PARK FISHING PIER & BOAT RAMP
59	0075	OLD HWY 90 FISHING BRIDGE
59	0085	OCEAN SPRINGS COMMUNITY PIER
59	0089	LAKE MARS PIER
59	0090	GULF ISLANDS NATIONAL

		SEASHORE
59	0091	FORT BAYOU PUBLIC FISHING PIER & RAMP
59	0112	BAYOU CASSOTTE PIER AND RAMP

Louisiana Site Listing

COUNTY	SITE NUMBER	SITE NAME
19	0030	PRIEN LAKE PARK
19	0060	DEVIL'S ELBOW LAUNCH
19	0062	INTERCOASTAL WATERWAY PARK
19	0262	INTERSTATE 210 BEACH LAUNCH
19	0266	LAKE CHARLES CIVIC CENTER SEAWALL
19	0272	I-10 BRIDGE LAUNCH
23	0024	BEACH BTW'N HOLLY BEACH\CONSTANCE BCH
23	0025	SABINE LAKE, BETWEEN TEXAS & LA LINE
23	0043	JOSEPH'S HARBOR
23	0044	ROCKEFELLER REFUGE LAUNCH
23	0046	GRAND CHENIER PARK
23	0049	RUTHERFORD BEACH PARK
23	0050	CAMERON JETTIES & RAMP
23	0053	HWY 27 ROADSIDE
23	0178	MONKEY ISLAND
23	0179	MERMENTAU RIVER AREA
23	0233	CAMERON SHIP CHANNEL
23	0298	HACKBERRY SHELL PILE AREA & BOAT RAMP
23	0305	HEBERT'S LANDING
45	0324	PORT OF IBERIA RAMP
45	0326	BAYOU PATOUT
51	0071	BONNABEL BOAT LAUNCH
51	0127	LAFITTE C-WAY MARINA
51	0140	BON VOYAGE MARINA
51	0141	BRIDGE SIDE MARINA
51	0143	CIGAR'S MARINA
51	0150	ABANDONED HWY 1 BRIDGE (WEST)
51	0151	ABANDONED HWY 1 BRIDGE (EAST)
51	0159	ELMER'S ISLAND CAMPING AND FISHING
51	0222	BANK ALONG HWY 1 ROADSIDE
51	0224	WILLIAMS BLVD BOAT RAMP
51	0255	PIRATES' COVE MARINA
51	0256	GRAND ISLE STATE PARK FISHING PIER
51	0268	GRAND ISLE BEACH AREA
51	0299	COCHIARAS MARINA
51	0316	SAND DOLLAR MARINA
51	0322	LAFITTE HARBOR
57	0008	ED'S BOAT LAUNCH
57	0130	CHARLIE HARDISONS PLACE BELLE PASS
57	0133	BUCKS LAUNCH
57	0135	BIG BAYOU BLUE MARINA
57	0169	LAFOURCHE BEACH
57	0230	MELANCON LAUNCH
57	0231	ROADSIDE ALONG SHOULDER OF HWY 1
57	0269	BOUDREAUX'S WATERFRONT MOTEL
57	0317	KAJUN SPORTSMAN MARINA

57	0323	Port Fourchon Marina
57	0328	BOBBY LYNN'S MARINA
57	0524	Oakridge Public Ramp
71	0155	WESTEND BOAT LAUNCH
71	0183	BAYOU BIENVENUE MARINA
71	0227	LOMBARD'S
71	0238	FORT PIKE STATE PARK-PUBLIC LAUNCH
71	0239	CHEF HARBOR
71	0287	FISHERMAN'S PARADISE
71	0306	SEABROOK LAUNCH & PIER
71	0333	FORT MACOMB
75	0006	VENICE MARINA
75	0073	MYRTLE GROVE MARINA
75	0074	PT LA HACHE MARINA, BESHEL BT LNCH
75	0121	HAPPY JACK'S MARINA
75	0122	HI RIDGE MARINA
75	0126	JOSHUA MARINA
75	0173	LAKE HERMITAGE LAUNCH
75	0232	DELTA MARINA
75	0257	FORT JACKSON
75	0311	CYPRESS COVE MARINA
87	0002	GULF OUTLET MARINA
87	0033	BLACKIE CAMPO'S BOAT LAUNCH
87	0040	DE POPES LAUNCH
87	0064	BRETON SOUND MARINA
87	0182	PIP'S PLACE
87	0274	SERIGNE'S BOAT LAUNCH
87	0277	END OF THE WORLD MARINA
87	0301	FISHERMAN'S LAUNCH
87	0318	REGGIO MARINA
87	0340	BAYOU BIENUENUE BOAT LAUNCH
101	0083	CYPREMONT POINT PUBLIC LAUNCH
101	0181	BURNS POINT RECREATIONAL AREA
101	0270	CYPREMONT POINT STATE PARK
103	0069	GILBERT'S PLACE
103	0070	RIGOLETS MARINA
103	0276	TITE'S PLACE
103	0296	PEARL RIVER RAMP (PUBLIC)
103	0297	LACOMBE BOAT RAMP
103	0300	MADISONVILLE RAMP
103	0319	MANDEVILLE HARBOR
105	0304	PASS MANCHAC RAMP
109	0067	CO CO MARINA
109	0079	T-IRV'S MARINA
109	0109	BOUDREAUX LANDING
109	0147	BAYOU DU LARGE MARINA
109	0152	SPORTSMAN'S PARADISE
109	0158	KOZY KAMPERS
109	0244	POINTE AUX CHENE MARINA

109	0278	BAYOU NEUF MARINA
109	0307	ISLE JEAN CHARLES RD
109	0320	POINT COCODRIE INN
109	0325	BAYOU DULARGE
109	0330	TERRY & BRENDA'S OLD LAUNCH
109	0331	POINT BARRE RAMP
109	0332	HARBOR LIGHT MARINA
109	0341	MONTEGUT RAMP
113	0021	INTRACSTL CITY PUB LNCH ON HWY 333
113	0023	ROLL OVER LANDING
113	0091	ACADIANA MARINA
113	0321	DON'S LAUNCH

Texas Site Listing

COUNTY	SITE NUMBER	SITE NAME
167	0001	Texas City Dike
039	0002	Freeport public ramp
167	0003	Galv. Causeway
167	0004	Galveston Yacht
355	0005	Port Aransas Public
355	0006	Woody's Sport Center
167	0007	Pier 19
039	0008	Brazoria Co. Ramp
167	0009	Teakwood Marina
039	0010	Action Charters
039	0011	Bridge Harbor Yacht Club
057	0013	Port O'Connor Public Ramp
057	0015	The Fishing Center
057	0016	Clark's Marina

Appendix F: Summary Statistics

Charter Boat Summary Statistics for trip and equipment expenditures by Alabama
coastal residents who did visit an oil/gas structure on the interview date

Variable	Label	N	Mean	Minimum	Maximum
TRANST	Transportation:Total	8	0.00	0.00	0.00
TRANSC	Transportation:Near-Coast	8	0.00	0.00	0.00
RCART	Rental Car:Total	8	0.00	0.00	0.00
RCARC	Rental Car:Near-Coast	8	0.00	0.00	0.00
LODGT	Lodging:Total	8	0.00	0.00	0.00
LODGC	Lodging:Near-Coast	8	0.00	0.00	0.00
GAST	Gasoline:Total	8	2.16	0.00	7.50
GASC	Gasoline:Near-Coast	8	2.16	0.00	7.50
FOODT	Other Food:Total	8	2.50	0.00	20.00
FOODC	Other Food:Near-Coast	8	2.50	0.00	20.00
GROCT	Groceries:Total	8	5.00	0.00	20.00
GROCC	Groceries:Near-Coast	8	5.00	0.00	20.00
BAITT	Bait:Total	8	3.75	0.00	20.00
BAITC	Bait:Near-Coast	8	3.75	0.00	20.00
FLICT	Fishing Licenses:Total	8	0.00	0.00	0.00
FLICC	Fishing Licenses:Near-Coast	8	0.00	0.00	0.00
TCKLT	Tackle:Total	8	0.00	0.00	0.00
TCKLC	Tackle:Near-Coast	8	0.00	0.00	0.00
OTHRNTT	Other Rentals:Total	8	0.00	0.00	0.00
OTHRNTC	Other Rentals:Near-Coast	8	0.00	0.00	0.00
CLTHT	Clothing:Total	8	0.00	0.00	0.00
CLTHC	Clothing:Near-Coast	8	0.00	0.00	0.00
OTHRTT	Other Trip Expenses:Total	8	0.00	0.00	0.00
OTHRTC	Other Trip Expenses:Near-Coast	8	0.00	0.00	0.00
CHFEEST	Charter/Party Fees:Total	8	0.00	0.00	0.00
CHFEESC	Charter/Party Fees:Near-Coast	8	0.00	0.00	0.00
RODC	Rods:Near-Coast	8	77.50	0.00	300.00
RODNC	Rods:Away-Coast	8	0.00	0.00	0.00
LINEC	Fishing Line:Near-Coast	8	33.13	0.00	200.00
LINENC	Fishing Line:Away-Coast	8	0.00	0.00	0.00
LUREC	Lures:Near-Coast	8	26.25	0.00	100.00
LURENC	Lures:Nonoastal	8	0.00	0.00	0.00
OTHCFC	Other Fishing:Near-Coast	8	0.00	0.00	0.00
OTHCFNC	Other Fishing:Away-Coast	8	0.00	0.00	0.00
BOOKC	Books:Near-Coast	8	3.75	0.00	30.00
BOOKNC	Books:Away-Coast	8	0.00	0.00	0.00
MEMBC	Memberships:Near-Coast	8	0.00	0.00	0.00
MEMBNC	Memberships:Away-Coast	8	0.00	0.00	0.00
CAMPC	Camping:Near-Coast	8	0.00	0.00	0.00
CAMPNC	Camping:Away-Coast	8	0.00	0.00	0.00
LICC	Licenses:Near-Coast	8	10.00	0.00	26.00
LICNC	Licenses:Away-Coast	8	0.00	0.00	0.00

Charter Boat Summary Statistics for trip and equipment expenditures by Alabama
noncoastal residents who did visit an oil/gas structure on the interview date

Variable	Label	N	Mean	Minimum	Maximum
TRANST	Transportation:Total	6	0.00	0.00	0.00
TRANSC	Transportation:Near-Coast	6	0.00	0.00	0.00
RCART	Rental Car:Total	6	0.00	0.00	0.00
RCARC	Rental Car:Near-Coast	6	0.00	0.00	0.00
LODGT	Lodging:Total	6	53.33	0.00	320.00
LODGC	Lodging:Near-Coast	6	53.33	0.00	320.00
GAST	Gasoline:Total	6	111.75	58.50	195.15
GASC	Gasoline:Near-Coast	6	0.00	0.00	0.00
FOODT	Other Food:Total	6	166.67	0.00	600.00
FOODC	Other Food:Near-Coast	6	166.67	0.00	600.00
GROCT	Groceries:Total	6	36.83	0.00	180.00
GROCC	Groceries:Near-Coast	6	36.83	0.00	180.00
BAITT	Bait:Total	6	10.67	0.00	36.00
BAITC	Bait:Near-Coast	6	10.67	0.00	36.00
FLICT	Fishing Licenses:Total	6	0.00	0.00	0.00
FLICC	Fishing Licenses:Near-Coast	6	0.00	0.00	0.00
TCKLT	Tackle:Total	6	0.00	0.00	0.00
TCKLC	Tackle:Near-Coast	6	0.00	0.00	0.00
OTHRNTT	Other Rentals:Total	6	0.00	0.00	0.00
OTHRNTC	Other Rentals:Near-Coast	6	0.00	0.00	0.00
CLTHT	Clothing:Total	6	0.00	0.00	0.00
CLTHC	Clothing:Near-Coast	6	0.00	0.00	0.00
OTHRTT	Other Trip Expenses:Total	6	0.33	0.00	2.00
OTHRTC	Other Trip Expenses:Near-Coast	6	0.33	0.00	2.00
CHFEEST	Charter/Party Fees:Total	6	570.83	0.00	1500.00
CHFEESC	Charter/Party Fees:Near-Coast	6	570.83	0.00	1500.00
RODC	Rods:Near-Coast	6	0.00	0.00	0.00
RODNC	Rods:Away-Coast	6	100.00	0.00	400.00
LINEC	Fishing Line:Near-Coast	6	0.00	0.00	0.00
LINENC	Fishing Line:Away-Coast	6	2.50	0.00	15.00
LUREC	Lures:Near-Coast	6	0.00	0.00	0.00
LURENC	Lures:Nonoastal	6	0.00	0.00	0.00
OTHCFC	Other Fishing:Near-Coast	6	8.33	0.00	50.00
OTHCFNC	Other Fishing:Away-Coast	6	0.00	0.00	0.00
BOOKC	Books:Near-Coast	6	0.00	0.00	0.00
BOOKNC	Books:Away-Coast	6	13.00	0.00	70.00
MEMBC	Memberships:Near-Coast	6	0.00	0.00	0.00
MEMBNC	Memberships:Away-Coast	6	0.00	0.00	0.00
CAMPC	Camping:Near-Coast	6	0.00	0.00	0.00
CAMPNC	Camping:Away-Coast	6	50.00	0.00	300.00
LICC	Licenses:Near-Coast	6	0.00	0.00	0.00
LICNC	Licenses:Away-Coast	6	7.00	0.00	31.00

C

harter Boat Summary Statistics for trip and equipment expenditures by Mississippi
coastal residents who did visit an oil/gas structure on the interview date

Variable	Label	N	Mean	Minimum	Maximum
TRANST	Transportation:Total	3	66.67	0.00	200.00
TRANSC	Transportation:Near-Coast	3	66.67	0.00	200.00
RCART	Rental Car:Total	3	0.00	0.00	0.00
RCARC	Rental Car:Near-Coast	3	0.00	0.00	0.00
LODGT	Lodging:Total	3	0.00	0.00	0.00
LODGC	Lodging:Near-Coast	3	0.00	0.00	0.00
GAST	Gasoline:Total	3	0.00	0.00	0.00
GASC	Gasoline:Near-Coast	3	0.00	0.00	0.00
FOODT	Other Food:Total	3	183.33	150.00	200.00
FOODC	Other Food:Near-Coast	3	183.33	150.00	200.00
GROCT	Groceries:Total	3	5.33	0.00	10.00
GROCC	Groceries:Near-Coast	3	5.33	0.00	10.00
BAITT	Bait:Total	3	2.00	0.00	6.00
BAITC	Bait:Near-Coast	3	2.00	0.00	6.00
FLICT	Fishing Licenses:Total	3	107.00	26.00	250.00
FLICC	Fishing Licenses:Near-Coast	3	107.00	26.00	250.00
TCKLT	Tackle:Total	3	200.00	0.00	600.00
TCKLC	Tackle:Near-Coast	3	200.00	0.00	600.00
OTHRNTT	Other Rentals:Total	3	0.00	0.00	0.00
OTHRNTC	Other Rentals:Near-Coast	3	0.00	0.00	0.00
CLTHT	Clothing:Total	3	0.00	0.00	0.00
CLTHC	Clothing:Near-Coast	3	0.00	0.00	0.00
OTHRTT	Other Trip Expenses:Total	3	105.33	0.00	276.00
OTHRTC	Other Trip Expenses:Near-Coast	3	105.33	0.00	276.00
CHFEEST	Charter/Party Fees:Total	3	0.00	0.00	0.00
CHFEESC	Charter/Party Fees:Near-Coast	3	0.00	0.00	0.00
RODC	Rods:Near-Coast	3	20.00	0.00	60.00
RODNC	Rods:Away-Coast	3	0.00	0.00	0.00
LINEC	Fishing Line:Near-Coast	3	101.67	0.00	300.00
LINENC	Fishing Line:Away-Coast	3	0.00	0.00	0.00
LUREC	Lures:Near-Coast	3	7.33	0.00	15.00
LURENC	Lures:Nonoastal	3	0.00	0.00	0.00
OTHCFC	Other Fishing:Near-Coast	3	0.00	0.00	0.00
OTHCFNC	Other Fishing:Away-Coast	3	0.00	0.00	0.00
BOOKC	Books:Near-Coast	3	33.67	0.00	100.00
BOOKNC	Books:Away-Coast	3	0.00	0.00	0.00
MEMBC	Memberships:Near-Coast	3	283.33	50.00	500.00
MEMBNC	Memberships:Away-Coast	3	0.00	0.00	0.00
CAMPC	Camping:Near-Coast	3	200.00	0.00	600.00
CAMPNC	Camping:Away-Coast	3	0.00	0.00	0.00
LICC	Licenses:Near-Coast	3	75.67	6.00	146.00
LICNC	Licenses:Away-Coast	3	0.00	0.00	0.00

Charter Boat Summary Statistics for trip and equipment expenditures by Mississippi
noncoastal residents who did visit an oil/gas structure on the interview date

Variable	Label	N	Mean	Minimum	Maximum
TRANST	Transportation:Total	8	0.00	0.00	0.00
TRANSC	Transportation:Near-Coast	8	0.00	0.00	0.00
RCART	Rental Car:Total	8	3.75	0.00	30.00
RCARC	Rental Car:Near-Coast	8	0.00	0.00	0.00
LODGT	Lodging:Total	8	105.00	0.00	450.00
LODGC	Lodging:Near-Coast	8	105.00	0.00	450.00
GAST	Gasoline:Total	8	33.79	0.00	60.00
GASC	Gasoline:Near-Coast	8	0.00	0.00	0.00
FOODT	Other Food:Total	8	51.25	0.00	210.00
FOODC	Other Food:Near-Coast	8	25.00	0.00	200.00
GROCT	Groceries:Total	8	100.00	0.00	600.00
GROCC	Groceries:Near-Coast	8	100.00	0.00	600.00
BAITT	Bait:Total	8	0.00	0.00	0.00
BAITC	Bait:Near-Coast	8	0.00	0.00	0.00
FLICT	Fishing Licenses:Total	8	7.50	0.00	45.00
FLICC	Fishing Licenses:Near-Coast	8	1.88	0.00	15.00
TCKLT	Tackle:Total	8	0.00	0.00	0.00
TCKLC	Tackle:Near-Coast	8	0.00	0.00	0.00
OTHRNTT	Other Rentals:Total	8	0.00	0.00	0.00
OTHRNTC	Other Rentals:Near-Coast	8	0.00	0.00	0.00
CLTHT	Clothing:Total	8	56.25	0.00	450.00
CLTHC	Clothing:Near-Coast	8	0.00	0.00	0.00
OTHRTT	Other Trip Expenses:Total	8	1.25	0.00	10.00
OTHRTC	Other Trip Expenses:Near-Coast	8	0.00	0.00	0.00
CHFEEST	Charter/Party Fees:Total	8	18.75	0.00	150.00
CHFEESC	Charter/Party Fees:Near-Coast	8	18.75	0.00	150.00
RODC	Rods:Near-Coast	8	0.00	0.00	0.00
RODNC	Rods:Away-Coast	8	72.50	0.00	400.00
LINEC	Fishing Line:Near-Coast	8	0.00	0.00	0.00
LINENC	Fishing Line:Away-Coast	8	19.13	0.00	100.00
LUREC	Lures:Near-Coast	8	0.00	0.00	0.00
LURENC	Lures:Nonoastal	8	6.88	0.00	50.00
OTHCFC	Other Fishing:Near-Coast	8	0.00	0.00	0.00
OTHCFNC	Other Fishing:Away-Coast	8	0.25	0.00	2.00
BOOKC	Books:Near-Coast	8	0.00	0.00	0.00
BOOKNC	Books:Away-Coast	8	5.13	0.00	40.00
MEMBC	Memberships:Near-Coast	8	0.00	0.00	0.00
MEMBNC	Memberships:Away-Coast	8	2.50	0.00	20.00
CAMPC	Camping:Near-Coast	8	0.00	0.00	0.00
CAMPNC	Camping:Away-Coast	8	0.00	0.00	0.00
LICC	Licenses:Near-Coast	8	0.00	0.00	0.00
LICNC	Licenses:Away-Coast	8	10.00	0.00	50.00

Charter Boat Summary Statistics for trip and equipment expenditures by Louisiana
coastal residents who did visit an oil/gas structure on the interview date

Variable	Label	N	Mean	Minimum	Maximum
TRANST	Transportation:Total	23	0.00	0.00	0.00
TRANSC	Transportation:Near-Coast	23	0.00	0.00	0.00
RCART	Rental Car:Total	23	0.00	0.00	0.00
RCARC	Rental Car:Near-Coast	23	0.00	0.00	0.00
LODGT	Lodging:Total	23	25.22	0.00	300.00
LODGC	Lodging:Near-Coast	23	25.22	0.00	300.00
GAST	Gasoline:Total	23	10.86	0.00	34.50
GASC	Gasoline:Near-Coast	23	10.86	0.00	34.50
FOODT	Other Food:Total	23	26.52	0.00	300.00
FOODC	Other Food:Near-Coast	23	26.52	0.00	300.00
GROCT	Groceries:Total	23	12.30	0.00	100.00
GROCC	Groceries:Near-Coast	23	12.30	0.00	100.00
BAITT	Bait:Total	23	14.00	0.00	300.00
BAITC	Bait:Near-Coast	23	14.00	0.00	300.00
FLICT	Fishing Licenses:Total	23	1.52	0.00	20.00
FLICC	Fishing Licenses:Near-Coast	23	1.52	0.00	20.00
TCKLT	Tackle:Total	23	1.48	0.00	25.00
TCKLC	Tackle:Near-Coast	23	1.48	0.00	25.00
OTHRNTT	Other Rentals:Total	23	13.04	0.00	300.00
OTHRNTC	Other Rentals:Near-Coast	23	13.04	0.00	300.00
CLTHT	Clothing:Total	23	6.52	0.00	100.00
CLTHC	Clothing:Near-Coast	23	6.52	0.00	100.00
OTHRTT	Other Trip Expenses:Total	23	2.22	0.00	30.00
OTHRTC	Other Trip Expenses:Near-Coast	23	2.22	0.00	30.00
CHFEEST	Charter/Party Fees:Total	23	61.74	0.00	1000.00
CHFEESC	Charter/Party Fees:Near-Coast	23	61.74	0.00	1000.00
RODC	Rods:Near-Coast	23	180.43	0.00	2000.00
RODNC	Rods:Away-Coast	23	99.78	0.00	1500.00
LINEC	Fishing Line:Near-Coast	23	13.74	0.00	100.00
LINENC	Fishing Line:Away-Coast	23	8.26	0.00	150.00
LUREC	Lures:Near-Coast	23	29.87	0.00	300.00
LURENC	Lures:Nonoastal	23	6.87	0.00	100.00
OTHCFC	Other Fishing:Near-Coast	23	122.61	0.00	2700.00
OTHCFNC	Other Fishing:Away-Coast	23	43.65	0.00	500.00
BOOKC	Books:Near-Coast	23	5.96	0.00	50.00
BOOKNC	Books:Away-Coast	23	0.00	0.00	0.00
MEMBC	Memberships:Near-Coast	23	2.61	0.00	60.00
MEMBNC	Memberships:Away-Coast	23	0.00	0.00	0.00
CAMPC	Camping:Near-Coast	23	28.70	0.00	600.00
CAMPNC	Camping:Away-Coast	23	0.00	0.00	0.00
LICC	Licenses:Near-Coast	23	11.30	0.00	65.00
LICNC	Licenses:Away-Coast	23	0.00	0.00	0.00

Charter Boat Summary Statistics for trip and equipment expenditures by Louisiana
noncoastal residents who did visit an oil/gas structure on the interview date

Variable	Label	N	Mean	Minimum	Maximum
TRANST	Transportation:Total	7	0.00	0.00	0.00
TRANSC	Transportation:Near-Coast	7	0.00	0.00	0.00
RCART	Rental Car:Total	7	0.00	0.00	0.00
RCARC	Rental Car:Near-Coast	7	0.00	0.00	0.00
LODGT	Lodging:Total	7	8.00	0.00	56.00
LODGC	Lodging:Near-Coast	7	8.00	0.00	56.00
GAST	Gasoline:Total	7	27.13	0.00	60.00
GASC	Gasoline:Near-Coast	7	0.00	0.00	0.00
FOODT	Other Food:Total	7	10.71	0.00	25.00
FOODC	Other Food:Near-Coast	7	0.71	0.00	5.00
GROCT	Groceries:Total	7	8.86	0.00	40.00
GROCC	Groceries:Near-Coast	7	0.00	0.00	0.00
BAITT	Bait:Total	7	4.29	0.00	15.00
BAITC	Bait:Near-Coast	7	3.57	0.00	15.00
FLICT	Fishing Licenses:Total	7	5.71	0.00	20.00
FLICC	Fishing Licenses:Near-Coast	7	2.86	0.00	10.00
TCKLT	Tackle:Total	7	0.00	0.00	0.00
TCKLC	Tackle:Near-Coast	7	0.00	0.00	0.00
OTHRNTT	Other Rentals:Total	7	0.00	0.00	0.00
OTHRNTC	Other Rentals:Near-Coast	7	0.00	0.00	0.00
CLTHT	Clothing:Total	7	0.43	0.00	3.00
CLTHC	Clothing:Near-Coast	7	0.00	0.00	0.00
OTHRTT	Other Trip Expenses:Total	7	2.86	0.00	15.00
OTHRTC	Other Trip Expenses:Near-Coast	7	0.71	0.00	5.00
CHFEEST	Charter/Party Fees:Total	7	82.71	0.00	190.00
CHFEESC	Charter/Party Fees:Near-Coast	7	82.71	0.00	190.00
RODC	Rods:Near-Coast	7	0.00	0.00	0.00
RODNC	Rods:Away-Coast	7	85.71	0.00	400.00
LINEC	Fishing Line:Near-Coast	7	0.00	0.00	0.00
LINENC	Fishing Line:Away-Coast	7	1.43	0.00	10.00
LUREC	Lures:Near-Coast	7	0.00	0.00	0.00
LURENC	Lures:Nonoastal	7	10.71	0.00	75.00
OTHCFC	Other Fishing:Near-Coast	7	0.00	0.00	0.00
OTHCFNC	Other Fishing:Away-Coast	7	0.00	0.00	0.00
BOOKC	Books:Near-Coast	7	0.00	0.00	0.00
BOOKNC	Books:Away-Coast	7	2.43	0.00	17.00
MEMBC	Memberships:Near-Coast	7	0.00	0.00	0.00
MEMBNC	Memberships:Away-Coast	7	0.00	0.00	0.00
CAMPC	Camping:Near-Coast	7	0.00	0.00	0.00
CAMPNC	Camping:Away-Coast	7	0.00	0.00	0.00
LICC	Licenses:Near-Coast	7	0.00	0.00	0.00
LICNC	Licenses:Away-Coast	7	2.29	0.00	10.00

Charter Boat Summary Statistics for trip and equipment expenditures by Texas
coastal residents who did visit an oil/gas structure on the interview date

Variable	Label	N	Mean	Minimum	Maximum
TRANST	Transportation:Total	14	0.00	0.00	0.00
TRANSC	Transportation:Near-Coast	14	0.00	0.00	0.00
RCART	Rental Car:Total	14	0.00	0.00	0.00
RCARC	Rental Car:Near-Coast	14	0.00	0.00	0.00
LODGT	Lodging:Total	14	0.00	0.00	0.00
LODGC	Lodging:Near-Coast	14	0.00	0.00	0.00
GAST	Gasoline:Total	14	5.03	0.00	12.75
GASC	Gasoline:Near-Coast	14	5.03	0.00	12.75
FOODT	Other Food:Total	14	16.43	0.00	100.00
FOODC	Other Food:Near-Coast	14	16.43	0.00	100.00
GROCT	Groceries:Total	14	29.64	0.00	200.00
GROCC	Groceries:Near-Coast	14	29.64	0.00	200.00
BAITT	Bait:Total	14	1.07	0.00	15.00
BAITC	Bait:Near-Coast	14	1.07	0.00	15.00
FLICT	Fishing Licenses:Total	14	0.00	0.00	0.00
FLICC	Fishing Licenses:Near-Coast	14	0.00	0.00	0.00
TCKLT	Tackle:Total	14	7.86	0.00	100.00
TCKLC	Tackle:Near-Coast	14	7.86	0.00	100.00
OTHRNTT	Other Rentals:Total	14	0.00	0.00	0.00
OTHRNTC	Other Rentals:Near-Coast	14	0.00	0.00	0.00
CLTHT	Clothing:Total	14	0.00	0.00	0.00
CLTHC	Clothing:Near-Coast	14	0.00	0.00	0.00
OTHRTT	Other Trip Expenses:Total	14	3.07	0.00	30.00
OTHRTC	Other Trip Expenses:Near-Coast	14	3.07	0.00	30.00
CHFEEST	Charter/Party Fees:Total	14	116.43	0.00	750.00
CHFEESC	Charter/Party Fees:Near-Coast	14	116.43	0.00	750.00
RODC	Rods:Near-Coast	14	323.21	0.00	1500.00
RODNC	Rods:Away-Coast	14	37.50	0.00	300.00
LINEC	Fishing Line:Near-Coast	14	49.93	0.00	300.00
LINENC	Fishing Line:Away-Coast	14	1.79	0.00	25.00
LUREC	Lures:Near-Coast	14	1.29	0.00	10.00
LURENC	Lures:Nonoastal	14	0.29	0.00	3.00
OTHCFC	Other Fishing:Near-Coast	14	2.14	0.00	30.00
OTHCFNC	Other Fishing:Away-Coast	14	3.57	0.00	50.00
BOOKC	Books:Near-Coast	14	24.79	0.00	120.00
BOOKNC	Books:Away-Coast	14	0.00	0.00	0.00
MEMBC	Memberships:Near-Coast	14	18.21	0.00	100.00
MEMBNC	Memberships:Away-Coast	14	0.00	0.00	0.00
CAMPC	Camping:Near-Coast	14	136.00	0.00	1000.00
CAMPNC	Camping:Away-Coast	14	0.00	0.00	0.00
LICC	Licenses:Near-Coast	14	39.14	0.00	230.00
LICNC	Licenses:Away-Coast	14	0.00	0.00	0.00

Charter Boat Summary Statistics for trip and equipment expenditures by Texas
noncoastal residents who did visit an oil/gas structure on the interview date

Variable	Label	N	Mean	Minimum	Maximum
TRANST	Transportation:Total	6	0.00	0.00	0.00
TRANSC	Transportation:Near-Coast	6	0.00	0.00	0.00
RCART	Rental Car:Total	6	20.83	0.00	125.00
RCARC	Rental Car:Near-Coast	6	0.00	0.00	0.00
LODGT	Lodging:Total	6	13.33	0.00	80.00
LODGC	Lodging:Near-Coast	6	13.33	0.00	80.00
GAST	Gasoline:Total	6	32.08	0.00	98.55
GASC	Gasoline:Near-Coast	6	0.00	0.00	0.00
FOODT	Other Food:Total	6	30.00	0.00	180.00
FOODC	Other Food:Near-Coast	6	30.00	0.00	180.00
GROCT	Groceries:Total	6	15.00	0.00	90.00
GROCC	Groceries:Near-Coast	6	15.00	0.00	90.00
BAITT	Bait:Total	6	0.00	0.00	0.00
BAITC	Bait:Near-Coast	6	0.00	0.00	0.00
FLICT	Fishing Licenses:Total	6	4.00	0.00	24.00
FLICC	Fishing Licenses:Near-Coast	6	4.00	0.00	24.00
TCKLT	Tackle:Total	6	0.00	0.00	0.00
TCKLC	Tackle:Near-Coast	6	0.00	0.00	0.00
OTHRNTT	Other Rentals:Total	6	0.00	0.00	0.00
OTHRNTC	Other Rentals:Near-Coast	6	0.00	0.00	0.00
CLTHT	Clothing:Total	6	0.00	0.00	0.00
CLTHC	Clothing:Near-Coast	6	0.00	0.00	0.00
OTHRTT	Other Trip Expenses:Total	6	7.67	0.00	40.00
OTHRTC	Other Trip Expenses:Near-Coast	6	7.67	0.00	40.00
CHFEEST	Charter/Party Fees:Total	6	191.67	0.00	1000.00
CHFEESC	Charter/Party Fees:Near-Coast	6	191.67	0.00	1000.00
RODC	Rods:Near-Coast	6	0.00	0.00	0.00
RODNC	Rods:Away-Coast	6	25.00	0.00	150.00
LINEC	Fishing Line:Near-Coast	6	0.00	0.00	0.00
LINENC	Fishing Line:Away-Coast	6	1.17	0.00	7.00
LUREC	Lures:Near-Coast	6	0.00	0.00	0.00
LURENC	Lures:Nonoastal	6	10.83	0.00	50.00
OTHCFC	Other Fishing:Near-Coast	6	0.00	0.00	0.00
OTHCFNC	Other Fishing:Away-Coast	6	0.00	0.00	0.00
BOOKC	Books:Near-Coast	6	0.00	0.00	0.00
BOOKNC	Books:Away-Coast	6	6.67	0.00	40.00
MEMBC	Memberships:Near-Coast	6	0.00	0.00	0.00
MEMBNC	Memberships:Away-Coast	6	0.00	0.00	0.00
CAMPC	Camping:Near-Coast	6	0.00	0.00	0.00
CAMPNC	Camping:Away-Coast	6	5.00	0.00	30.00
LICC	Licenses:Near-Coast	6	0.00	0.00	0.00
LICNC	Licenses:Away-Coast	6	14.50	0.00	54.00

Charter Boat Summary Statistics for trip and equipment expenditures by Alabama
coastal residents who did't visit an oil/gas structure on the interview date

Variable	Label	N	Mean	Minimum	Maximum
TRANST	Transportation:Total	12	0.00	0.00	0.00
TRANSC	Transportation:Near-Coast	12	0.00	0.00	0.00
RCART	Rental Car:Total	12	0.00	0.00	0.00
RCARC	Rental Car:Near-Coast	12	0.00	0.00	0.00
LODGT	Lodging:Total	12	87.92	0.00	450.00
LODGC	Lodging:Near-Coast	12	87.92	0.00	450.00
GAST	Gasoline:Total	12	10.76	0.15	30.60
GASC	Gasoline:Near-Coast	12	10.76	0.15	30.60
FOODT	Other Food:Total	12	21.67	0.00	200.00
FOODC	Other Food:Near-Coast	12	21.67	0.00	200.00
GROCT	Groceries:Total	12	15.42	0.00	100.00
GROCC	Groceries:Near-Coast	12	15.42	0.00	100.00
BAITT	Bait:Total	12	5.00	0.00	50.00
BAITC	Bait:Near-Coast	12	5.00	0.00	50.00
FLICT	Fishing Licenses:Total	12	0.00	0.00	0.00
FLICC	Fishing Licenses:Near-Coast	12	0.00	0.00	0.00
TCKLT	Tackle:Total	12	0.00	0.00	0.00
TCKLC	Tackle:Near-Coast	12	0.00	0.00	0.00
OTHRNTT	Other Rentals:Total	12	0.00	0.00	0.00
OTHRNTC	Other Rentals:Near-Coast	12	0.00	0.00	0.00
CLTHT	Clothing:Total	12	2.00	0.00	24.00
CLTHC	Clothing:Near-Coast	12	2.00	0.00	24.00
OTHRTT	Other Trip Expenses:Total	12	3.08	0.00	31.00
OTHRTC	Other Trip Expenses:Near-Coast	12	3.08	0.00	31.00
CHFEEST	Charter/Party Fees:Total	12	41.50	0.00	200.00
CHFEESC	Charter/Party Fees:Near-Coast	12	41.50	0.00	200.00
RODC	Rods:Near-Coast	12	102.50	0.00	600.00
RODNC	Rods:Away-Coast	12	25.00	0.00	300.00
LINEC	Fishing Line:Near-Coast	12	16.83	0.00	100.00
LINENC	Fishing Line:Away-Coast	12	1.67	0.00	20.00
LUREC	Lures:Near-Coast	12	9.83	0.00	50.00
LURENC	Lures:Nonoastal	12	2.50	0.00	30.00
OTHCFC	Other Fishing:Near-Coast	12	0.00	0.00	0.00
OTHCFNC	Other Fishing:Away-Coast	12	916.67	0.00	11000.00
BOOKC	Books:Near-Coast	12	3.58	0.00	16.00
BOOKNC	Books:Away-Coast	12	0.00	0.00	0.00
MEMBC	Memberships:Near-Coast	12	4.17	0.00	50.00
MEMBNC	Memberships:Away-Coast	12	0.00	0.00	0.00
CAMPC	Camping:Near-Coast	12	83.33	0.00	1000.00
CAMPNC	Camping:Away-Coast	12	0.00	0.00	0.00
LICC	Licenses:Near-Coast	12	14.42	0.00	72.00
LICNC	Licenses:Away-Coast	12	0.00	0.00	0.00

Charter Boat Summary Statistics for trip and equipment expenditures by Alabama
noncoastal residents who did't visit an oil/gas structure on the interview date

Variable	Label	N	Mean	Minimum	Maximum
TRANST	Transportation:Total	22	0.00	0.00	0.00
TRANSC	Transportation:Near-Coast	22	0.00	0.00	0.00
RCART	Rental Car:Total	22	0.00	0.00	0.00
RCARC	Rental Car:Near-Coast	22	0.00	0.00	0.00
LODGT	Lodging:Total	22	174.09	0.00	1800.00
LODGC	Lodging:Near-Coast	22	174.09	0.00	1800.00
GAST	Gasoline:Total	22	47.18	0.00	165.60
GASC	Gasoline:Near-Coast	22	0.00	0.00	0.00
FOODT	Other Food:Total	22	47.73	0.00	350.00
FOODC	Other Food:Near-Coast	22	47.73	0.00	350.00
GROCT	Groceries:Total	22	56.59	0.00	700.00
GROCC	Groceries:Near-Coast	22	56.14	0.00	700.00
BAITT	Bait:Total	22	4.55	0.00	70.00
BAITC	Bait:Near-Coast	22	4.55	0.00	70.00
FLICT	Fishing Licenses:Total	22	5.27	0.00	56.00
FLICC	Fishing Licenses:Near-Coast	22	5.27	0.00	56.00
TCKLT	Tackle:Total	22	0.00	0.00	0.00
TCKLC	Tackle:Near-Coast	22	0.00	0.00	0.00
OTHRNTT	Other Rentals:Total	22	0.00	0.00	0.00
OTHRNTC	Other Rentals:Near-Coast	22	0.00	0.00	0.00
CLTHT	Clothing:Total	22	0.91	0.00	20.00
CLTHC	Clothing:Near-Coast	22	0.91	0.00	20.00
OTHRTT	Other Trip Expenses:Total	22	5.36	0.00	30.00
OTHRTC	Other Trip Expenses:Near-Coast	22	5.36	0.00	30.00
CHFEEST	Charter/Party Fees:Total	22	95.68	0.00	400.00
CHFEESC	Charter/Party Fees:Near-Coast	22	95.68	0.00	400.00
RODC	Rods:Near-Coast	22	11.36	0.00	250.00
RODNC	Rods:Away-Coast	22	101.82	0.00	1000.00
LINEC	Fishing Line:Near-Coast	22	0.23	0.00	5.00
LINENC	Fishing Line:Away-Coast	22	8.86	0.00	100.00
LUREC	Lures:Near-Coast	22	0.55	0.00	12.00
LURENC	Lures:Nonoastal	22	9.45	0.00	50.00
OTHCFC	Other Fishing:Near-Coast	22	0.00	0.00	0.00
OTHCFNC	Other Fishing:Away-Coast	22	45.68	0.00	1000.00
BOOKC	Books:Near-Coast	22	0.00	0.00	0.00
BOOKNC	Books:Away-Coast	22	13.36	0.00	150.00
MEMBC	Memberships:Near-Coast	22	0.00	0.00	0.00
MEMBNC	Memberships:Away-Coast	22	2.27	0.00	50.00
CAMPC	Camping:Near-Coast	22	0.00	0.00	0.00
CAMPNC	Camping:Away-Coast	22	68.18	0.00	1500.00
LICC	Licenses:Near-Coast	22	0.00	0.00	0.00
LICNC	Licenses:Away-Coast	22	6.41	0.00	40.00

Charter Boat Summary Statistics for trip and equipment expenditures by Mississippi
coastal residents who did't visit an oil/gas structure on the interview date

Variable	Label	N	Mean	Minimum	Maximum
TRANST	Transportation:Total	10	0.00	0.00	0.00
TRANSC	Transportation:Near-Coast	10	0.00	0.00	0.00
RCART	Rental Car:Total	10	0.00	0.00	0.00
RCARC	Rental Car:Near-Coast	10	0.00	0.00	0.00
LODGT	Lodging:Total	10	11.80	0.00	118.00
LODGC	Lodging:Near-Coast	10	11.80	0.00	118.00
GAST	Gasoline:Total	10	6.98	0.00	60.00
GASC	Gasoline:Near-Coast	10	6.98	0.00	60.00
FOODT	Other Food:Total	10	1.50	0.00	15.00
FOODC	Other Food:Near-Coast	10	1.50	0.00	15.00
GROCT	Groceries:Total	10	11.30	0.00	40.00
GROCC	Groceries:Near-Coast	10	11.30	0.00	40.00
BAITT	Bait:Total	10	3.80	0.00	10.00
BAITC	Bait:Near-Coast	10	3.80	0.00	10.00
FLICT	Fishing Licenses:Total	10	0.00	0.00	0.00
FLICC	Fishing Licenses:Near-Coast	10	0.00	0.00	0.00
TCKLT	Tackle:Total	10	3.00	0.00	30.00
TCKLC	Tackle:Near-Coast	10	3.00	0.00	30.00
OTHRNTT	Other Rentals:Total	10	0.00	0.00	0.00
OTHRNTC	Other Rentals:Near-Coast	10	0.00	0.00	0.00
CLTHT	Clothing:Total	10	0.00	0.00	0.00
CLTHC	Clothing:Near-Coast	10	0.00	0.00	0.00
OTHRTT	Other Trip Expenses:Total	10	2.70	0.00	17.00
OTHRTC	Other Trip Expenses:Near-Coast	10	2.70	0.00	17.00
CHFEEST	Charter/Party Fees:Total	10	35.00	0.00	350.00
CHFEESC	Charter/Party Fees:Near-Coast	10	35.00	0.00	350.00
RODC	Rods:Near-Coast	10	375.00	0.00	2500.00
RODNC	Rods:Away-Coast	10	85.00	0.00	450.00
LINEC	Fishing Line:Near-Coast	10	14.50	0.00	100.00
LINENC	Fishing Line:Away-Coast	10	10.00	0.00	80.00
LUREC	Lures:Near-Coast	10	14.20	0.00	75.00
LURENC	Lures:Nonoastal	10	5.20	0.00	50.00
OTHCFC	Other Fishing:Near-Coast	10	110.00	0.00	1000.00
OTHCFNC	Other Fishing:Away-Coast	10	50.00	0.00	500.00
BOOKC	Books:Near-Coast	10	8.10	0.00	35.00
BOOKNC	Books:Away-Coast	10	0.00	0.00	0.00
MEMBC	Memberships:Near-Coast	10	6.00	0.00	60.00
MEMBNC	Memberships:Away-Coast	10	0.00	0.00	0.00
CAMPC	Camping:Near-Coast	10	62.00	0.00	500.00
CAMPNC	Camping:Away-Coast	10	0.00	0.00	0.00
LICC	Licenses:Near-Coast	10	30.50	0.00	80.00
LICNC	Licenses:Away-Coast	10	0.00	0.00	0.00

Charter Boat Summary Statistics for trip and equipment expenditures by Mississippi noncoastal residents who did't visit an oil/gas structure on the interview date

Variable	Label	N	Mean	Minimum	Maximum
TRANST	Transportation:Total	11	0.00	0.00	0.00
TRANSC	Transportation:Near-Coast	11	0.00	0.00	0.00
RCART	Rental Car:Total	11	4.73	0.00	52.00
RCARC	Rental Car:Near-Coast	11	0.00	0.00	0.00
LODGT	Lodging:Total	11	13.64	0.00	150.00
LODGC	Lodging:Near-Coast	11	13.64	0.00	150.00
GAST	Gasoline:Total	11	40.34	0.00	82.80
GASC	Gasoline:Near-Coast	11	0.00	0.00	0.00
FOODT	Other Food:Total	11	48.18	0.00	300.00
FOODC	Other Food:Near-Coast	11	48.18	0.00	300.00
GROCT	Groceries:Total	11	60.91	0.00	500.00
GROCC	Groceries:Near-Coast	11	60.91	0.00	500.00
BAITT	Bait:Total	11	21.82	0.00	200.00
BAITC	Bait:Near-Coast	11	21.82	0.00	200.00
FLICT	Fishing Licenses:Total	11	3.64	0.00	40.00
FLICC	Fishing Licenses:Near-Coast	11	3.64	0.00	40.00
TCKLT	Tackle:Total	11	19.55	0.00	200.00
TCKLC	Tackle:Near-Coast	11	19.55	0.00	200.00
OTHRNTT	Other Rentals:Total	11	4.55	0.00	50.00
OTHRNTC	Other Rentals:Near-Coast	11	4.55	0.00	50.00
CLTHT	Clothing:Total	11	4.55	0.00	20.00
CLTHC	Clothing:Near-Coast	11	2.73	0.00	20.00
OTHRTT	Other Trip Expenses:Total	11	20.73	0.00	150.00
OTHRTC	Other Trip Expenses:Near-Coast	11	20.73	0.00	150.00
CHFEEST	Charter/Party Fees:Total	11	43.64	0.00	380.00
CHFEESC	Charter/Party Fees:Near-Coast	11	43.64	0.00	380.00
RODC	Rods:Near-Coast	11	9.09	0.00	100.00
RODNC	Rods:Away-Coast	11	218.18	0.00	2000.00
LINEC	Fishing Line:Near-Coast	11	1.82	0.00	20.00
LINENC	Fishing Line:Away-Coast	11	11.00	0.00	100.00
LUREC	Lures:Near-Coast	11	6.82	0.00	50.00
LURENC	Lures:Nonoastal	11	6.91	0.00	75.00
OTHCFC	Other Fishing:Near-Coast	11	0.00	0.00	0.00
OTHCFNC	Other Fishing:Away-Coast	11	640.91	0.00	6500.00
BOOKC	Books:Near-Coast	11	0.00	0.00	0.00
BOOKNC	Books:Away-Coast	11	1.82	0.00	20.00
MEMBC	Memberships:Near-Coast	11	0.00	0.00	0.00
MEMBNC	Memberships:Away-Coast	11	0.00	0.00	0.00
CAMPC	Camping:Near-Coast	11	0.00	0.00	0.00
CAMPNC	Camping:Away-Coast	11	3.64	0.00	40.00
LICC	Licenses:Near-Coast	11	0.00	0.00	0.00
LICNC	Licenses:Away-Coast	11	12.91	0.00	40.00

Charter Boat Summary Statistics for trip and equipment expenditures by Louisiana
coastal residents who did't visit an oil/gas structure on the interview date

Variable	Label	N	Mean	Minimum	Maximum
TRANST	Transportation:Total	26	0.19	0.00	5.00
TRANSC	Transportation:Near-Coast	26	0.19	0.00	5.00
RCART	Rental Car:Total	26	0.00	0.00	0.00
RCARC	Rental Car:Near-Coast	26	0.00	0.00	0.00
LODGT	Lodging:Total	26	18.85	0.00	250.00
LODGC	Lodging:Near-Coast	26	18.85	0.00	250.00
GAST	Gasoline:Total	26	11.47	0.00	52.50
GASC	Gasoline:Near-Coast	26	11.47	0.00	52.50
FOODT	Other Food:Total	26	9.81	0.00	100.00
FOODC	Other Food:Near-Coast	26	9.81	0.00	100.00
GROCT	Groceries:Total	26	6.38	0.00	100.00
GROCC	Groceries:Near-Coast	26	6.38	0.00	100.00
BAITT	Bait:Total	26	3.85	0.00	60.00
BAITC	Bait:Near-Coast	26	3.85	0.00	60.00
FLICT	Fishing Licenses:Total	26	0.19	0.00	5.00
FLICC	Fishing Licenses:Near-Coast	26	0.19	0.00	5.00
TCKLT	Tackle:Total	26	2.50	0.00	30.00
TCKLC	Tackle:Near-Coast	26	2.50	0.00	30.00
OTHRNTT	Other Rentals:Total	26	4.81	0.00	125.00
OTHRNTC	Other Rentals:Near-Coast	26	4.81	0.00	125.00
CLTHT	Clothing:Total	26	1.54	0.00	40.00
CLTHC	Clothing:Near-Coast	26	1.54	0.00	40.00
OTHRTT	Other Trip Expenses:Total	26	0.46	0.00	7.00
OTHRTC	Other Trip Expenses:Near-Coast	26	0.46	0.00	7.00
CHFEEST	Charter/Party Fees:Total	26	19.04	0.00	150.00
CHFEESC	Charter/Party Fees:Near-Coast	26	19.04	0.00	150.00
RODC	Rods:Near-Coast	26	148.15	0.00	2000.00
RODNC	Rods:Away-Coast	26	118.46	0.00	2000.00
LINEC	Fishing Line:Near-Coast	26	13.08	0.00	200.00
LINENC	Fishing Line:Away-Coast	26	8.38	0.00	200.00
LUREC	Lures:Near-Coast	26	39.23	0.00	500.00
LURENC	Lures:Nonoastal	26	3.85	0.00	60.00
OTHCFC	Other Fishing:Near-Coast	26	961.54	0.00	25000.00
OTHCFNC	Other Fishing:Away-Coast	26	3.85	0.00	100.00
BOOKC	Books:Near-Coast	26	15.38	0.00	200.00
BOOKNC	Books:Away-Coast	26	0.00	0.00	0.00
MEMBC	Memberships:Near-Coast	26	2.31	0.00	35.00
MEMBNC	Memberships:Away-Coast	26	0.00	0.00	0.00
CAMPC	Camping:Near-Coast	26	115.38	0.00	3000.00
CAMPNC	Camping:Away-Coast	26	0.00	0.00	0.00
LICC	Licenses:Near-Coast	26	12.46	0.00	50.00
LICNC	Licenses:Away-Coast	26	0.00	0.00	0.00

Charter Boat Summary Statistics for trip and equipment expenditures by Louisiana
noncoastal residents who did't visit an oil/gas structure on the interview date

Variable	Label	N	Mean	Minimum	Maximum
TRANST	Transportation:Total	6	0.00	0.00	0.00
TRANSC	Transportation:Near-Coast	6	0.00	0.00	0.00
RCART	Rental Car:Total	6	0.00	0.00	0.00
RCARC	Rental Car:Near-Coast	6	0.00	0.00	0.00
LODGT	Lodging:Total	6	12.50	0.00	75.00
LODGC	Lodging:Near-Coast	6	12.50	0.00	75.00
GAST	Gasoline:Total	6	39.20	0.15	112.65
GASC	Gasoline:Near-Coast	6	0.00	0.00	0.00
FOODT	Other Food:Total	6	98.33	0.00	300.00
FOODC	Other Food:Near-Coast	6	54.17	0.00	300.00
GROCT	Groceries:Total	6	72.50	0.00	300.00
GROCC	Groceries:Near-Coast	6	64.17	0.00	300.00
BAITT	Bait:Total	6	9.17	0.00	40.00
BAITC	Bait:Near-Coast	6	9.17	0.00	40.00
FLICT	Fishing Licenses:Total	6	4.67	0.00	13.00
FLICC	Fishing Licenses:Near-Coast	6	2.50	0.00	10.00
TCKLT	Tackle:Total	6	4.00	0.00	20.00
TCKLC	Tackle:Near-Coast	6	0.67	0.00	4.00
OTHRNTT	Other Rentals:Total	6	0.00	0.00	0.00
OTHRNTC	Other Rentals:Near-Coast	6	0.00	0.00	0.00
CLTHT	Clothing:Total	6	0.00	0.00	0.00
CLTHC	Clothing:Near-Coast	6	0.00	0.00	0.00
OTHRTT	Other Trip Expenses:Total	6	0.83	0.00	5.00
OTHRTC	Other Trip Expenses:Near-Coast	6	0.00	0.00	0.00
CHFEEST	Charter/Party Fees:Total	6	222.50	0.00	700.00
CHFEESC	Charter/Party Fees:Near-Coast	6	222.50	0.00	700.00
RODC	Rods:Near-Coast	6	83.33	0.00	500.00
RODNC	Rods:Away-Coast	6	43.33	0.00	200.00
LINEC	Fishing Line:Near-Coast	6	0.00	0.00	0.00
LINENC	Fishing Line:Away-Coast	6	11.67	0.00	50.00
LUREC	Lures:Near-Coast	6	0.17	0.00	1.00
LURENC	Lures:Nonoastal	6	56.67	0.00	300.00
OTHCFC	Other Fishing:Near-Coast	6	0.00	0.00	0.00
OTHCFNC	Other Fishing:Away-Coast	6	0.00	0.00	0.00
BOOKC	Books:Near-Coast	6	0.00	0.00	0.00
BOOKNC	Books:Away-Coast	6	5.33	0.00	17.00
MEMBC	Memberships:Near-Coast	6	0.00	0.00	0.00
MEMBNC	Memberships:Away-Coast	6	4.17	0.00	25.00
CAMPC	Camping:Near-Coast	6	0.00	0.00	0.00
CAMPNC	Camping:Away-Coast	6	83.33	0.00	500.00
LICC	Licenses:Near-Coast	6	0.00	0.00	0.00
LICNC	Licenses:Away-Coast	6	11.00	0.00	40.00

Charter Boat Summary Statistics for trip and equipment expenditures by Texas
coastal residents who did't visit an oil/gas structure on the interview date

Variable	Label	N	Mean	Minimum	Maximum
TRANST	Transportation:Total	2	0.00	0.00	0.00
TRANSC	Transportation:Near-Coast	2	0.00	0.00	0.00
RCART	Rental Car:Total	2	0.00	0.00	0.00
RCARC	Rental Car:Near-Coast	2	0.00	0.00	0.00
LODGT	Lodging:Total	2	0.00	0.00	0.00
LODGC	Lodging:Near-Coast	2	0.00	0.00	0.00
GAST	Gasoline:Total	2	9.38	7.50	11.25
GASC	Gasoline:Near-Coast	2	9.38	7.50	11.25
FOODT	Other Food:Total	2	0.00	0.00	0.00
FOODC	Other Food:Near-Coast	2	0.00	0.00	0.00
GROCT	Groceries:Total	2	2.50	0.00	5.00
GROCC	Groceries:Near-Coast	2	2.50	0.00	5.00
BAITT	Bait:Total	2	0.00	0.00	0.00
BAITC	Bait:Near-Coast	2	0.00	0.00	0.00
FLICT	Fishing Licenses:Total	2	0.00	0.00	0.00
FLICC	Fishing Licenses:Near-Coast	2	0.00	0.00	0.00
TCKLT	Tackle:Total	2	0.00	0.00	0.00
TCKLC	Tackle:Near-Coast	2	0.00	0.00	0.00
OTHRNTT	Other Rentals:Total	2	0.00	0.00	0.00
OTHRNTC	Other Rentals:Near-Coast	2	0.00	0.00	0.00
CLTHT	Clothing:Total	2	0.00	0.00	0.00
CLTHC	Clothing:Near-Coast	2	0.00	0.00	0.00
OTHRTT	Other Trip Expenses:Total	2	0.00	0.00	0.00
OTHRTC	Other Trip Expenses:Near-Coast	2	0.00	0.00	0.00
CHFEEST	Charter/Party Fees:Total	2	0.00	0.00	0.00
CHFEESC	Charter/Party Fees:Near-Coast	2	0.00	0.00	0.00
RODC	Rods:Near-Coast	2	0.00	0.00	0.00
RODNC	Rods:Away-Coast	2	0.00	0.00	0.00
LINEC	Fishing Line:Near-Coast	2	0.00	0.00	0.00
LINENC	Fishing Line:Away-Coast	2	0.00	0.00	0.00
LUREC	Lures:Near-Coast	2	0.00	0.00	0.00
LURENC	Lures:Nonoastal	2	0.00	0.00	0.00
OTHCFC	Other Fishing:Near-Coast	2	0.00	0.00	0.00
OTHCFNC	Other Fishing:Away-Coast	2	0.00	0.00	0.00
BOOKC	Books:Near-Coast	2	0.00	0.00	0.00
BOOKNC	Books:Away-Coast	2	0.00	0.00	0.00
MEMBC	Memberships:Near-Coast	2	0.00	0.00	0.00
MEMBNC	Memberships:Away-Coast	2	0.00	0.00	0.00
CAMPC	Camping:Near-Coast	2	0.00	0.00	0.00
CAMPNC	Camping:Away-Coast	2	0.00	0.00	0.00
LICC	Licenses:Near-Coast	2	9.50	0.00	19.00
LICNC	Licenses:Away-Coast	2	0.00	0.00	0.00

Charter Boat Summary Statistics for trip and equipment expenditures by Texas
noncoastal residents who did't visit an oil/gas structure on the interview date

Variable	Label	N	Mean	Minimum	Maximum
TRANST	Transportation:Total	3	0.00	0.00	0.00
TRANSC	Transportation:Near-Coast	3	0.00	0.00	0.00
RCART	Rental Car:Total	3	0.00	0.00	0.00
RCARC	Rental Car:Near-Coast	3	0.00	0.00	0.00
LODGT	Lodging:Total	3	18.33	0.00	55.00
LODGC	Lodging:Near-Coast	3	18.33	0.00	55.00
GAST	Gasoline:Total	3	52.60	37.50	60.15
GASC	Gasoline:Near-Coast	3	0.00	0.00	0.00
FOODT	Other Food:Total	3	100.00	0.00	300.00
FOODC	Other Food:Near-Coast	3	100.00	0.00	300.00
GROCT	Groceries:Total	3	100.00	0.00	300.00
GROCC	Groceries:Near-Coast	3	100.00	0.00	300.00
BAITT	Bait:Total	3	0.00	0.00	0.00
BAITC	Bait:Near-Coast	3	0.00	0.00	0.00
FLICT	Fishing Licenses:Total	3	0.00	0.00	0.00
FLICC	Fishing Licenses:Near-Coast	3	0.00	0.00	0.00
TCKLT	Tackle:Total	3	30.00	0.00	90.00
TCKLC	Tackle:Near-Coast	3	30.00	0.00	90.00
OTHRNTT	Other Rentals:Total	3	0.00	0.00	0.00
OTHRNTC	Other Rentals:Near-Coast	3	0.00	0.00	0.00
CLTHT	Clothing:Total	3	0.00	0.00	0.00
CLTHC	Clothing:Near-Coast	3	0.00	0.00	0.00
OTHRTT	Other Trip Expenses:Total	3	5.00	0.00	15.00
OTHRTC	Other Trip Expenses:Near-Coast	3	5.00	0.00	15.00
CHFEEST	Charter/Party Fees:Total	3	133.33	0.00	400.00
CHFEESC	Charter/Party Fees:Near-Coast	3	133.33	0.00	400.00
RODC	Rods:Near-Coast	3	0.00	0.00	0.00
RODNC	Rods:Away-Coast	3	0.00	0.00	0.00
LINEC	Fishing Line:Near-Coast	3	0.00	0.00	0.00
LINENC	Fishing Line:Away-Coast	3	0.00	0.00	0.00
LUREC	Lures:Near-Coast	3	10.00	0.00	30.00
LURENC	Lures:Nonoastal	3	0.00	0.00	0.00
OTHCFC	Other Fishing:Near-Coast	3	0.00	0.00	0.00
OTHCFNC	Other Fishing:Away-Coast	3	0.00	0.00	0.00
BOOKC	Books:Near-Coast	3	0.00	0.00	0.00
BOOKNC	Books:Away-Coast	3	8.33	0.00	25.00
MEMBC	Memberships:Near-Coast	3	0.00	0.00	0.00
MEMBNC	Memberships:Away-Coast	3	0.00	0.00	0.00
CAMPC	Camping:Near-Coast	3	0.00	0.00	0.00
CAMPNC	Camping:Away-Coast	3	0.00	0.00	0.00
LICC	Licenses:Near-Coast	3	0.00	0.00	0.00
LICNC	Licenses:Away-Coast	3	19.00	0.00	50.00

Private Diving Summary Statistics for trip and equipment expenditures by Alabama
coastal residents who did visit an oil/gas structure on the interview date

Variable	Label	N	Mean	Minimum	Maximum
TRANSC	Transportation:Near-Coast	3	0.00	0.00	0.00
RCART	Rental Car:Total	3	0.00	0.00	0.00
RCARC	Rental Car:Near-Coast	3	0.00	0.00	0.00
LODGT	Lodging:Total	3	0.00	0.00	0.00
LODGC	Lodging:Near-Coast	3	0.00	0.00	0.00
GAST	Gasoline:Total	3	18.60	4.50	45.30
GASC	Gasoline:Near-Coast	3	18.60	4.50	45.30
FOODT	Other Food:Total	3	8.33	0.00	15.00
FOODC	Other Food:Near-Coast	3	8.33	0.00	15.00
GROCT	Groceries:Total	3	8.33	0.00	15.00
GROCC	Groceries:Near-Coast	3	8.33	0.00	15.00
FUELT	Fuel:Total	3	16.67	0.00	50.00
FUELC	Fuel:Near-Coast	3	16.67	0.00	50.00
BRNTT	Boat Rentals:Total	3	0.00	0.00	0.00
BRNTC	Boat Rentals:Near-Coast	3	0.00	0.00	0.00
LNCHT	Launch Fees:Total	3	0.00	0.00	0.00
LNCHC	Launch Fees:Near-Coast	3	0.00	0.00	0.00
DOCKT	Dockage Fees:Total	3	0.00	0.00	0.00
DOCKC	Dockage Fees:Near-Coast	3	0.00	0.00	0.00
TREPRT	Trip Repairs:Total	3	0.00	0.00	0.00
TREPRC	Trip Repairs:Near-Coast	3	0.00	0.00	0.00
DFEET	Dive Fees:Total	3	0.00	0.00	0.00
DFEEC	Dive Fees:Near-Coast	3	0.00	0.00	0.00
TCKLT	Tackle:Total	3	3.33	0.00	10.00
TCKLC	Tackle:Near-Coast	3	3.33	0.00	10.00
OTHRNTT	Other Rentals:Total	3	0.00	0.00	0.00
OTHRNTC	Other Rentals:Near-Coast	3	0.00	0.00	0.00
GUIDT	Guide Fees:Total	3	0.00	0.00	0.00
GUIDC	Guide Fees:Near-Coast	3	0.00	0.00	0.00
CLTHT	Clothing:Total	3	0.00	0.00	0.00
CLTHC	Clothing:Near-Coast	3	0.00	0.00	0.00
OTHRTT	Other Trip Expenses:Total	3	2.33	0.00	7.00
OTHRTC	Other Trip Expenses:Near-Coast	3	2.33	0.00	7.00
AIRFT	Air Fees:Total	3	3.33	0.00	10.00
AIRFC	Air Fees:Near-Coast	3	3.33	0.00	10.00
BOATNC	Boats:Away-Coast	3	0.00	0.00	0.00
BOATC	Boats:Near-Coast	3	0.00	0.00	0.00
MOTORNC	Motors:Away-Coast	3	0.00	0.00	0.00
MOTORC	Motors:Near-Coast	3	0.00	0.00	0.00
TRAILNC	Trailers:Away-Coast	3	0.00	0.00	0.00
TRAILC	Trailers:Near-Coast	3	0.00	0.00	0.00
AEQPNC	Electronics:Away-Coast	3	66.67	0.00	200.00
AEQPC	Electronics:Near-Coast	3	0.00	0.00	0.00
DFITNC	Diving Outfit:Away-Coast	3	0.00	0.00	0.00
DFITC	Diving Outfit:Near-Coast	3	0.00	0.00	0.00
REPRNC	Capital Repairs:Away-Coast	3	0.00	0.00	0.00
REPRC	Capital Repairs:Near-Coast	3	0.00	0.00	0.00
DEQPNC	Dive Equipment:Away-Coast	3	0.00	0.00	0.00
DEQPC	Dive Equipment:Near-Coast	3	0.00	0.00	0.00

LESSNC	Dive Lessons:Away-Coast	3	0.00	0.00	0.00
LESSC	Dive Lessons:Near-Coast	3	0.00	0.00	0.00
OTHDNC	Other Diving:Away-Coast	3	0.00	0.00	0.00
OTHDC	Other Diving:Near-Coast	3	0.00	0.00	0.00
BOOKNC	Books:Away-Coast	3	0.00	0.00	0.00
BOOKC	Books:Near-Coast	3	3.33	0.00	10.00
MEMBNC	Memberships:Away-Coast	3	0.00	0.00	0.00
MEMBC	Memberships:Near-Coast	3	0.00	0.00	0.00
CAMPNC	Camping:Away-Coast	3	0.00	0.00	0.00
CAMPC	Camping:Near-Coast	3	0.00	0.00	0.00
LICNC	Licenses:Away-Coast	3	0.00	0.00	0.00
LICC	Licenses:Near-Coast	3	11.00	0.00	33.00

Private Diving Summary Statistics for trip and equipment expenditures by Mississippi
coastal residents who did visit an oil/gas structure on the interview date

Variable	Label	N	Mean	Minimum	Maximum
TRANSC	Transportation:Near-Coast	2	0.00	0.00	0.00
RCART	Rental Car:Total	2	0.00	0.00	0.00
RCARC	Rental Car:Near-Coast	2	0.00	0.00	0.00
LODGT	Lodging:Total	2	0.00	0.00	0.00
LODGC	Lodging:Near-Coast	2	0.00	0.00	0.00
GAST	Gasoline:Total	2	0.83	0.15	1.50
GASC	Gasoline:Near-Coast	2	0.83	0.15	1.50
FOODT	Other Food:Total	2	10.00	0.00	20.00
FOODC	Other Food:Near-Coast	2	10.00	0.00	20.00
GROCT	Groceries:Total	2	22.50	20.00	25.00
GROCC	Groceries:Near-Coast	2	22.50	20.00	25.00
FUELT	Fuel:Total	2	47.50	20.00	75.00
FUELC	Fuel:Near-Coast	2	47.50	20.00	75.00
BRNTT	Boat Rentals:Total	2	0.00	0.00	0.00
BRNTC	Boat Rentals:Near-Coast	2	0.00	0.00	0.00
LNCHT	Launch Fees:Total	2	0.00	0.00	0.00
LNCHC	Launch Fees:Near-Coast	2	0.00	0.00	0.00
DOCKT	Dockage Fees:Total	2	50.00	0.00	100.00
DOCKC	Dockage Fees:Near-Coast	2	50.00	0.00	100.00
TREPRT	Trip Repairs:Total	2	0.00	0.00	0.00
TREPRC	Trip Repairs:Near-Coast	2	0.00	0.00	0.00
DFEET	Dive Fees:Total	2	0.00	0.00	0.00
DFEEC	Dive Fees:Near-Coast	2	0.00	0.00	0.00
TCKLT	Tackle:Total	2	10.00	0.00	20.00
TCKLC	Tackle:Near-Coast	2	10.00	0.00	20.00
OTHRNTT	Other Rentals:Total	2	45.00	20.00	70.00
OTHRNTC	Other Rentals:Near-Coast	2	45.00	20.00	70.00
GUIDT	Guide Fees:Total	2	0.00	0.00	0.00
GUIDC	Guide Fees:Near-Coast	2	0.00	0.00	0.00
CLTHT	Clothing:Total	2	0.00	0.00	0.00
CLTHC	Clothing:Near-Coast	2	0.00	0.00	0.00
OTHRTT	Other Trip Expenses:Total	2	2.50	0.00	5.00
OTHRTC	Other Trip Expenses:Near-Coast	2	2.50	0.00	5.00
AIRFT	Air Fees:Total	2	10.00	10.00	10.00
AIRFC	Air Fees:Near-Coast	2	10.00	10.00	10.00
BOATNC	Boats:Away-Coast	2	0.00	0.00	0.00
BOATC	Boats:Near-Coast	2	0.00	0.00	0.00
MOTORNC	Motors:Away-Coast	2	0.00	0.00	0.00
MOTORC	Motors:Near-Coast	2	0.00	0.00	0.00
TRAILNC	Trailers:Away-Coast	2	0.00	0.00	0.00
TRAILC	Trailers:Near-Coast	2	0.00	0.00	0.00
AEQPNC	Electronics:Away-Coast	2	0.00	0.00	0.00
AEQPC	Electronics:Near-Coast	2	0.00	0.00	0.00
DFITNC	Diving Outfit:Away-Coast	2	0.00	0.00	0.00
DFITC	Diving Outfit:Near-Coast	2	500.00	0.00	1000.00
REPRNC	Capital Repairs:Away-Coast	2	0.00	0.00	0.00
REPRC	Capital Repairs:Near-Coast	2	50.00	0.00	100.00
DEQPNC	Dive Equipment:Away-Coast	2	0.00	0.00	0.00
DEQPC	Dive Equipment:Near-Coast	2	0.00	0.00	0.00

LESSNC	DIve Lessons:Away-Coast	2	0.00	0.00	0.00
LESSC	Dive Lessons:Near-Coast	2	62.50	0.00	125.00
OTHDNC	Other Diving:Away-Coast	2	0.00	0.00	0.00
OTHDC	Other Diving:Near-Coast	2	0.00	0.00	0.00
BOOKNC	Books:Away-Coast	2	0.00	0.00	0.00
BOOKC	Books:Near-Coast	2	0.00	0.00	0.00
MEMBNC	Memberships:Away-Coast	2	0.00	0.00	0.00
MEMBC	Memberships:Near-Coast	2	0.00	0.00	0.00
CAMPNC	Camping:Away-Coast	2	0.00	0.00	0.00
CAMPC	Camping:Near-Coast	2	0.00	0.00	0.00
LICNC	Licenses:Away-Coast	2	0.00	0.00	0.00
LICC	Licenses:Near-Coast	2	5.00	0.00	10.00

Private Diving Summary Statistics for trip and equipment expenditures by Mississippi
noncoastal residents who did visit an oil/gas structure on the interview date

Variable	Label	N	Mean	Minimum	Maximum
TRANSC	Transportation:Near-Coast	3	0.00	0.00	0.00
RCART	Rental Car:Total	3	0.00	0.00	0.00
RCARC	Rental Car:Near-Coast	3	0.00	0.00	0.00
LODGT	Lodging:Total	3	0.00	0.00	0.00
LODGC	Lodging:Near-Coast	3	0.00	0.00	0.00
GAST	Gasoline:Total	3	7.00	0.00	21.00
GASC	Gasoline:Near-Coast	3	0.00	0.00	0.00
FOODT	Other Food:Total	3	100.00	0.00	300.00
FOODC	Other Food:Near-Coast	3	0.00	0.00	0.00
GROCT	Groceries:Total	3	0.00	0.00	0.00
GROCC	Groceries:Near-Coast	3	0.00	0.00	0.00
FUELT	Fuel:Total	3	100.00	0.00	300.00
FUELC	Fuel:Near-Coast	3	0.00	0.00	0.00
BRNTT	Boat Rentals:Total	3	0.00	0.00	0.00
BRNTC	Boat Rentals:Near-Coast	3	0.00	0.00	0.00
LNCHT	Launch Fees:Total	3	0.00	0.00	0.00
LNCHC	Launch Fees:Near-Coast	3	0.00	0.00	0.00
DOCKT	Dockage Fees:Total	3	0.00	0.00	0.00
DOCKC	Dockage Fees:Near-Coast	3	0.00	0.00	0.00
TREPRT	Trip Repairs:Total	3	0.00	0.00	0.00
TREPRC	Trip Repairs:Near-Coast	3	0.00	0.00	0.00
DFEET	Dive Fees:Total	3	350.00	0.00	1050.00
DFEEC	Dive Fees:Near-Coast	3	350.00	0.00	1050.00
TCKLT	Tackle:Total	3	0.00	0.00	0.00
TCKLC	Tackle:Near-Coast	3	0.00	0.00	0.00
OTHRNTT	Other Rentals:Total	3	0.00	0.00	0.00
OTHRNTC	Other Rentals:Near-Coast	3	0.00	0.00	0.00
GUIDT	Guide Fees:Total	3	0.00	0.00	0.00
GUIDC	Guide Fees:Near-Coast	3	0.00	0.00	0.00
CLTHT	Clothing:Total	3	0.00	0.00	0.00
CLTHC	Clothing:Near-Coast	3	0.00	0.00	0.00
OTHRTT	Other Trip Expenses:Total	3	0.00	0.00	0.00
OTHRTC	Other Trip Expenses:Near-Coast	3	0.00	0.00	0.00
AIRFT	Air Fees:Total	3	0.00	0.00	0.00
AIRFC	Air Fees:Near-Coast	3	0.00	0.00	0.00
BOATNC	Boats:Away-Coast	3	0.00	0.00	0.00
BOATC	Boats:Near-Coast	3	0.00	0.00	0.00
MOTORNC	Motors:Away-Coast	3	0.00	0.00	0.00
MOTORC	Motors:Near-Coast	3	0.00	0.00	0.00
TRAILNC	Trailers:Away-Coast	3	0.00	0.00	0.00
TRAILC	Trailers:Near-Coast	3	0.00	0.00	0.00
AEQPNC	Electronics:Away-Coast	3	0.00	0.00	0.00
AEQPC	Electronics:Near-Coast	3	0.00	0.00	0.00
DFITNC	Diving Outfit:Away-Coast	3	0.00	0.00	0.00
DFITC	Diving Outfit:Near-Coast	3	0.00	0.00	0.00
REPRNC	Capital Repairs:Away-Coast	3	0.00	0.00	0.00
REPRC	Capital Repairs:Near-Coast	3	0.00	0.00	0.00
DEQPNC	Dive Equipment:Away-Coast	3	0.00	0.00	0.00
DEQPC	Dive Equipment:Near-Coast	3	0.00	0.00	0.00

LESSNC	DIve Lessons:Away-Coast	3	50.00	0.00	150.00
LESSC	Dive Lessons:Near-Coast	3	0.00	0.00	0.00
OTHDNC	Other Diving:Away-Coast	3	0.00	0.00	0.00
OTHDC	Other Diving:Near-Coast	3	0.00	0.00	0.00
BOOKNC	Books:Away-Coast	3	0.00	0.00	0.00
BOOKC	Books:Near-Coast	3	0.00	0.00	0.00
MEMBNC	Memberships:Away-Coast	3	30.00	0.00	75.00
MEMBC	Memberships:Near-Coast	3	0.00	0.00	0.00
CAMPNC	Camping:Away-Coast	3	0.00	0.00	0.00
CAMPC	Camping:Near-Coast	3	0.00	0.00	0.00
LICNC	Licenses:Away-Coast	3	7.00	0.00	15.00
LICC	Licenses:Near-Coast	3	0.00	0.00	0.00

Private Diving Summary Statistics for trip and equipment expenditures by Louisiana
coastal residents who did visit an oil/gas structure on the interview date

Variable	Label	N	Mean	Minimum	Maximum
TRANSC	Transportation:Near-Coast	1	0.00	0.00	0.00
RCART	Rental Car:Total	1	0.00	0.00	0.00
RCARC	Rental Car:Near-Coast	1	0.00	0.00	0.00
LODGT	Lodging:Total	1	0.00	0.00	0.00
LODGC	Lodging:Near-Coast	1	0.00	0.00	0.00
GAST	Gasoline:Total	1	6.00	6.00	6.00
GASC	Gasoline:Near-Coast	1	6.00	6.00	6.00
FOODT	Other Food:Total	1	50.00	50.00	50.00
FOODC	Other Food:Near-Coast	1	50.00	50.00	50.00
GROCT	Groceries:Total	1	50.00	50.00	50.00
GROCC	Groceries:Near-Coast	1	50.00	50.00	50.00
FUELT	Fuel:Total	1	50.00	50.00	50.00
FUELC	Fuel:Near-Coast	1	50.00	50.00	50.00
BRNTT	Boat Rentals:Total	1	0.00	0.00	0.00
BRNTC	Boat Rentals:Near-Coast	1	0.00	0.00	0.00
LNCHT	Launch Fees:Total	1	0.00	0.00	0.00
LNCHC	Launch Fees:Near-Coast	1	0.00	0.00	0.00
DOCKT	Dockage Fees:Total	1	0.00	0.00	0.00
DOCKC	Dockage Fees:Near-Coast	1	0.00	0.00	0.00
TREPRT	Trip Repairs:Total	1	0.00	0.00	0.00
TREPRC	Trip Repairs:Near-Coast	1	0.00	0.00	0.00
DFEET	Dive Fees:Total	1	0.00	0.00	0.00
DFEEC	Dive Fees:Near-Coast	1	0.00	0.00	0.00
TCKLT	Tackle:Total	1	15.00	15.00	15.00
TCKLC	Tackle:Near-Coast	1	15.00	15.00	15.00
OTHRNTT	Other Rentals:Total	1	0.00	0.00	0.00
OTHRNTC	Other Rentals:Near-Coast	1	0.00	0.00	0.00
GUIDT	Guide Fees:Total	1	0.00	0.00	0.00
GUIDC	Guide Fees:Near-Coast	1	0.00	0.00	0.00
CLTHT	Clothing:Total	1	0.00	0.00	0.00
CLTHC	Clothing:Near-Coast	1	0.00	0.00	0.00
OTHRTT	Other Trip Expenses:Total	1	0.00	0.00	0.00
OTHRTC	Other Trip Expenses:Near-Coast	1	0.00	0.00	0.00
AIRFT	Air Fees:Total	1	50.00	50.00	50.00
AIRFC	Air Fees:Near-Coast	1	50.00	50.00	50.00
BOATNC	Boats:Away-Coast	1	0.00	0.00	0.00
BOATC	Boats:Near-Coast	1	0.00	0.00	0.00
MOTORNC	Motors:Away-Coast	1	0.00	0.00	0.00
MOTORC	Motors:Near-Coast	1	0.00	0.00	0.00
TRAILNC	Trailers:Away-Coast	1	0.00	0.00	0.00
TRAILC	Trailers:Near-Coast	1	0.00	0.00	0.00
AEQPNC	Electronics:Away-Coast	1	0.00	0.00	0.00
AEQPC	Electronics:Near-Coast	1	0.00	0.00	0.00
DFITNC	Diving Outfit:Away-Coast	1	0.00	0.00	0.00
DFITC	Diving Outfit:Near-Coast	1	0.00	0.00	0.00
REPRNC	Capital Repairs:Away-Coast	1	2000.00	2000.00	2000.00
REPRC	Capital Repairs:Near-Coast	1	0.00	0.00	0.00
DEQPNC	Dive Equipment:Away-Coast	1	0.00	0.00	0.00
DEQPC	Dive Equipment:Near-Coast	1	0.00	0.00	0.00

LESSNC	DIve Lessons:Away-Coast	1	150.00	150.00	150.00
LESSC	Dive Lessons:Near-Coast	1	0.00	0.00	0.00
OTHDNC	Other Diving:Away-Coast	1	100.00	100.00	100.00
OTHDC	Other Diving:Near-Coast	1	0.00	0.00	0.00
BOOKNC	Books:Away-Coast	1	0.00	0.00	0.00
BOOKC	Books:Near-Coast	1	0.00	0.00	0.00
MEMBNC	Memberships:Away-Coast	1	0.00	0.00	0.00
MEMBC	Memberships:Near-Coast	1	40.00	40.00	40.00
CAMPNC	Camping:Away-Coast	1	0.00	0.00	0.00
CAMPC	Camping:Near-Coast	1	0.00	0.00	0.00
LICNC	Licenses:Away-Coast	1	0.00	0.00	0.00
LICC	Licenses:Near-Coast	1	11.00	11.00	11.00

- -

Private Diving Summary Statistics for trip and equipment expenditures by Louisiana
noncoastal residents who did visit an oil/gas structure on the interview date

Variable	Label	N	Mean	Minimum	Maximum
TRANSC	Transportation:Near-Coast	1	0.00	0.00	0.00
RCART	Rental Car:Total	1	0.00	0.00	0.00
RCARC	Rental Car:Near-Coast	1	0.00	0.00	0.00
LODGT	Lodging:Total	1	104.00	104.00	104.00
LODGC	Lodging:Near-Coast	1	104.00	104.00	104.00
GAST	Gasoline:Total	1	0.00	0.00	0.00
GASC	Gasoline:Near-Coast	1	0.00	0.00	0.00
FOODT	Other Food:Total	1	15.00	15.00	15.00
FOODC	Other Food:Near-Coast	1	0.00	0.00	0.00
GROCT	Groceries:Total	1	15.00	15.00	15.00
GROCC	Groceries:Near-Coast	1	15.00	15.00	15.00
FUELT	Fuel:Total	1	30.00	30.00	30.00
FUELC	Fuel:Near-Coast	1	30.00	30.00	30.00
BRNTT	Boat Rentals:Total	1	0.00	0.00	0.00
BRNTC	Boat Rentals:Near-Coast	1	0.00	0.00	0.00
LNCHT	Launch Fees:Total	1	0.00	0.00	0.00
LNCHC	Launch Fees:Near-Coast	1	0.00	0.00	0.00
DOCKT	Dockage Fees:Total	1	0.00	0.00	0.00
DOCKC	Dockage Fees:Near-Coast	1	0.00	0.00	0.00
TREPRT	Trip Repairs:Total	1	0.00	0.00	0.00
TREPRC	Trip Repairs:Near-Coast	1	0.00	0.00	0.00
DFEET	Dive Fees:Total	1	0.00	0.00	0.00
DFEEC	Dive Fees:Near-Coast	1	0.00	0.00	0.00
TCKLT	Tackle:Total	1	0.00	0.00	0.00
TCKLC	Tackle:Near-Coast	1	0.00	0.00	0.00
OTHRNTT	Other Rentals:Total	1	0.00	0.00	0.00
OTHRNTC	Other Rentals:Near-Coast	1	0.00	0.00	0.00
GUIDT	Guide Fees:Total	1	0.00	0.00	0.00
GUIDC	Guide Fees:Near-Coast	1	0.00	0.00	0.00
CLTHT	Clothing:Total	1	0.00	0.00	0.00
CLTHC	Clothing:Near-Coast	1	0.00	0.00	0.00
OTHRTT	Other Trip Expenses:Total	1	0.00	0.00	0.00
OTHRTC	Other Trip Expenses:Near-Coast	1	0.00	0.00	0.00
AIRFT	Air Fees:Total	1	64.00	64.00	64.00
AIRFC	Air Fees:Near-Coast	1	0.00	0.00	0.00
BOATNC	Boats:Away-Coast	1	0.00	0.00	0.00
BOATC	Boats:Near-Coast	1	0.00	0.00	0.00
MOTORNC	Motors:Away-Coast	1	0.00	0.00	0.00
MOTORC	Motors:Near-Coast	1	0.00	0.00	0.00
TRAILNC	Trailers:Away-Coast	1	0.00	0.00	0.00
TRAILC	Trailers:Near-Coast	1	0.00	0.00	0.00
AEQPNC	Electronics:Away-Coast	1	0.00	0.00	0.00
AEQPC	Electronics:Near-Coast	1	0.00	0.00	0.00
DFITNC	Diving Outfit:Away-Coast	1	0.00	0.00	0.00
DFITC	Diving Outfit:Near-Coast	1	0.00	0.00	0.00
REPRNC	Capital Repairs:Away-Coast	1	0.00	0.00	0.00
REPRC	Capital Repairs:Near-Coast	1	0.00	0.00	0.00
DEQPNC	Dive Equipment:Away-Coast	1	0.00	0.00	0.00
DEQPC	Dive Equipment:Near-Coast	1	0.00	0.00	0.00

LESSNC	DIve Lessons:Away-Coast	1	0.00	0.00	0.00
LESSC	Dive Lessons:Near-Coast	1	0.00	0.00	0.00
OTHDNC	Other Diving:Away-Coast	1	110.00	110.00	110.00
OTHDC	Other Diving:Near-Coast	1	0.00	0.00	0.00
BOOKNC	Books:Away-Coast	1	0.00	0.00	0.00
BOOKC	Books:Near-Coast	1	0.00	0.00	0.00
MEMBNC	Memberships:Away-Coast	1	0.00	0.00	0.00
MEMBC	Memberships:Near-Coast	1	0.00	0.00	0.00
CAMPNC	Camping:Away-Coast	1	0.00	0.00	0.00
CAMPC	Camping:Near-Coast	1	0.00	0.00	0.00
LICNC	Licenses:Away-Coast	1	6.00	6.00	6.00
LICC	Licenses:Near-Coast	1	0.00	0.00	0.00

Private Diving Summary Statistics for trip and equipment expenditures by Alabama
coastal residents who did't visit an oil/gas structure on the interview date

Variable	Label	N	Mean	Minimum	Maximum
TRANSC	Transportation:Near-Coast	4	0.00	0.00	0.00
RCART	Rental Car:Total	4	0.00	0.00	0.00
RCARC	Rental Car:Near-Coast	4	0.00	0.00	0.00
LODGT	Lodging:Total	4	0.00	0.00	0.00
LODGC	Lodging:Near-Coast	4	0.00	0.00	0.00
GAST	Gasoline:Total	4	1.05	0.45	2.25
GASC	Gasoline:Near-Coast	4	1.05	0.45	2.25
FOODT	Other Food:Total	4	25.00	0.00	100.00
FOODC	Other Food:Near-Coast	4	25.00	0.00	100.00
GROCT	Groceries:Total	4	0.00	0.00	0.00
GROCC	Groceries:Near-Coast	4	0.00	0.00	0.00
FUELT	Fuel:Total	4	0.00	0.00	0.00
FUELC	Fuel:Near-Coast	4	0.00	0.00	0.00
BRNTT	Boat Rentals:Total	4	5.75	0.00	23.00
BRNTC	Boat Rentals:Near-Coast	4	5.75	0.00	23.00
LNCHT	Launch Fees:Total	4	0.00	0.00	0.00
LNCHC	Launch Fees:Near-Coast	4	0.00	0.00	0.00
DOCKT	Dockage Fees:Total	4	0.00	0.00	0.00
DOCKC	Dockage Fees:Near-Coast	4	0.00	0.00	0.00
TREPRT	Trip Repairs:Total	4	0.00	0.00	0.00
TREPRC	Trip Repairs:Near-Coast	4	0.00	0.00	0.00
DFEET	Dive Fees:Total	4	0.00	0.00	0.00
DFEEC	Dive Fees:Near-Coast	4	0.00	0.00	0.00
TCKLT	Tackle:Total	4	0.00	0.00	0.00
TCKLC	Tackle:Near-Coast	4	0.00	0.00	0.00
OTHRNTT	Other Rentals:Total	4	0.00	0.00	0.00
OTHRNTC	Other Rentals:Near-Coast	4	0.00	0.00	0.00
GUIDT	Guide Fees:Total	4	0.00	0.00	0.00
GUIDC	Guide Fees:Near-Coast	4	0.00	0.00	0.00
CLTHT	Clothing:Total	4	57.50	0.00	230.00
CLTHC	Clothing:Near-Coast	4	57.50	0.00	230.00
OTHRTT	Other Trip Expenses:Total	4	1.25	0.00	5.00
OTHRTC	Other Trip Expenses:Near-Coast	4	1.25	0.00	5.00
AIRFT	Air Fees:Total	4	0.00	0.00	0.00
AIRFC	Air Fees:Near-Coast	4	0.00	0.00	0.00
BOATNC	Boats:Away-Coast	4	0.00	0.00	0.00
BOATC	Boats:Near-Coast	4	0.00	0.00	0.00
MOTORNC	Motors:Away-Coast	4	0.00	0.00	0.00
MOTORC	Motors:Near-Coast	4	0.00	0.00	0.00
TRAILNC	Trailers:Away-Coast	4	0.00	0.00	0.00
TRAILC	Trailers:Near-Coast	4	0.00	0.00	0.00
AEQPNC	Electronics:Away-Coast	4	0.00	0.00	0.00
AEQPC	Electronics:Near-Coast	4	0.00	0.00	0.00
DFITNC	Diving Outfit:Away-Coast	4	0.00	0.00	0.00
DFITC	Diving Outfit:Near-Coast	4	0.00	0.00	0.00
REPRNC	Capital Repairs:Away-Coast	4	0.00	0.00	0.00
REPRC	Capital Repairs:Near-Coast	4	0.00	0.00	0.00
DEQPNC	Dive Equipment:Away-Coast	4	0.00	0.00	0.00
DEQPC	Dive Equipment:Near-Coast	4	0.00	0.00	0.00

LESSNC	DIve Lessons:Away-Coast	4	0.00	0.00	0.00
LESSC	Dive Lessons:Near-Coast	4	62.50	0.00	250.00
OTHDNC	Other Diving:Away-Coast	4	0.00	0.00	0.00
OTHDC	Other Diving:Near-Coast	4	0.00	0.00	0.00
BOOKNC	Books:Away-Coast	4	0.00	0.00	0.00
BOOKC	Books:Near-Coast	4	30.00	0.00	70.00
MEMBNC	Memberships:Away-Coast	4	0.00	0.00	0.00
MEMBC	Memberships:Near-Coast	4	28.75	0.00	100.00
CAMPNC	Camping:Away-Coast	4	0.00	0.00	0.00
CAMPC	Camping:Near-Coast	4	0.00	0.00	0.00
LICNC	Licenses:Away-Coast	4	0.00	0.00	0.00
LICC	Licenses:Near-Coast	4	20.25	15.00	25.00

- -

Private Diving Summary Statistics for trip and equipment expenditures by Alabama
noncoastal residents who did't visit an oil/gas structure on the interview date

Variable	Label	N	Mean	Minimum	Maximum
TRANSC	Transportation:Near-Coast	2	0.00	0.00	0.00
RCART	Rental Car:Total	2	0.00	0.00	0.00
RCARC	Rental Car:Near-Coast	2	0.00	0.00	0.00
LODGT	Lodging:Total	2	0.00	0.00	0.00
LODGC	Lodging:Near-Coast	2	0.00	0.00	0.00
GAST	Gasoline:Total	2	7.95	0.00	15.90
GASC	Gasoline:Near-Coast	2	0.00	0.00	0.00
FOODT	Other Food:Total	2	0.00	0.00	0.00
FOODC	Other Food:Near-Coast	2	0.00	0.00	0.00
GROCT	Groceries:Total	2	0.00	0.00	0.00
GROCC	Groceries:Near-Coast	2	0.00	0.00	0.00
FUELT	Fuel:Total	2	0.00	0.00	0.00
FUELC	Fuel:Near-Coast	2	0.00	0.00	0.00
BRNTT	Boat Rentals:Total	2	0.00	0.00	0.00
BRNTC	Boat Rentals:Near-Coast	2	0.00	0.00	0.00
LNCHT	Launch Fees:Total	2	0.00	0.00	0.00
LNCHC	Launch Fees:Near-Coast	2	0.00	0.00	0.00
DOCKT	Dockage Fees:Total	2	0.00	0.00	0.00
DOCKC	Dockage Fees:Near-Coast	2	0.00	0.00	0.00
TREPRT	Trip Repairs:Total	2	0.00	0.00	0.00
TREPRC	Trip Repairs:Near-Coast	2	0.00	0.00	0.00
DFEET	Dive Fees:Total	2	0.00	0.00	0.00
DFEEC	Dive Fees:Near-Coast	2	0.00	0.00	0.00
TCKLT	Tackle:Total	2	0.00	0.00	0.00
TCKLC	Tackle:Near-Coast	2	0.00	0.00	0.00
OTHRNTT	Other Rentals:Total	2	0.00	0.00	0.00
OTHRNTC	Other Rentals:Near-Coast	2	0.00	0.00	0.00
GUIDT	Guide Fees:Total	2	0.00	0.00	0.00
GUIDC	Guide Fees:Near-Coast	2	0.00	0.00	0.00
CLTHT	Clothing:Total	2	0.00	0.00	0.00
CLTHC	Clothing:Near-Coast	2	0.00	0.00	0.00
OTHRTT	Other Trip Expenses:Total	2	0.00	0.00	0.00
OTHRTC	Other Trip Expenses:Near-Coast	2	0.00	0.00	0.00
AIRFT	Air Fees:Total	2	0.00	0.00	0.00
AIRFC	Air Fees:Near-Coast	2	0.00	0.00	0.00
BOATNC	Boats:Away-Coast	2	0.00	0.00	0.00
BOATC	Boats:Near-Coast	2	0.00	0.00	0.00
MOTORNC	Motors:Away-Coast	2	0.00	0.00	0.00
MOTORC	Motors:Near-Coast	2	0.00	0.00	0.00
TRAILNC	Trailers:Away-Coast	2	0.00	0.00	0.00
TRAILC	Trailers:Near-Coast	2	0.00	0.00	0.00
AEQPNC	Electronics:Away-Coast	2	0.00	0.00	0.00
AEQPC	Electronics:Near-Coast	2	0.00	0.00	0.00
DFITNC	Diving Outfit:Away-Coast	2	0.00	0.00	0.00
DFITC	Diving Outfit:Near-Coast	2	0.00	0.00	0.00
REPRNC	Capital Repairs:Away-Coast	2	0.00	0.00	0.00
REPRC	Capital Repairs:Near-Coast	2	0.00	0.00	0.00
DEQPNC	Dive Equipment:Away-Coast	2	0.00	0.00	0.00
DEQPC	Dive Equipment:Near-Coast	2	0.00	0.00	0.00

LESSNC	Dive Lessons:Away-Coast	2	0.00	0.00	0.00
LESSC	Dive Lessons:Near-Coast	2	0.00	0.00	0.00
OTHDNC	Other Diving:Away-Coast	2	0.00	0.00	0.00
OTHDC	Other Diving:Near-Coast	2	0.00	0.00	0.00
BOOKNC	Books:Away-Coast	2	0.00	0.00	0.00
BOOKC	Books:Near-Coast	2	0.00	0.00	0.00
MEMBNC	Memberships:Away-Coast	2	50.00	0.00	100.00
MEMBC	Memberships:Near-Coast	2	0.00	0.00	0.00
CAMPNC	Camping:Away-Coast	2	0.00	0.00	0.00
CAMPC	Camping:Near-Coast	2	0.00	0.00	0.00
LICNC	Licenses:Away-Coast	2	0.00	0.00	0.00
LICC	Licenses:Near-Coast	2	0.00	0.00	0.00

Party Boat Summary Statistics for trip and equipment expenditures by Mississippi
coastal residents who did visit an oil/gas structure on the interview date

Variable	Label	Mean	Minimum	Maximum
TRANST	Transportation:Total	0.00	0.00	0.00
TRANSC	Transportation:Near-Coast	0.00	0.00	0.00
RCART	Rental Car:Total	0.00	0.00	0.00
RCARC	Rental Car:Near-Coast	0.00	0.00	0.00
LODGT	Lodging:Total	0.00	0.00	0.00
LODGC	Lodging:Near-Coast	0.00	0.00	0.00
GAST	Gasoline:Total	15.00	15.00	15.00
GASC	Gasoline:Near-Coast	15.00	15.00	15.00
FOODT	Other Food:Total	0.00	0.00	0.00
FOODC	Other Food:Near-Coast	0.00	0.00	0.00
GROCT	Groceries:Total	60.00	60.00	60.00
GROCC	Groceries:Near-Coast	60.00	60.00	60.00
BAITT	Bait:Total	0.00	0.00	0.00
BAITC	Bait:Near-Coast	0.00	0.00	0.00
FLICT	Fishing Licenses:Total	0.00	0.00	0.00
FLICC	Fishing Licenses:Near-Coast	0.00	0.00	0.00
TCKLT	Tackle:Total	0.00	0.00	0.00
TCKLC	Tackle:Near-Coast	0.00	0.00	0.00
OTHRNTT	Other Rentals:Total	0.00	0.00	0.00
OTHRNTC	Other Rentals:Near-Coast	0.00	0.00	0.00
CLTHT	Clothing:Total	0.00	0.00	0.00
CLTHC	Clothing:Near-Coast	0.00	0.00	0.00
OTHRTT	Other Trip Expenses:Total	0.00	0.00	0.00
OTHRTC	Other Trip Expenses:Near-Coast	0.00	0.00	0.00
CHFEEST	Charter/Party Fees:Total	100.00	100.00	100.00
CHFEESC	Charter/Party Fees:Near-Coast	100.00	100.00	100.00
RODC	Rods:Near-Coast	0.00	0.00	0.00
RODNC	Rods:Away-Coast	0.00	0.00	0.00
LINEC	Fishing Line:Near-Coast	0.00	0.00	0.00
LINENC	Fishing Line:Away-Coast	0.00	0.00	0.00
LUREC	Lures:Near-Coast	0.00	0.00	0.00
LURENC	Lures:Nonoastal	0.00	0.00	0.00
OTHCFC	Other Fishing:Near-Coast	0.00	0.00	0.00
OTHCFNC	Other Fishing:Away-Coast	0.00	0.00	0.00
BOOKC	Books:Near-Coast	0.00	0.00	0.00
BOOKNC	Books:Away-Coast	0.00	0.00	0.00
MEMBC	Memberships:Near-Coast	0.00	0.00	0.00
MEMBNC	Memberships:Away-Coast	0.00	0.00	0.00
CAMPC	Camping:Near-Coast	0.00	0.00	0.00
CAMPNC	Camping:Away-Coast	0.00	0.00	0.00
LICC	Licenses:Near-Coast	25.00	25.00	25.00
LICNC	Licenses:Away-Coast	0.00	0.00	0.00

Party Boat Summary Statistics for trip and equipment expenditures by Louisiana
coastal residents who did visit an oil/gas structure on the interview date

Variable	Label	Mean	Minimum	Maximum
TRANST	Transportation:Total	0.00	0.00	0.00
TRANSC	Transportation:Near-Coast	0.00	0.00	0.00
RCART	Rental Car:Total	0.00	0.00	0.00
RCARC	Rental Car:Near-Coast	0.00	0.00	0.00
LODGT	Lodging:Total	36.50	0.00	225.00
LODGC	Lodging:Near-Coast	36.50	0.00	225.00
GAST	Gasoline:Total	17.40	6.75	30.00
GASC	Gasoline:Near-Coast	17.40	6.75	30.00
FOODT	Other Food:Total	22.00	0.00	125.00
FOODC	Other Food:Near-Coast	22.00	0.00	125.00
GROCT	Groceries:Total	20.00	0.00	100.00
GROCC	Groceries:Near-Coast	20.00	0.00	100.00
BAITT	Bait:Total	0.00	0.00	0.00
BAITC	Bait:Near-Coast	0.00	0.00	0.00
FLICT	Fishing Licenses:Total	0.00	0.00	0.00
FLICC	Fishing Licenses:Near-Coast	0.00	0.00	0.00
TCKLT	Tackle:Total	1.00	0.00	10.00
TCKLC	Tackle:Near-Coast	1.00	0.00	10.00
OTHRNTT	Other Rentals:Total	0.00	0.00	0.00
OTHRNTC	Other Rentals:Near-Coast	0.00	0.00	0.00
CLTHT	Clothing:Total	0.00	0.00	0.00
CLTHC	Clothing:Near-Coast	0.00	0.00	0.00
OTHRTT	Other Trip Expenses:Total	3.80	0.00	28.00
OTHRTC	Other Trip Expenses:Near-Coast	3.80	0.00	28.00
CHFEEST	Charter/Party Fees:Total	61.50	0.00	240.00
CHFEESC	Charter/Party Fees:Near-Coast	61.50	0.00	240.00
RODC	Rods:Near-Coast	0.00	0.00	0.00
RODNC	Rods:Away-Coast	75.00	0.00	600.00
LINEC	Fishing Line:Near-Coast	0.00	0.00	0.00
LINENC	Fishing Line:Away-Coast	2.60	0.00	15.00
LUREC	Lures:Near-Coast	0.00	0.00	0.00
LURENC	Lures:Nonoastal	6.00	0.00	30.00
OTHCFC	Other Fishing:Near-Coast	0.00	0.00	0.00
OTHCFNC	Other Fishing:Away-Coast	2.50	0.00	25.00
BOOKC	Books:Near-Coast	2.10	0.00	16.00
BOOKNC	Books:Away-Coast	0.00	0.00	0.00
MEMBC	Memberships:Near-Coast	0.00	0.00	0.00
MEMBNC	Memberships:Away-Coast	0.00	0.00	0.00
CAMPC	Camping:Near-Coast	6.00	0.00	60.00
CAMPNC	Camping:Away-Coast	0.00	0.00	0.00
LICC	Licenses:Near-Coast	13.00	0.00	44.00
LICNC	Licenses:Away-Coast	0.00	0.00	0.00

Party Boat Summary Statistics for trip and equipment expenditures by Louisiana
noncoastal residents who did visit an oil/gas structure on the interview date

Variable	Label	Mean	Minimum	Maximum
TRANST	Transportation:Total	0.00	0.00	0.00
TRANSC	Transportation:Near-Coast	0.00	0.00	0.00
RCART	Rental Car:Total	0.00	0.00	0.00
RCARC	Rental Car:Near-Coast	0.00	0.00	0.00
LODGT	Lodging:Total	3.33	0.00	10.00
LODGC	Lodging:Near-Coast	3.33	0.00	10.00
GAST	Gasoline:Total	11.60	0.30	19.50
GASC	Gasoline:Near-Coast	0.00	0.00	0.00
FOODT	Other Food:Total	83.33	10.00	200.00
FOODC	Other Food:Near-Coast	13.33	0.00	40.00
GROCT	Groceries:Total	11.67	0.00	25.00
GROCC	Groceries:Near-Coast	0.00	0.00	0.00
BAITT	Bait:Total	20.00	0.00	40.00
BAITC	Bait:Near-Coast	13.33	0.00	40.00
FLICT	Fishing Licenses:Total	0.00	0.00	0.00
FLICC	Fishing Licenses:Near-Coast	0.00	0.00	0.00
TCKLT	Tackle:Total	0.67	0.00	2.00
TCKLC	Tackle:Near-Coast	0.00	0.00	0.00
OTHRNTT	Other Rentals:Total	0.00	0.00	0.00
OTHRNTC	Other Rentals:Near-Coast	0.00	0.00	0.00
CLTHT	Clothing:Total	0.00	0.00	0.00
CLTHC	Clothing:Near-Coast	0.00	0.00	0.00
OTHRTT	Other Trip Expenses:Total	0.00	0.00	0.00
OTHRTC	Other Trip Expenses:Near-Coast	0.00	0.00	0.00
CHFEEST	Charter/Party Fees:Total	81.67	0.00	125.00
CHFEESC	Charter/Party Fees:Near-Coast	81.67	0.00	125.00
RODC	Rods:Near-Coast	0.00	0.00	0.00
RODNC	Rods:Away-Coast	200.00	0.00	400.00
LINEC	Fishing Line:Near-Coast	0.00	0.00	0.00
LINENC	Fishing Line:Away-Coast	33.33	0.00	50.00
LUREC	Lures:Near-Coast	0.00	0.00	0.00
LURENC	Lures:Nonoastal	66.67	0.00	100.00
OTHCFC	Other Fishing:Near-Coast	0.00	0.00	0.00
OTHCFNC	Other Fishing:Away-Coast	17.00	0.00	51.00
BOOKC	Books:Near-Coast	0.00	0.00	0.00
BOOKNC	Books:Away-Coast	0.00	0.00	0.00
MEMBC	Memberships:Near-Coast	0.00	0.00	0.00
MEMBNC	Memberships:Away-Coast	8.33	0.00	25.00
CAMPC	Camping:Near-Coast	0.00	0.00	0.00
CAMPNC	Camping:Away-Coast	0.00	0.00	0.00
LICC	Licenses:Near-Coast	0.00	0.00	0.00
LICNC	Licenses:Away-Coast	7.33	5.00	11.00

Party Boat Summary Statistics for trip and equipment expenditures by Texas
coastal residents who did visit an oil/gas structure on the interview date

Variable	Label	Mean	Minimum	Maximum
TRANST	Transportation:Total	0.00	0.00	0.00
TRANSC	Transportation:Near-Coast	0.00	0.00	0.00
RCART	Rental Car:Total	0.00	0.00	0.00
RCARC	Rental Car:Near-Coast	0.00	0.00	0.00
LODGT	Lodging:Total	0.00	0.00	0.00
LODGC	Lodging:Near-Coast	0.00	0.00	0.00
GAST	Gasoline:Total	7.05	0.00	15.15
GASC	Gasoline:Near-Coast	7.05	0.00	15.15
FOODT	Other Food:Total	12.00	0.00	20.00
FOODC	Other Food:Near-Coast	12.00	0.00	20.00
GROCT	Groceries:Total	15.00	0.00	25.00
GROCC	Groceries:Near-Coast	15.00	0.00	25.00
BAITT	Bait:Total	17.00	0.00	26.00
BAITC	Bait:Near-Coast	17.00	0.00	26.00
FLICT	Fishing Licenses:Total	0.00	0.00	0.00
FLICC	Fishing Licenses:Near-Coast	0.00	0.00	0.00
TCKLT	Tackle:Total	5.00	0.00	15.00
TCKLC	Tackle:Near-Coast	5.00	0.00	15.00
OTHRNTT	Other Rentals:Total	0.00	0.00	0.00
OTHRNTC	Other Rentals:Near-Coast	0.00	0.00	0.00
CLTHT	Clothing:Total	0.00	0.00	0.00
CLTHC	Clothing:Near-Coast	0.00	0.00	0.00
OTHRTT	Other Trip Expenses:Total	10.00	0.00	22.00
OTHRTC	Other Trip Expenses:Near-Coast	10.00	0.00	22.00
CHFEEST	Charter/Party Fees:Total	63.33	0.00	130.00
CHFEESC	Charter/Party Fees:Near-Coast	63.33	0.00	130.00
RODC	Rods:Near-Coast	933.33	0.00	1500.00
RODNC	Rods:Away-Coast	0.00	0.00	0.00
LINEC	Fishing Line:Near-Coast	43.00	0.00	129.00
LINENC	Fishing Line:Away-Coast	0.00	0.00	0.00
LUREC	Lures:Near-Coast	83.33	0.00	250.00
LURENC	Lures:Nonoastal	0.00	0.00	0.00
OTHCFC	Other Fishing:Near-Coast	0.00	0.00	0.00
OTHCFNC	Other Fishing:Away-Coast	0.00	0.00	0.00
BOOKC	Books:Near-Coast	53.33	0.00	90.00
BOOKNC	Books:Away-Coast	0.00	0.00	0.00
MEMBC	Memberships:Near-Coast	40.00	0.00	80.00
MEMBNC	Memberships:Away-Coast	0.00	0.00	0.00
CAMPC	Camping:Near-Coast	25.00	0.00	75.00
CAMPNC	Camping:Away-Coast	0.00	0.00	0.00
LICC	Licenses:Near-Coast	32.33	20.00	49.00
LICNC	Licenses:Away-Coast	0.00	0.00	0.00

Party Boat Summary Statistics for trip and equipment expenditures by Texas
noncoastal residents who did visit an oil/gas structure on the interview date

Variable	Label	Mean	Minimum	Maximum
TRANST	Transportation:Total	0.00	0.00	0.00
TRANSC	Transportation:Near-Coast	0.00	0.00	0.00
RCART	Rental Car:Total	0.00	0.00	0.00
RCARC	Rental Car:Near-Coast	0.00	0.00	0.00
LODGT	Lodging:Total	0.00	0.00	0.00
LODGC	Lodging:Near-Coast	0.00	0.00	0.00
GAST	Gasoline:Total	21.75	13.50	30.00
GASC	Gasoline:Near-Coast	0.00	0.00	0.00
FOODT	Other Food:Total	47.50	15.00	80.00
FOODC	Other Food:Near-Coast	42.50	5.00	80.00
GROCT	Groceries:Total	7.50	0.00	15.00
GROCC	Groceries:Near-Coast	7.50	0.00	15.00
BAITT	Bait:Total	5.00	0.00	10.00
BAITC	Bait:Near-Coast	5.00	0.00	10.00
FLICT	Fishing Licenses:Total	0.00	0.00	0.00
FLICC	Fishing Licenses:Near-Coast	0.00	0.00	0.00
TCKLT	Tackle:Total	0.00	0.00	0.00
TCKLC	Tackle:Near-Coast	0.00	0.00	0.00
OTHRNTT	Other Rentals:Total	0.00	0.00	0.00
OTHRNTC	Other Rentals:Near-Coast	0.00	0.00	0.00
CLTHT	Clothing:Total	0.00	0.00	0.00
CLTHC	Clothing:Near-Coast	0.00	0.00	0.00
OTHRTT	Other Trip Expenses:Total	0.00	0.00	0.00
OTHRTC	Other Trip Expenses:Near-Coast	0.00	0.00	0.00
CHFEEST	Charter/Party Fees:Total	37.50	0.00	75.00
CHFEESC	Charter/Party Fees:Near-Coast	37.50	0.00	75.00
RODC	Rods:Near-Coast	0.00	0.00	0.00
RODNC	Rods:Away-Coast	0.00	0.00	0.00
LINEC	Fishing Line:Near-Coast	0.00	0.00	0.00
LINENC	Fishing Line:Away-Coast	0.00	0.00	0.00
LUREC	Lures:Near-Coast	0.00	0.00	0.00
LURENC	Lures:Nonoastal	75.00	0.00	150.00
OTHCFC	Other Fishing:Near-Coast	0.00	0.00	0.00
OTHCFNC	Other Fishing:Away-Coast	0.00	0.00	0.00
BOOKC	Books:Near-Coast	0.00	0.00	0.00
BOOKNC	Books:Away-Coast	23.00	0.00	46.00
MEMBC	Memberships:Near-Coast	0.00	0.00	0.00
MEMBNC	Memberships:Away-Coast	0.00	0.00	0.00
CAMPC	Camping:Near-Coast	0.00	0.00	0.00
CAMPNC	Camping:Away-Coast	0.00	0.00	0.00
LICC	Licenses:Near-Coast	0.00	0.00	0.00
LICNC	Licenses:Away-Coast	25.00	0.00	50.00

Party Boat Summary Statistics for trip and equipment expenditures by Alabama
coastal residents who did't visit an oil/gas structure on the interview date

Variable	Label	Mean	Minimum	Maximum
TRANST	Transportation:Total	0.00	0.00	0.00
TRANSC	Transportation:Near-Coast	0.00	0.00	0.00
RCART	Rental Car:Total	0.00	0.00	0.00
RCARC	Rental Car:Near-Coast	0.00	0.00	0.00
LODGT	Lodging:Total	106.67	0.00	320.00
LODGC	Lodging:Near-Coast	106.67	0.00	320.00
GAST	Gasoline:Total	18.75	1.50	32.25
GASC	Gasoline:Near-Coast	18.75	1.50	32.25
FOODT	Other Food:Total	66.67	0.00	200.00
FOODC	Other Food:Near-Coast	66.67	0.00	200.00
GROCT	Groceries:Total	25.00	0.00	75.00
GROCC	Groceries:Near-Coast	25.00	0.00	75.00
BAITT	Bait:Total	1.33	0.00	4.00
BAITC	Bait:Near-Coast	1.33	0.00	4.00
FLICT	Fishing Licenses:Total	0.00	0.00	0.00
FLICC	Fishing Licenses:Near-Coast	0.00	0.00	0.00
TCKLT	Tackle:Total	0.00	0.00	0.00
TCKLC	Tackle:Near-Coast	0.00	0.00	0.00
OTHRNTT	Other Rentals:Total	0.00	0.00	0.00
OTHRNTC	Other Rentals:Near-Coast	0.00	0.00	0.00
CLTHT	Clothing:Total	0.00	0.00	0.00
CLTHC	Clothing:Near-Coast	0.00	0.00	0.00
OTHRTT	Other Trip Expenses:Total	1.67	0.00	5.00
OTHRTC	Other Trip Expenses:Near-Coast	1.67	0.00	5.00
CHFEEST	Charter/Party Fees:Total	100.00	0.00	300.00
CHFEESC	Charter/Party Fees:Near-Coast	100.00	0.00	300.00
RODC	Rods:Near-Coast	0.00	0.00	0.00
RODNC	Rods:Away-Coast	0.00	0.00	0.00
LINEC	Fishing Line:Near-Coast	0.00	0.00	0.00
LINENC	Fishing Line:Away-Coast	1.33	0.00	4.00
LUREC	Lures:Near-Coast	0.00	0.00	0.00
LURENC	Lures:Nonoastal	26.67	0.00	40.00
OTHCFC	Other Fishing:Near-Coast	0.00	0.00	0.00
OTHCFNC	Other Fishing:Away-Coast	0.00	0.00	0.00
BOOKC	Books:Near-Coast	6.67	0.00	20.00
BOOKNC	Books:Away-Coast	0.00	0.00	0.00
MEMBC	Memberships:Near-Coast	0.00	0.00	0.00
MEMBNC	Memberships:Away-Coast	0.00	0.00	0.00
CAMPC	Camping:Near-Coast	0.00	0.00	0.00
CAMPNC	Camping:Away-Coast	0.00	0.00	0.00
LICC	Licenses:Near-Coast	11.67	0.00	35.00
LICNC	Licenses:Away-Coast	0.00	0.00	0.00

Party Boat Summary Statistics for trip and equipment expenditures by Alabama
noncoastal residents who did't visit an oil/gas structure on the interview date

Variable	Label	Mean	Minimum	Maximum
TRANST	Transportation:Total	0.00	0.00	0.00
TRANSC	Transportation:Near-Coast	0.00	0.00	0.00
RCART	Rental Car:Total	51.11	0.00	230.00
RCARC	Rental Car:Near-Coast	0.00	0.00	0.00
LODGT	Lodging:Total	414.11	0.00	1752.00
LODGC	Lodging:Near-Coast	414.11	0.00	1752.00
GAST	Gasoline:Total	82.40	0.00	183.00
GASC	Gasoline:Near-Coast	0.00	0.00	0.00
FOODT	Other Food:Total	25.56	0.00	100.00
FOODC	Other Food:Near-Coast	11.11	0.00	100.00
GROCT	Groceries:Total	8.89	0.00	60.00
GROCC	Groceries:Near-Coast	8.89	0.00	60.00
BAITT	Bait:Total	1.67	0.00	10.00
BAITC	Bait:Near-Coast	1.67	0.00	10.00
FLICT	Fishing Licenses:Total	1.11	0.00	10.00
FLICC	Fishing Licenses:Near-Coast	1.11	0.00	10.00
TCKLT	Tackle:Total	2.22	0.00	20.00
TCKLC	Tackle:Near-Coast	2.22	0.00	20.00
OTHRNTT	Other Rentals:Total	0.00	0.00	0.00
OTHRNTC	Other Rentals:Near-Coast	0.00	0.00	0.00
CLTHT	Clothing:Total	0.00	0.00	0.00
CLTHC	Clothing:Near-Coast	0.00	0.00	0.00
OTHRTT	Other Trip Expenses:Total	13.44	0.00	110.00
OTHRTC	Other Trip Expenses:Near-Coast	1.22	0.00	6.00
CHFEEST	Charter/Party Fees:Total	34.44	0.00	120.00
CHFEESC	Charter/Party Fees:Near-Coast	34.44	0.00	120.00
RODC	Rods:Near-Coast	5.56	0.00	50.00
RODNC	Rods:Away-Coast	0.00	0.00	0.00
LINEC	Fishing Line:Near-Coast	0.44	0.00	4.00
LINENC	Fishing Line:Away-Coast	0.00	0.00	0.00
LUREC	Lures:Near-Coast	1.78	0.00	10.00
LURENC	Lures:Nonoastal	0.00	0.00	0.00
OTHCFC	Other Fishing:Near-Coast	0.00	0.00	0.00
OTHCFNC	Other Fishing:Away-Coast	0.00	0.00	0.00
BOOKC	Books:Near-Coast	0.00	0.00	0.00
BOOKNC	Books:Away-Coast	0.00	0.00	0.00
MEMBC	Memberships:Near-Coast	0.00	0.00	0.00
MEMBNC	Memberships:Away-Coast	0.00	0.00	0.00
CAMPC	Camping:Near-Coast	0.00	0.00	0.00
CAMPNC	Camping:Away-Coast	33.33	0.00	300.00
LICC	Licenses:Near-Coast	0.00	0.00	0.00
LICNC	Licenses:Away-Coast	3.11	0.00	13.00

Party Boat Summary Statistics for trip and equipment expenditures by Texas
noncoastal residents who did't visit an oil/gas structure on the interview date

Variable	Label	Mean	Minimum	Maximum
TRANST	Transportation:Total	0.00	0.00	0.00
TRANSC	Transportation:Near-Coast	0.00	0.00	0.00
RCART	Rental Car:Total	0.00	0.00	0.00
RCARC	Rental Car:Near-Coast	0.00	0.00	0.00
LODGT	Lodging:Total	112.50	0.00	600.00
LODGC	Lodging:Near-Coast	112.50	0.00	600.00
GAST	Gasoline:Total	60.55	42.00	82.50
GASC	Gasoline:Near-Coast	0.00	0.00	0.00
FOODT	Other Food:Total	38.33	0.00	100.00
FOODC	Other Food:Near-Coast	33.33	0.00	100.00
GROCT	Groceries:Total	25.00	0.00	100.00
GROCC	Groceries:Near-Coast	25.00	0.00	100.00
BAITT	Bait:Total	4.17	0.00	15.00
BAITC	Bait:Near-Coast	1.67	0.00	10.00
FLICT	Fishing Licenses:Total	0.00	0.00	0.00
FLICC	Fishing Licenses:Near-Coast	0.00	0.00	0.00
TCKLT	Tackle:Total	0.00	0.00	0.00
TCKLC	Tackle:Near-Coast	0.00	0.00	0.00
OTHRNTT	Other Rentals:Total	0.00	0.00	0.00
OTHRNTC	Other Rentals:Near-Coast	0.00	0.00	0.00
CLTHT	Clothing:Total	0.00	0.00	0.00
CLTHC	Clothing:Near-Coast	0.00	0.00	0.00
OTHRTT	Other Trip Expenses:Total	20.83	0.00	120.00
OTHRTC	Other Trip Expenses:Near-Coast	20.00	0.00	120.00
CHFEEST	Charter/Party Fees:Total	47.50	0.00	200.00
CHFEESC	Charter/Party Fees:Near-Coast	47.50	0.00	200.00
RODC	Rods:Near-Coast	0.00	0.00	0.00
RODNC	Rods:Away-Coast	71.67	0.00	400.00
LINEC	Fishing Line:Near-Coast	0.00	0.00	0.00
LINENC	Fishing Line:Away-Coast	5.00	0.00	30.00
LUREC	Lures:Near-Coast	0.00	0.00	0.00
LURENC	Lures:Nonoastal	18.67	0.00	100.00
OTHCFC	Other Fishing:Near-Coast	0.00	0.00	0.00
OTHCFNC	Other Fishing:Away-Coast	0.83	0.00	5.00
BOOKC	Books:Near-Coast	0.00	0.00	0.00
BOOKNC	Books:Away-Coast	52.33	0.00	300.00
MEMBC	Memberships:Near-Coast	0.00	0.00	0.00
MEMBNC	Memberships:Away-Coast	24.17	0.00	100.00
CAMPC	Camping:Near-Coast	0.00	0.00	0.00
CAMPNC	Camping:Away-Coast	10.00	0.00	60.00
LICC	Licenses:Near-Coast	0.00	0.00	0.00
LICNC	Licenses:Away-Coast	3.17	0.00	19.00

Private Fishing Summary Statistics for trip and equipment expenditures by Alabama
coastal residents who did visit an oil/gas structure on the interview date

Variable	Label	N	Mean	Minimum	Maximum
TRANST	Transportation:Total	88	0.00	0.00	0.00
TRANSC	Transportation:Near-Coast	88	0.00	0.00	0.00
RCART	Rental Car:Total	88	0.00	0.00	0.00
RCARC	Rental Car:Near-Coast	88	0.00	0.00	0.00
LODGT	Lodging:Total	88	9.41	0.00	360.00
LODGC	Lodging:Near-Coast	88	9.41	0.00	360.00
GAST	Gasoline:Total	88	4.61	0.00	30.00
GASC	Gasoline:Near-Coast	88	4.61	0.00	30.00
FOODT	Other Food:Total	88	7.53	0.00	100.00
FOODC	Other Food:Near-Coast	88	7.53	0.00	100.00
GROCT	Groceries:Total	88	11.16	0.00	100.00
GROCC	Groceries:Near-Coast	88	11.16	0.00	100.00
FUELT	Fuel:Total	88	22.76	0.00	150.00
FUELC	Fuel:Near-Coast	88	22.76	0.00	150.00
BRNTT	Boat Rentals:Total	88	0.34	0.00	30.00
BRNTC	Boat Rentals:Near-Coast	88	0.34	0.00	30.00
LNCHT	Launch Fees:Total	88	0.48	0.00	30.00
LNCHC	Launch Fees:Near-Coast	88	0.48	0.00	30.00
DOCKT	Dockage Fees:Total	88	0.00	0.00	0.00
DOCKC	Dockage Fees:Near-Coast	88	0.00	0.00	0.00
TREPRT	Trip Repairs:Total	88	2.27	0.00	200.00
TREPRC	Trip Repairs:Near-Coast	88	2.27	0.00	200.00
BAITT	Bait:Total	88	12.86	0.00	96.00
BAITC	Bait:Near-Coast	88	12.86	0.00	96.00
FLICT	Fishing Licenses:Total	88	1.22	0.00	26.00
FLICC	Fishing Licenses:Near-Coast	88	1.22	0.00	26.00
TCKLT	Tackle:Total	88	5.25	0.00	100.00
TCKLC	Tackle:Near-Coast	88	5.25	0.00	100.00
OTHRNTT	Other Rentals:Total	88	0.00	0.00	0.00
OTHRNTC	Other Rentals:Near-Coast	88	0.00	0.00	0.00
CLTHT	Clothing:Total	88	0.00	0.00	0.00
CLTHC	Clothing:Near-Coast	88	0.00	0.00	0.00
GUIDT	Guide Fees:Total	88	0.00	0.00	0.00
GUIDC	Guide Fees:Near-Coast	88	0.00	0.00	0.00
OTHRTT	Other Trip Expenses:Total	88	1.92	0.00	31.00
OTHRTC	Other Trip Expenses:Near-Coast	88	1.92	0.00	31.00
BOATNC	Boats:Away-Coast	88	170.45	0.00	15000.00
BOATC	Boats:Near-Coast	88	1418.69	0.00	45000.00
MOTORNC	Motors:Away-Coast	88	131.82	0.00	10000.00
MOTORC	Motors:Near-Coast	88	397.73	0.00	20000.00
TRAILNC	Trailers:Away-Coast	88	28.41	0.00	2500.00
TRAILC	Trailers:Near-Coast	88	34.09	0.00	3000.00
AEQPNC	Electronics:Away-Coast	88	180.09	0.00	3000.00
AEQPC	Electronics:Near-Coast	88	0.00	0.00	0.00
BFITNC	Fishing Outfit:Away-Coast	88	38.07	0.00	2000.00
BFITC	Fishing Outfit:Near-Coast	88	0.00	0.00	0.00
RODC	Rods:Near-Coast	88	182.73	0.00	1600.00
RODNC	Rods:Away-Coast	88	9.32	0.00	400.00
LINEC	Fishing Line:Near-Coast	88	27.25	0.00	200.00

LINENC	Fishing Line:Away-Coast	88	3.52	0.00	200.00
LUREC	Lures:Near-Coast	88	44.84	0.00	600.00
LURENC	Lures:Nonoastal	88	6.53	0.00	200.00
REPRNC	Capital Repairs:Away-Coast	88	38.18	0.00	2200.00
REPRC	Capital Repairs:Near-Coast	88	106.25	0.00	5000.00
OTHCFNC	Other Fishing:Away-Coast	88	0.80	0.00	40.00
OTHCFC	Other Fishing:Near-Coast	88	8.75	0.00	180.00
BOOKNC	Books:Away-Coast	88	0.00	0.00	0.00
BOOKC	Books:Near-Coast	88	6.11	0.00	60.00
MEMBNC	Memberships:Away-Coast	88	0.00	0.00	0.00
MEMBC	Memberships:Near-Coast	88	6.88	0.00	100.00
CAMPNC	Camping:Away-Coast	88	0.00	0.00	0.00
CAMPC	Camping:Near-Coast	88	3.73	0.00	150.00
LICNC	Licenses:Away-Coast	88	0.00	0.00	0.00
LICC	Licenses:Near-Coast	88	15.83	0.00	110.00

Private Fishing Summary Statistics for trip and equipment expenditures by Alabama
noncoastal residents who did visit an oil/gas structure on the interview date

Variable	Label	N	Mean	Minimum	Maximum
TRANST	Transportation:Total	5	0.00	0.00	0.00
TRANSC	Transportation:Near-Coast	5	0.00	0.00	0.00
RCART	Rental Car:Total	5	0.00	0.00	0.00
RCARC	Rental Car:Near-Coast	5	0.00	0.00	0.00
LODGT	Lodging:Total	5	20.00	0.00	100.00
LODGC	Lodging:Near-Coast	5	20.00	0.00	100.00
GAST	Gasoline:Total	5	51.00	31.50	78.00
GASC	Gasoline:Near-Coast	5	0.00	0.00	0.00
FOODT	Other Food:Total	5	5.00	0.00	25.00
FOODC	Other Food:Near-Coast	5	0.00	0.00	0.00
GROCT	Groceries:Total	5	10.00	0.00	30.00
GROCC	Groceries:Near-Coast	5	6.00	0.00	30.00
FUELT	Fuel:Total	5	10.00	0.00	50.00
FUELC	Fuel:Near-Coast	5	10.00	0.00	50.00
BRNTT	Boat Rentals:Total	5	0.00	0.00	0.00
BRNTC	Boat Rentals:Near-Coast	5	0.00	0.00	0.00
LNCHT	Launch Fees:Total	5	0.00	0.00	0.00
LNCHC	Launch Fees:Near-Coast	5	0.00	0.00	0.00
DOCKT	Dockage Fees:Total	5	0.00	0.00	0.00
DOCKC	Dockage Fees:Near-Coast	5	0.00	0.00	0.00
TREPRT	Trip Repairs:Total	5	0.00	0.00	0.00
TREPRC	Trip Repairs:Near-Coast	5	0.00	0.00	0.00
BAITT	Bait:Total	5	9.00	0.00	30.00
BAITC	Bait:Near-Coast	5	9.00	0.00	30.00
FLICT	Fishing Licenses:Total	5	0.00	0.00	0.00
FLICC	Fishing Licenses:Near-Coast	5	0.00	0.00	0.00
TCKLT	Tackle:Total	5	0.00	0.00	0.00
TCKLC	Tackle:Near-Coast	5	0.00	0.00	0.00
OTHRNTT	Other Rentals:Total	5	0.00	0.00	0.00
OTHRNTC	Other Rentals:Near-Coast	5	0.00	0.00	0.00
CLTHT	Clothing:Total	5	0.00	0.00	0.00
CLTHC	Clothing:Near-Coast	5	0.00	0.00	0.00
GUIDT	Guide Fees:Total	5	0.00	0.00	0.00
GUIDC	Guide Fees:Near-Coast	5	0.00	0.00	0.00
OTHRTT	Other Trip Expenses:Total	5	1.00	0.00	5.00
OTHRTC	Other Trip Expenses:Near-Coast	5	0.00	0.00	0.00
BOATNC	Boats:Away-Coast	5	0.00	0.00	0.00
BOATC	Boats:Near-Coast	5	0.00	0.00	0.00
MOTORNC	Motors:Away-Coast	5	0.00	0.00	0.00
MOTORC	Motors:Near-Coast	5	0.00	0.00	0.00
TRAILNC	Trailers:Away-Coast	5	0.00	0.00	0.00
TRAILC	Trailers:Near-Coast	5	0.00	0.00	0.00
AEQPNC	Electronics:Away-Coast	5	0.00	0.00	0.00
AEQPC	Electronics:Near-Coast	5	0.00	0.00	0.00
BFITNC	Fishing Outfit:Away-Coast	5	0.00	0.00	0.00
BFITC	Fishing Outfit:Near-Coast	5	0.00	0.00	0.00
RODC	Rods:Near-Coast	5	0.00	0.00	0.00
RODNC	Rods:Away-Coast	5	0.00	0.00	0.00
LINEC	Fishing Line:Near-Coast	5	0.00	0.00	0.00

LINENC	Fishing Line:Away-Coast	5	0.60	0.00	3.00
LUREC	Lures:Near-Coast	5	0.00	0.00	0.00
LURENC	Lures:Nonoastal	5	35.00	0.00	150.00
REPRNC	Capital Repairs:Away-Coast	5	0.00	0.00	0.00
REPRC	Capital Repairs:Near-Coast	5	0.00	0.00	0.00
OTHCFNC	Other Fishing:Away-Coast	5	0.00	0.00	0.00
OTHCFC	Other Fishing:Near-Coast	5	0.00	0.00	0.00
BOOKNC	Books:Away-Coast	5	22.00	0.00	60.00
BOOKC	Books:Near-Coast	5	0.00	0.00	0.00
MEMBNC	Memberships:Away-Coast	5	0.00	0.00	0.00
MEMBC	Memberships:Near-Coast	5	0.00	0.00	0.00
CAMPNC	Camping:Away-Coast	5	0.00	0.00	0.00
CAMPC	Camping:Near-Coast	5	0.00	0.00	0.00
LICNC	Licenses:Away-Coast	5	19.20	0.00	40.00
LICC	Licenses:Near-Coast	5	0.00	0.00	0.00

Private Fishing Summary Statistics for trip and equipment expenditures by Mississippi
coastal residents who did visit an oil/gas structure on the interview date

Variable	Label	N	Mean	Minimum	Maximum
TRANST	Transportation:Total	28	0.00	0.00	0.00
TRANSC	Transportation:Near-Coast	28	0.00	0.00	0.00
RCART	Rental Car:Total	28	0.00	0.00	0.00
RCARC	Rental Car:Near-Coast	28	0.00	0.00	0.00
LODGT	Lodging:Total	28	4.86	0.00	136.00
LODGC	Lodging:Near-Coast	28	4.86	0.00	136.00
GAST	Gasoline:Total	28	2.11	0.00	10.50
GASC	Gasoline:Near-Coast	28	2.11	0.00	10.50
FOODT	Other Food:Total	28	18.07	0.00	300.00
FOODC	Other Food:Near-Coast	28	18.07	0.00	300.00
GROCT	Groceries:Total	28	19.39	0.00	100.00
GROCC	Groceries:Near-Coast	28	19.39	0.00	100.00
FUELT	Fuel:Total	28	72.86	0.00	900.00
FUELC	Fuel:Near-Coast	28	72.86	0.00	900.00
BRNTT	Boat Rentals:Total	28	0.36	0.00	10.00
BRNTC	Boat Rentals:Near-Coast	28	0.36	0.00	10.00
LNCHT	Launch Fees:Total	28	0.64	0.00	16.00
LNCHC	Launch Fees:Near-Coast	28	0.64	0.00	16.00
DOCKT	Dockage Fees:Total	28	0.57	0.00	16.00
DOCKC	Dockage Fees:Near-Coast	28	0.57	0.00	16.00
TREPRT	Trip Repairs:Total	28	0.00	0.00	0.00
TREPRC	Trip Repairs:Near-Coast	28	0.00	0.00	0.00
BAITT	Bait:Total	28	13.82	0.00	100.00
BAITC	Bait:Near-Coast	28	13.82	0.00	100.00
FLICT	Fishing Licenses:Total	28	9.86	0.00	150.00
FLICC	Fishing Licenses:Near-Coast	28	9.86	0.00	150.00
TCKLT	Tackle:Total	28	7.32	0.00	75.00
TCKLC	Tackle:Near-Coast	28	7.32	0.00	75.00
OTHRNTT	Other Rentals:Total	28	0.00	0.00	0.00
OTHRNTC	Other Rentals:Near-Coast	28	0.00	0.00	0.00
CLTHT	Clothing:Total	28	4.46	0.00	50.00
CLTHC	Clothing:Near-Coast	28	4.46	0.00	50.00
GUIDT	Guide Fees:Total	28	0.00	0.00	0.00
GUIDC	Guide Fees:Near-Coast	28	0.00	0.00	0.00
OTHRTT	Other Trip Expenses:Total	28	4.64	0.00	30.00
OTHRTC	Other Trip Expenses:Near-Coast	28	4.64	0.00	30.00
BOATNC	Boats:Away-Coast	28	0.00	0.00	0.00
BOATC	Boats:Near-Coast	28	0.00	0.00	0.00
MOTORNC	Motors:Away-Coast	28	0.00	0.00	0.00
MOTORC	Motors:Near-Coast	28	714.29	0.00	20000.00
TRAILNC	Trailers:Away-Coast	28	0.00	0.00	0.00
TRAILC	Trailers:Near-Coast	28	0.00	0.00	0.00
AEQPNC	Electronics:Away-Coast	28	512.50	0.00	6000.00
AEQPC	Electronics:Near-Coast	28	0.00	0.00	0.00
BFITNC	Fishing Outfit:Away-Coast	28	48.21	0.00	1000.00
BFITC	Fishing Outfit:Near-Coast	28	0.00	0.00	0.00
RODC	Rods:Near-Coast	28	308.57	0.00	5000.00
RODNC	Rods:Away-Coast	28	117.86	0.00	1100.00
LINEC	Fishing Line:Near-Coast	28	62.75	0.00	500.00

LINENC	Fishing Line:Away-Coast	28	1.00	0.00	25.00
LUREC	Lures:Near-Coast	28	369.46	0.00	7000.00
LURENC	Lures:Nonoastal	28	5.36	0.00	100.00
REPRNC	Capital Repairs:Away-Coast	28	17.86	0.00	500.00
REPRC	Capital Repairs:Near-Coast	28	376.79	0.00	6000.00
OTHCFNC	Other Fishing:Away-Coast	28	0.00	0.00	0.00
OTHCFC	Other Fishing:Near-Coast	28	110.00	0.00	2500.00
BOOKNC	Books:Away-Coast	28	0.00	0.00	0.00
BOOKC	Books:Near-Coast	28	13.89	0.00	90.00
MEMBNC	Memberships:Away-Coast	28	0.00	0.00	0.00
MEMBC	Memberships:Near-Coast	28	27.50	0.00	200.00
CAMPNC	Camping:Away-Coast	28	0.00	0.00	0.00
CAMPC	Camping:Near-Coast	28	27.86	0.00	400.00
LICNC	Licenses:Away-Coast	28	0.00	0.00	0.00
LICC	Licenses:Near-Coast	28	22.50	0.00	100.00

Private Fishing Summary Statistics for trip and equipment expenditures by Mississippi
noncoastal residents who did visit an oil/gas structure on the interview date

Variable	Label	N	Mean	Minimum	Maximum
TRANST	Transportation:Total	3	0.00	0.00	0.00
TRANSC	Transportation:Near-Coast	3	0.00	0.00	0.00
RCART	Rental Car:Total	3	0.00	0.00	0.00
RCARC	Rental Car:Near-Coast	3	0.00	0.00	0.00
LODGT	Lodging:Total	3	19.33	0.00	58.00
LODGC	Lodging:Near-Coast	3	19.33	0.00	58.00
GAST	Gasoline:Total	3	34.70	19.95	46.50
GASC	Gasoline:Near-Coast	3	0.00	0.00	0.00
FOODT	Other Food:Total	3	34.00	0.00	90.00
FOODC	Other Food:Near-Coast	3	30.00	0.00	90.00
GROCT	Groceries:Total	3	17.67	0.00	40.00
GROCC	Groceries:Near-Coast	3	17.67	0.00	40.00
FUELT	Fuel:Total	3	43.33	0.00	120.00
FUELC	Fuel:Near-Coast	3	40.00	0.00	120.00
BRNTT	Boat Rentals:Total	3	1.33	0.00	4.00
BRNTC	Boat Rentals:Near-Coast	3	1.33	0.00	4.00
LNCHT	Launch Fees:Total	3	1.33	0.00	4.00
LNCHC	Launch Fees:Near-Coast	3	1.33	0.00	4.00
DOCKT	Dockage Fees:Total	3	0.00	0.00	0.00
DOCKC	Dockage Fees:Near-Coast	3	0.00	0.00	0.00
TREPRT	Trip Repairs:Total	3	0.00	0.00	0.00
TREPRC	Trip Repairs:Near-Coast	3	0.00	0.00	0.00
BAITT	Bait:Total	3	10.00	0.00	30.00
BAITC	Bait:Near-Coast	3	10.00	0.00	30.00
FLICT	Fishing Licenses:Total	3	0.00	0.00	0.00
FLICC	Fishing Licenses:Near-Coast	3	0.00	0.00	0.00
TCKLT	Tackle:Total	3	0.00	0.00	0.00
TCKLC	Tackle:Near-Coast	3	0.00	0.00	0.00
OTHRNTT	Other Rentals:Total	3	0.00	0.00	0.00
OTHRNTC	Other Rentals:Near-Coast	3	0.00	0.00	0.00
CLTHT	Clothing:Total	3	0.00	0.00	0.00
CLTHC	Clothing:Near-Coast	3	0.00	0.00	0.00
GUIDT	Guide Fees:Total	3	0.00	0.00	0.00
GUIDC	Guide Fees:Near-Coast	3	0.00	0.00	0.00
OTHRTT	Other Trip Expenses:Total	3	1.00	0.00	3.00
OTHRTC	Other Trip Expenses:Near-Coast	3	0.00	0.00	0.00
BOATNC	Boats:Away-Coast	3	5333.33	0.00	16000.00
BOATC	Boats:Near-Coast	3	0.00	0.00	0.00
MOTORNC	Motors:Away-Coast	3	0.00	0.00	0.00
MOTORC	Motors:Near-Coast	3	0.00	0.00	0.00
TRAILNC	Trailers:Away-Coast	3	0.00	0.00	0.00
TRAILC	Trailers:Near-Coast	3	0.00	0.00	0.00
AEQPNC	Electronics:Away-Coast	3	0.00	0.00	0.00
AEQPC	Electronics:Near-Coast	3	0.00	0.00	0.00
BFITNC	Fishing Outfit:Away-Coast	3	0.00	0.00	0.00
BFITC	Fishing Outfit:Near-Coast	3	0.00	0.00	0.00
RODC	Rods:Near-Coast	3	166.67	0.00	500.00
RODNC	Rods:Away-Coast	3	0.00	0.00	0.00
LINEC	Fishing Line:Near-Coast	3	0.00	0.00	0.00

LINENC	Fishing Line:Away-Coast	3	0.00	0.00	0.00
LUREC	Lures:Near-Coast	3	20.00	0.00	60.00
LURENC	Lures:Nonoastal	3	0.00	0.00	0.00
REPRNC	Capital Repairs:Away-Coast	3	0.00	0.00	0.00
REPRC	Capital Repairs:Near-Coast	3	0.00	0.00	0.00
OTHCFNC	Other Fishing:Away-Coast	3	0.00	0.00	0.00
OTHCFC	Other Fishing:Near-Coast	3	0.00	0.00	0.00
BOOKNC	Books:Away-Coast	3	13.33	0.00	40.00
BOOKC	Books:Near-Coast	3	0.00	0.00	0.00
MEMBNC	Memberships:Away-Coast	3	0.00	0.00	0.00
MEMBC	Memberships:Near-Coast	3	0.00	0.00	0.00
CAMPNC	Camping:Away-Coast	3	0.00	0.00	0.00
CAMPC	Camping:Near-Coast	3	0.00	0.00	0.00
LICNC	Licenses:Away-Coast	3	16.33	0.00	46.00
LICC	Licenses:Near-Coast	3	0.00	0.00	0.00

Private Fishing Summary Statistics for trip and equipment expenditures by Louisiana
coastal residents who did visit an oil/gas structure on the interview date

Variable	Label	N	Mean	Minimum	Maximum
TRANST	Transportation:Total	71	3.52	0.00	250.00
TRANSC	Transportation:Near-Coast	71	3.52	0.00	250.00
RCART	Rental Car:Total	71	0.00	0.00	0.00
RCARC	Rental Car:Near-Coast	71	0.00	0.00	0.00
LODGT	Lodging:Total	71	9.96	0.00	500.00
LODGC	Lodging:Near-Coast	71	9.96	0.00	500.00
GAST	Gasoline:Total	71	6.87	0.00	38.70
GASC	Gasoline:Near-Coast	71	6.87	0.00	38.70
FOODT	Other Food:Total	71	18.28	0.00	600.00
FOODC	Other Food:Near-Coast	71	18.28	0.00	600.00
GROCT	Groceries:Total	71	19.58	0.00	300.00
GROCC	Groceries:Near-Coast	71	19.58	0.00	300.00
FUELT	Fuel:Total	71	35.75	0.00	400.00
FUELC	Fuel:Near-Coast	71	35.75	0.00	400.00
BRNTT	Boat Rentals:Total	71	0.42	0.00	10.00
BRNTC	Boat Rentals:Near-Coast	71	0.42	0.00	10.00
LNCHT	Launch Fees:Total	71	2.92	0.00	30.00
LNCHC	Launch Fees:Near-Coast	71	2.92	0.00	30.00
DOCKT	Dockage Fees:Total	71	1.46	0.00	60.00
DOCKC	Dockage Fees:Near-Coast	71	1.46	0.00	60.00
TREPRT	Trip Repairs:Total	71	0.00	0.00	0.00
TREPRC	Trip Repairs:Near-Coast	71	0.00	0.00	0.00
BAITT	Bait:Total	71	13.56	0.00	90.00
BAITC	Bait:Near-Coast	71	13.56	0.00	90.00
FLICT	Fishing Licenses:Total	71	2.96	0.00	75.00
FLICC	Fishing Licenses:Near-Coast	71	2.96	0.00	75.00
TCKLT	Tackle:Total	71	2.80	0.00	25.00
TCKLC	Tackle:Near-Coast	71	2.80	0.00	25.00
OTHRNTT	Other Rentals:Total	71	0.00	0.00	0.00
OTHRNTC	Other Rentals:Near-Coast	71	0.00	0.00	0.00
CLTHT	Clothing:Total	71	0.00	0.00	0.00
CLTHC	Clothing:Near-Coast	71	0.00	0.00	0.00
GUIDT	Guide Fees:Total	71	0.00	0.00	0.00
GUIDC	Guide Fees:Near-Coast	71	0.00	0.00	0.00
OTHRTT	Other Trip Expenses:Total	71	1.72	0.00	18.00
OTHRTC	Other Trip Expenses:Near-Coast	71	1.72	0.00	18.00
BOATNC	Boats:Away-Coast	71	330.99	0.00	16000.00
BOATC	Boats:Near-Coast	71	1323.94	0.00	31000.00
MOTORNC	Motors:Away-Coast	71	523.94	0.00	10000.00
MOTORC	Motors:Near-Coast	71	126.76	0.00	9000.00
TRAILNC	Trailers:Away-Coast	71	112.68	0.00	4000.00
TRAILC	Trailers:Near-Coast	71	39.44	0.00	1500.00
AEQPNC	Electronics:Away-Coast	71	69.11	0.00	1500.00
AEQPC	Electronics:Near-Coast	71	0.00	0.00	0.00
BFITNC	Fishing Outfit:Away-Coast	71	2.82	0.00	200.00
BFITC	Fishing Outfit:Near-Coast	71	0.00	0.00	0.00
RODC	Rods:Near-Coast	71	185.28	0.00	5000.00
RODNC	Rods:Away-Coast	71	83.80	0.00	3000.00
LINEC	Fishing Line:Near-Coast	71	72.30	0.00	3000.00

LINENC	Fishing Line:Away-Coast	71	2.08	0.00	30.00
LUREC	Lures:Near-Coast	71	70.70	0.00	700.00
LURENC	Lures:Nonoastal	71	52.82	0.00	1500.00
REPRNC	Capital Repairs:Away-Coast	71	28.52	0.00	800.00
REPRC	Capital Repairs:Near-Coast	71	130.35	0.00	3000.00
OTHCFNC	Other Fishing:Away-Coast	71	2.54	0.00	120.00
OTHCFC	Other Fishing:Near-Coast	71	31.62	0.00	900.00
BOOKNC	Books:Away-Coast	71	0.00	0.00	0.00
BOOKC	Books:Near-Coast	71	6.06	0.00	100.00
MEMBNC	Memberships:Away-Coast	71	0.00	0.00	0.00
MEMBC	Memberships:Near-Coast	71	30.38	0.00	1500.00
CAMPNC	Camping:Away-Coast	71	0.00	0.00	0.00
CAMPC	Camping:Near-Coast	71	10.56	0.00	400.00
LICNC	Licenses:Away-Coast	71	0.00	0.00	0.00
LICC	Licenses:Near-Coast	71	21.45	0.00	550.00

Private Fishing Summary Statistics for trip and equipment expenditures by Louisiana
noncoastal residents who did visit an oil/gas structure on the interview date

Variable	Label	N	Mean	Minimum	Maximum
TRANST	Transportation:Total	13	0.00	0.00	0.00
TRANSC	Transportation:Near-Coast	13	0.00	0.00	0.00
RCART	Rental Car:Total	13	0.00	0.00	0.00
RCARC	Rental Car:Near-Coast	13	0.00	0.00	0.00
LODGT	Lodging:Total	13	44.23	0.00	325.00
LODGC	Lodging:Near-Coast	13	44.23	0.00	325.00
GAST	Gasoline:Total	13	35.99	3.00	75.60
GASC	Gasoline:Near-Coast	13	0.00	0.00	0.00
FOODT	Other Food:Total	13	41.54	0.00	200.00
FOODC	Other Food:Near-Coast	13	25.15	0.00	120.00
GROCT	Groceries:Total	13	61.92	0.00	500.00
GROCC	Groceries:Near-Coast	13	53.62	0.00	500.00
FUELT	Fuel:Total	13	87.38	0.00	650.00
FUELC	Fuel:Near-Coast	13	76.62	0.00	650.00
BRNTT	Boat Rentals:Total	13	0.00	0.00	0.00
BRNTC	Boat Rentals:Near-Coast	13	0.00	0.00	0.00
LNCHT	Launch Fees:Total	13	0.00	0.00	0.00
LNCHC	Launch Fees:Near-Coast	13	0.00	0.00	0.00
DOCKT	Dockage Fees:Total	13	0.00	0.00	0.00
DOCKC	Dockage Fees:Near-Coast	13	0.00	0.00	0.00
TREPRT	Trip Repairs:Total	13	0.00	0.00	0.00
TREPRC	Trip Repairs:Near-Coast	13	0.00	0.00	0.00
BAITT	Bait:Total	13	23.77	0.00	150.00
BAITC	Bait:Near-Coast	13	23.15	0.00	150.00
FLICT	Fishing Licenses:Total	13	0.00	0.00	0.00
FLICC	Fishing Licenses:Near-Coast	13	0.00	0.00	0.00
TCKLT	Tackle:Total	13	10.38	0.00	30.00
TCKLC	Tackle:Near-Coast	13	8.23	0.00	30.00
OTHRNTT	Other Rentals:Total	13	0.00	0.00	0.00
OTHRNTC	Other Rentals:Near-Coast	13	0.00	0.00	0.00
CLTHT	Clothing:Total	13	0.00	0.00	0.00
CLTHC	Clothing:Near-Coast	13	0.00	0.00	0.00
GUIDT	Guide Fees:Total	13	0.00	0.00	0.00
GUIDC	Guide Fees:Near-Coast	13	0.00	0.00	0.00
OTHRTT	Other Trip Expenses:Total	13	5.31	0.00	15.00
OTHRTC	Other Trip Expenses:Near-Coast	13	0.00	0.00	0.00
BOATNC	Boats:Away-Coast	13	92.31	0.00	1200.00
BOATC	Boats:Near-Coast	13	0.00	0.00	0.00
MOTORNC	Motors:Away-Coast	13	0.00	0.00	0.00
MOTORC	Motors:Near-Coast	13	0.00	0.00	0.00
TRAILNC	Trailers:Away-Coast	13	153.85	0.00	2000.00
TRAILC	Trailers:Near-Coast	13	0.00	0.00	0.00
AEQPNC	Electronics:Away-Coast	13	76.92	0.00	400.00
AEQPC	Electronics:Near-Coast	13	0.00	0.00	0.00
BFITNC	Fishing Outfit:Away-Coast	13	0.00	0.00	0.00
BFITC	Fishing Outfit:Near-Coast	13	0.00	0.00	0.00
RODC	Rods:Near-Coast	13	0.00	0.00	0.00
RODNC	Rods:Away-Coast	13	53.85	0.00	300.00
LINEC	Fishing Line:Near-Coast	13	3.08	0.00	30.00

LINENC	Fishing Line:Away-Coast	13	12.31	0.00	50.00
LUREC	Lures:Near-Coast	13	3.85	0.00	30.00
LURENC	Lures:Nonoastal	13	29.23	0.00	100.00
REPRNC	Capital Repairs:Away-Coast	13	150.00	0.00	1000.00
REPRC	Capital Repairs:Near-Coast	13	0.00	0.00	0.00
OTHCFNC	Other Fishing:Away-Coast	13	30.77	0.00	400.00
OTHCFC	Other Fishing:Near-Coast	13	0.00	0.00	0.00
BOOKNC	Books:Away-Coast	13	22.69	0.00	100.00
BOOKC	Books:Near-Coast	13	0.00	0.00	0.00
MEMBNC	Memberships:Away-Coast	13	2.62	0.00	20.00
MEMBC	Memberships:Near-Coast	13	0.00	0.00	0.00
CAMPNC	Camping:Away-Coast	13	99.23	0.00	500.00
CAMPC	Camping:Near-Coast	13	0.00	0.00	0.00
LICNC	Licenses:Away-Coast	13	13.38	0.00	60.00
LICC	Licenses:Near-Coast	13	0.00	0.00	0.00

Private Fishing Summary Statistics for trip and equipment expenditures by Texas
coastal residents who did visit an oil/gas structure on the interview date

Variable	Label	N	Mean	Minimum	Maximum
TRANST	Transportation:Total	48	0.00	0.00	0.00
TRANSC	Transportation:Near-Coast	48	0.00	0.00	0.00
RCART	Rental Car:Total	48	0.00	0.00	0.00
RCARC	Rental Car:Near-Coast	48	0.00	0.00	0.00
LODGT	Lodging:Total	48	13.85	0.00	300.00
LODGC	Lodging:Near-Coast	48	13.85	0.00	300.00
GAST	Gasoline:Total	48	9.78	0.00	37.95
GASC	Gasoline:Near-Coast	48	9.78	0.00	37.95
FOODT	Other Food:Total	48	14.15	0.00	225.00
FOODC	Other Food:Near-Coast	48	14.15	0.00	225.00
GROCT	Groceries:Total	48	23.46	0.00	200.00
GROCC	Groceries:Near-Coast	48	23.46	0.00	200.00
FUELT	Fuel:Total	48	56.50	0.00	400.00
FUELC	Fuel:Near-Coast	48	56.50	0.00	400.00
BRNTT	Boat Rentals:Total	48	0.94	0.00	30.00
BRNTC	Boat Rentals:Near-Coast	48	0.94	0.00	30.00
LNCHT	Launch Fees:Total	48	1.81	0.00	20.00
LNCHC	Launch Fees:Near-Coast	48	1.81	0.00	20.00
DOCKT	Dockage Fees:Total	48	0.00	0.00	0.00
DOCKC	Dockage Fees:Near-Coast	48	0.00	0.00	0.00
TREPRT	Trip Repairs:Total	48	0.21	0.00	10.00
TREPRC	Trip Repairs:Near-Coast	48	0.21	0.00	10.00
BAITT	Bait:Total	48	23.71	0.00	300.00
BAITC	Bait:Near-Coast	48	23.71	0.00	300.00
FLICT	Fishing Licenses:Total	48	0.52	0.00	25.00
FLICC	Fishing Licenses:Near-Coast	48	0.52	0.00	25.00
TCKLT	Tackle:Total	48	8.54	0.00	100.00
TCKLC	Tackle:Near-Coast	48	8.54	0.00	100.00
OTHRNTT	Other Rentals:Total	48	0.00	0.00	0.00
OTHRNTC	Other Rentals:Near-Coast	48	0.00	0.00	0.00
CLTHT	Clothing:Total	48	1.46	0.00	60.00
CLTHC	Clothing:Near-Coast	48	1.46	0.00	60.00
GUIDT	Guide Fees:Total	48	0.00	0.00	0.00
GUIDC	Guide Fees:Near-Coast	48	0.00	0.00	0.00
OTHRTT	Other Trip Expenses:Total	48	4.69	0.00	75.00
OTHRTC	Other Trip Expenses:Near-Coast	48	4.69	0.00	75.00
BOATNC	Boats:Away-Coast	48	0.00	0.00	0.00
BOATC	Boats:Near-Coast	48	458.33	0.00	22000.00
MOTORNC	Motors:Away-Coast	48	0.00	0.00	0.00
MOTORC	Motors:Near-Coast	48	0.00	0.00	0.00
TRAILNC	Trailers:Away-Coast	48	0.00	0.00	0.00
TRAILC	Trailers:Near-Coast	48	0.00	0.00	0.00
AEQPNC	Electronics:Away-Coast	48	160.63	0.00	3000.00
AEQPC	Electronics:Near-Coast	48	0.00	0.00	0.00
BFITNC	Fishing Outfit:Away-Coast	48	24.17	0.00	600.00
BFITC	Fishing Outfit:Near-Coast	48	0.00	0.00	0.00
RODC	Rods:Near-Coast	48	268.02	0.00	4000.00
RODNC	Rods:Away-Coast	48	30.21	0.00	600.00
LINEC	Fishing Line:Near-Coast	48	33.79	0.00	300.00

LINENC	Fishing Line:Away-Coast	48	9.90	0.00	150.00
LUREC	Lures:Near-Coast	48	97.29	0.00	600.00
LURENC	Lures:Nonoastal	48	19.06	0.00	300.00
REPRNC	Capital Repairs:Away-Coast	48	114.58	0.00	1500.00
REPRC	Capital Repairs:Near-Coast	48	204.90	0.00	2000.00
OTHCFNC	Other Fishing:Away-Coast	48	63.54	0.00	2000.00
OTHCFC	Other Fishing:Near-Coast	48	284.58	0.00	10000.00
BOOKNC	Books:Away-Coast	48	0.00	0.00	0.00
BOOKC	Books:Near-Coast	48	18.23	0.00	100.00
MEMBNC	Memberships:Away-Coast	48	0.00	0.00	0.00
MEMBC	Memberships:Near-Coast	48	10.50	0.00	100.00
CAMPNC	Camping:Away-Coast	48	0.00	0.00	0.00
CAMPC	Camping:Near-Coast	48	26.56	0.00	325.00
LICNC	Licenses:Away-Coast	48	0.00	0.00	0.00
LICC	Licenses:Near-Coast	48	24.58	0.00	65.00

Private Fishing Summary Statistics for trip and equipment expenditures by Texas
noncoastal residents who did visit an oil/gas structure on the interview date

Variable	Label	N	Mean	Minimum	Maximum
TRANST	Transportation:Total	7	0.00	0.00	0.00
TRANSC	Transportation:Near-Coast	7	0.00	0.00	0.00
RCART	Rental Car:Total	7	0.00	0.00	0.00
RCARC	Rental Car:Near-Coast	7	0.00	0.00	0.00
LODGT	Lodging:Total	7	196.43	0.00	500.00
LODGC	Lodging:Near-Coast	7	196.43	0.00	500.00
GAST	Gasoline:Total	7	37.16	17.25	69.75
GASC	Gasoline:Near-Coast	7	0.00	0.00	0.00
FOODT	Other Food:Total	7	181.71	0.00	900.00
FOODC	Other Food:Near-Coast	7	181.71	0.00	900.00
GROCT	Groceries:Total	7	92.86	0.00	400.00
GROCC	Groceries:Near-Coast	7	35.71	0.00	100.00
FUELT	Fuel:Total	7	102.86	0.00	600.00
FUELC	Fuel:Near-Coast	7	102.86	0.00	600.00
BRNTT	Boat Rentals:Total	7	0.00	0.00	0.00
BRNTC	Boat Rentals:Near-Coast	7	0.00	0.00	0.00
LNCHT	Launch Fees:Total	7	0.00	0.00	0.00
LNCHC	Launch Fees:Near-Coast	7	0.00	0.00	0.00
DOCKT	Dockage Fees:Total	7	0.00	0.00	0.00
DOCKC	Dockage Fees:Near-Coast	7	0.00	0.00	0.00
TREPRT	Trip Repairs:Total	7	0.00	0.00	0.00
TREPRC	Trip Repairs:Near-Coast	7	0.00	0.00	0.00
BAITT	Bait:Total	7	47.86	0.00	140.00
BAITC	Bait:Near-Coast	7	47.86	0.00	140.00
FLICT	Fishing Licenses:Total	7	2.86	0.00	20.00
FLICC	Fishing Licenses:Near-Coast	7	0.00	0.00	0.00
TCKLT	Tackle:Total	7	14.29	0.00	60.00
TCKLC	Tackle:Near-Coast	7	14.29	0.00	60.00
OTHRNTT	Other Rentals:Total	7	0.00	0.00	0.00
OTHRNTC	Other Rentals:Near-Coast	7	0.00	0.00	0.00
CLTHT	Clothing:Total	7	50.71	0.00	280.00
CLTHC	Clothing:Near-Coast	7	20.00	0.00	140.00
GUIDT	Guide Fees:Total	7	0.00	0.00	0.00
GUIDC	Guide Fees:Near-Coast	7	0.00	0.00	0.00
OTHRTT	Other Trip Expenses:Total	7	5.00	0.00	20.00
OTHRTC	Other Trip Expenses:Near-Coast	7	0.00	0.00	0.00
BOATNC	Boats:Away-Coast	7	2000.00	0.00	14000.00
BOATC	Boats:Near-Coast	7	0.00	0.00	0.00
MOTORNC	Motors:Away-Coast	7	3285.71	0.00	19000.00
MOTORC	Motors:Near-Coast	7	0.00	0.00	0.00
TRAILNC	Trailers:Away-Coast	7	571.43	0.00	4000.00
TRAILC	Trailers:Near-Coast	7	0.00	0.00	0.00
AEQPNC	Electronics:Away-Coast	7	1000.00	0.00	6000.00
AEQPC	Electronics:Near-Coast	7	0.00	0.00	0.00
BFITNC	Fishing Outfit:Away-Coast	7	1714.29	0.00	12000.00
BFITC	Fishing Outfit:Near-Coast	7	0.00	0.00	0.00
RODC	Rods:Near-Coast	7	285.71	0.00	2000.00
RODNC	Rods:Away-Coast	7	285.71	0.00	1000.00
LINEC	Fishing Line:Near-Coast	7	14.29	0.00	100.00

LINENC	Fishing Line:Away-Coast	7	50.29	0.00	300.00
LUREC	Lures:Near-Coast	7	5.71	0.00	40.00
LURENC	Lures:Nonoastal	7	64.29	0.00	200.00
REPRNC	Capital Repairs:Away-Coast	7	0.00	0.00	0.00
REPRC	Capital Repairs:Near-Coast	7	71.43	0.00	500.00
OTHCFNC	Other Fishing:Away-Coast	7	0.00	0.00	0.00
OTHCFC	Other Fishing:Near-Coast	7	0.00	0.00	0.00
BOOKNC	Books:Away-Coast	7	8.14	0.00	25.00
BOOKC	Books:Near-Coast	7	0.00	0.00	0.00
MEMBNC	Memberships:Away-Coast	7	19.29	0.00	70.00
MEMBC	Memberships:Near-Coast	7	0.00	0.00	0.00
CAMPNC	Camping:Away-Coast	7	71.43	0.00	400.00
CAMPC	Camping:Near-Coast	7	0.00	0.00	0.00
LICNC	Licenses:Away-Coast	7	26.57	0.00	50.00
LICC	Licenses:Near-Coast	7	0.00	0.00	0.00

- -

Private Fishing Summary Statistics for trip and equipment expenditures by Alabama
coastal residents who did't visit an oil/gas structure on the interview date

Variable	Label	N	Mean	Minimum	Maximum
TRANST	Transportation:Total	61	0.00	0.00	0.00
TRANSC	Transportation:Near-Coast	61	0.00	0.00	0.00
RCART	Rental Car:Total	61	0.00	0.00	0.00
RCARC	Rental Car:Near-Coast	61	0.00	0.00	0.00
LODGT	Lodging:Total	61	0.00	0.00	0.00
LODGC	Lodging:Near-Coast	61	0.00	0.00	0.00
GAST	Gasoline:Total	61	3.42	0.00	15.30
GASC	Gasoline:Near-Coast	61	3.42	0.00	15.30
FOODT	Other Food:Total	61	46.64	0.00	2500.00
FOODC	Other Food:Near-Coast	61	46.64	0.00	2500.00
GROCT	Groceries:Total	61	16.61	0.00	500.00
GROCC	Groceries:Near-Coast	61	16.61	0.00	500.00
FUELT	Fuel:Total	61	16.62	0.00	100.00
FUELC	Fuel:Near-Coast	61	16.62	0.00	100.00
BRNTT	Boat Rentals:Total	61	0.00	0.00	0.00
BRNTC	Boat Rentals:Near-Coast	61	0.00	0.00	0.00
LNCHT	Launch Fees:Total	61	0.75	0.00	17.00
LNCHC	Launch Fees:Near-Coast	61	0.75	0.00	17.00
DOCKT	Dockage Fees:Total	61	0.00	0.00	0.00
DOCKC	Dockage Fees:Near-Coast	61	0.00	0.00	0.00
TREPRT	Trip Repairs:Total	61	0.00	0.00	0.00
TREPRC	Trip Repairs:Near-Coast	61	0.00	0.00	0.00
BAITT	Bait:Total	61	9.87	0.00	100.00
BAITC	Bait:Near-Coast	61	9.87	0.00	100.00
FLICT	Fishing Licenses:Total	61	0.80	0.00	26.00
FLICC	Fishing Licenses:Near-Coast	61	0.80	0.00	26.00
TCKLT	Tackle:Total	61	2.70	0.00	30.00
TCKLC	Tackle:Near-Coast	61	2.70	0.00	30.00
OTHRNTT	Other Rentals:Total	61	0.00	0.00	0.00
OTHRNTC	Other Rentals:Near-Coast	61	0.00	0.00	0.00
CLTHT	Clothing:Total	61	0.00	0.00	0.00
CLTHC	Clothing:Near-Coast	61	0.00	0.00	0.00
GUIDT	Guide Fees:Total	61	0.00	0.00	0.00
GUIDC	Guide Fees:Near-Coast	61	0.00	0.00	0.00
OTHRTT	Other Trip Expenses:Total	61	2.54	0.00	100.00
OTHRTC	Other Trip Expenses:Near-Coast	61	2.54	0.00	100.00
BOATNC	Boats:Away-Coast	61	0.00	0.00	0.00
BOATC	Boats:Near-Coast	61	114.75	0.00	7000.00
MOTORNC	Motors:Away-Coast	61	0.00	0.00	0.00
MOTORC	Motors:Near-Coast	61	98.36	0.00	6000.00
TRAILNC	Trailers:Away-Coast	61	0.00	0.00	0.00
TRAILC	Trailers:Near-Coast	61	68.85	0.00	3000.00
AEQPNC	Electronics:Away-Coast	61	159.02	0.00	8000.00
AEQPC	Electronics:Near-Coast	61	0.00	0.00	0.00
BFITNC	Fishing Outfit:Away-Coast	61	78.69	0.00	3000.00
BFITC	Fishing Outfit:Near-Coast	61	0.00	0.00	0.00
RODC	Rods:Near-Coast	61	205.49	0.00	3000.00
RODNC	Rods:Away-Coast	61	10.57	0.00	300.00
LINEC	Fishing Line:Near-Coast	61	18.54	0.00	500.00

LINENC	Fishing Line:Away-Coast	61	9.34	0.00	300.00
LUREC	Lures:Near-Coast	61	44.39	0.00	1000.00
LURENC	Lures:Nonoastal	61	27.13	0.00	1000.00
REPRNC	Capital Repairs:Away-Coast	61	11.97	0.00	300.00
REPRC	Capital Repairs:Near-Coast	61	142.95	0.00	5000.00
OTHCFNC	Other Fishing:Away-Coast	61	37.30	0.00	1500.00
OTHCFC	Other Fishing:Near-Coast	61	29.38	0.00	500.00
BOOKNC	Books:Away-Coast	61	0.00	0.00	0.00
BOOKC	Books:Near-Coast	61	8.72	0.00	100.00
MEMBNC	Memberships:Away-Coast	61	0.00	0.00	0.00
MEMBC	Memberships:Near-Coast	61	4.59	0.00	95.00
CAMPNC	Camping:Away-Coast	61	0.00	0.00	0.00
CAMPC	Camping:Near-Coast	61	16.39	0.00	300.00
LICNC	Licenses:Away-Coast	61	0.00	0.00	0.00
LICC	Licenses:Near-Coast	61	14.11	0.00	32.00

Private Fishing Summary Statistics for trip and equipment expenditures by Alabama
noncoastal residents who did't visit an oil/gas structure on the interview date

Variable	Label	N	Mean	Minimum	Maximum
TRANST	Transportation:Total	12	0.00	0.00	0.00
TRANSC	Transportation:Near-Coast	12	0.00	0.00	0.00
RCART	Rental Car:Total	12	0.00	0.00	0.00
RCARC	Rental Car:Near-Coast	12	0.00	0.00	0.00
LODGT	Lodging:Total	12	115.00	0.00	750.00
LODGC	Lodging:Near-Coast	12	115.00	0.00	750.00
GAST	Gasoline:Total	12	45.65	0.00	183.00
GASC	Gasoline:Near-Coast	12	0.00	0.00	0.00
FOODT	Other Food:Total	12	15.83	0.00	75.00
FOODC	Other Food:Near-Coast	12	15.83	0.00	75.00
GROCT	Groceries:Total	12	5.83	0.00	40.00
GROCC	Groceries:Near-Coast	12	5.83	0.00	40.00
FUELT	Fuel:Total	12	22.08	0.00	100.00
FUELC	Fuel:Near-Coast	12	20.42	0.00	100.00
BRNTT	Boat Rentals:Total	12	15.83	0.00	100.00
BRNTC	Boat Rentals:Near-Coast	12	15.83	0.00	100.00
LNCHT	Launch Fees:Total	12	0.00	0.00	0.00
LNCHC	Launch Fees:Near-Coast	12	0.00	0.00	0.00
DOCKT	Dockage Fees:Total	12	0.00	0.00	0.00
DOCKC	Dockage Fees:Near-Coast	12	0.00	0.00	0.00
TREPRT	Trip Repairs:Total	12	0.00	0.00	0.00
TREPRC	Trip Repairs:Near-Coast	12	0.00	0.00	0.00
BAITT	Bait:Total	12	19.83	0.00	60.00
BAITC	Bait:Near-Coast	12	19.83	0.00	60.00
FLICT	Fishing Licenses:Total	12	11.83	0.00	50.00
FLICC	Fishing Licenses:Near-Coast	12	9.50	0.00	50.00
TCKLT	Tackle:Total	12	16.67	0.00	180.00
TCKLC	Tackle:Near-Coast	12	16.67	0.00	180.00
OTHRNTT	Other Rentals:Total	12	0.00	0.00	0.00
OTHRNTC	Other Rentals:Near-Coast	12	0.00	0.00	0.00
CLTHT	Clothing:Total	12	10.00	0.00	120.00
CLTHC	Clothing:Near-Coast	12	10.00	0.00	120.00
GUIDT	Guide Fees:Total	12	0.00	0.00	0.00
GUIDC	Guide Fees:Near-Coast	12	0.00	0.00	0.00
OTHRTT	Other Trip Expenses:Total	12	1.67	0.00	12.00
OTHRTC	Other Trip Expenses:Near-Coast	12	0.00	0.00	0.00
BOATNC	Boats:Away-Coast	12	0.00	0.00	0.00
BOATC	Boats:Near-Coast	12	0.00	0.00	0.00
MOTORNC	Motors:Away-Coast	12	0.00	0.00	0.00
MOTORC	Motors:Near-Coast	12	0.00	0.00	0.00
TRAILNC	Trailers:Away-Coast	12	0.00	0.00	0.00
TRAILC	Trailers:Near-Coast	12	0.00	0.00	0.00
AEQPNC	Electronics:Away-Coast	12	14.58	0.00	175.00
AEQPC	Electronics:Near-Coast	12	0.00	0.00	0.00
BFITNC	Fishing Outfit:Away-Coast	12	0.00	0.00	0.00
BFITC	Fishing Outfit:Near-Coast	12	0.00	0.00	0.00
RODC	Rods:Near-Coast	12	83.33	0.00	1000.00
RODNC	Rods:Away-Coast	12	50.00	0.00	400.00
LINEC	Fishing Line:Near-Coast	12	1.83	0.00	12.00

LINENC	Fishing Line:Away-Coast	12	10.25	0.00	100.00
LUREC	Lures:Near-Coast	12	0.00	0.00	0.00
LURENC	Lures:Nonoastal	12	10.83	0.00	100.00
REPRNC	Capital Repairs:Away-Coast	12	208.33	0.00	1500.00
REPRC	Capital Repairs:Near-Coast	12	0.00	0.00	0.00
OTHCFNC	Other Fishing:Away-Coast	12	24.08	0.00	150.00
OTHCFC	Other Fishing:Near-Coast	12	3.33	0.00	20.00
BOOKNC	Books:Away-Coast	12	6.17	0.00	30.00
BOOKC	Books:Near-Coast	12	0.00	0.00	0.00
MEMBNC	Memberships:Away-Coast	12	0.00	0.00	0.00
MEMBC	Memberships:Near-Coast	12	0.00	0.00	0.00
CAMPNC	Camping:Away-Coast	12	0.00	0.00	0.00
CAMPC	Camping:Near-Coast	12	0.00	0.00	0.00
LICNC	Licenses:Away-Coast	12	18.42	0.00	70.00
LICC	Licenses:Near-Coast	12	0.00	0.00	0.00

- -

Private Fishing Summary Statistics for trip and equipment expenditures by Mississippi
coastal residents who did't visit an oil/gas structure on the interview date

Variable	Label	N	Mean	Minimum	Maximum
TRANST	Transportation:Total	30	7.83	0.00	80.00
TRANSC	Transportation:Near-Coast	30	7.83	0.00	80.00
RCART	Rental Car:Total	30	0.00	0.00	0.00
RCARC	Rental Car:Near-Coast	30	0.00	0.00	0.00
LODGT	Lodging:Total	30	0.00	0.00	0.00
LODGC	Lodging:Near-Coast	30	0.00	0.00	0.00
GAST	Gasoline:Total	30	2.24	0.00	17.25
GASC	Gasoline:Near-Coast	30	2.24	0.00	17.25
FOODT	Other Food:Total	30	1.20	0.00	20.00
FOODC	Other Food:Near-Coast	30	1.20	0.00	20.00
GROCT	Groceries:Total	30	13.07	0.00	75.00
GROCC	Groceries:Near-Coast	30	13.07	0.00	75.00
FUELT	Fuel:Total	30	22.33	0.00	170.00
FUELC	Fuel:Near-Coast	30	22.33	0.00	170.00
BRNTT	Boat Rentals:Total	30	0.00	0.00	0.00
BRNTC	Boat Rentals:Near-Coast	30	0.00	0.00	0.00
LNCHT	Launch Fees:Total	30	0.00	0.00	0.00
LNCHC	Launch Fees:Near-Coast	30	0.00	0.00	0.00
DOCKT	Dockage Fees:Total	30	1.67	0.00	50.00
DOCKC	Dockage Fees:Near-Coast	30	1.67	0.00	50.00
TREPRT	Trip Repairs:Total	30	193.33	0.00	5800.00
TREPRC	Trip Repairs:Near-Coast	30	193.33	0.00	5800.00
BAITT	Bait:Total	30	9.23	0.00	50.00
BAITC	Bait:Near-Coast	30	9.23	0.00	50.00
FLICT	Fishing Licenses:Total	30	2.37	0.00	48.00
FLICC	Fishing Licenses:Near-Coast	30	2.37	0.00	48.00
TCKLT	Tackle:Total	30	1.77	0.00	28.00
TCKLC	Tackle:Near-Coast	30	1.77	0.00	28.00
OTHRNTT	Other Rentals:Total	30	0.00	0.00	0.00
OTHRNTC	Other Rentals:Near-Coast	30	0.00	0.00	0.00
CLTHT	Clothing:Total	30	3.90	0.00	110.00
CLTHC	Clothing:Near-Coast	30	3.90	0.00	110.00
GUIDT	Guide Fees:Total	30	0.00	0.00	0.00
GUIDC	Guide Fees:Near-Coast	30	0.00	0.00	0.00
OTHRTT	Other Trip Expenses:Total	30	1.77	0.00	18.00
OTHRTC	Other Trip Expenses:Near-Coast	30	1.77	0.00	18.00
BOATNC	Boats:Away-Coast	30	1600.00	0.00	37000.00
BOATC	Boats:Near-Coast	30	1966.67	0.00	38000.00
MOTORNC	Motors:Away-Coast	30	166.67	0.00	5000.00
MOTORC	Motors:Near-Coast	30	466.67	0.00	14000.00
TRAILNC	Trailers:Away-Coast	30	166.67	0.00	5000.00
TRAILC	Trailers:Near-Coast	30	93.33	0.00	2800.00
AEQPNC	Electronics:Away-Coast	30	796.07	0.00	21000.00
AEQPC	Electronics:Near-Coast	30	0.00	0.00	0.00
BFITNC	Fishing Outfit:Away-Coast	30	378.67	0.00	10000.00
BFITC	Fishing Outfit:Near-Coast	30	0.00	0.00	0.00
RODC	Rods:Near-Coast	30	91.67	0.00	1000.00
RODNC	Rods:Away-Coast	30	295.07	0.00	6000.00
LINEC	Fishing Line:Near-Coast	30	60.93	0.00	1000.00

LINENC	Fishing Line:Away-Coast	30	6.10	0.00	100.00
LUREC	Lures:Near-Coast	30	205.33	0.00	5000.00
LURENC	Lures:Nonoastal	30	14.67	0.00	200.00
REPRNC	Capital Repairs:Away-Coast	30	26.67	0.00	800.00
REPRC	Capital Repairs:Near-Coast	30	211.10	0.00	2950.00
OTHCFNC	Other Fishing:Away-Coast	30	0.00	0.00	0.00
OTHCFC	Other Fishing:Near-Coast	30	102.50	0.00	2000.00
BOOKNC	Books:Away-Coast	30	0.00	0.00	0.00
BOOKC	Books:Near-Coast	30	38.90	0.00	1000.00
MEMBNC	Memberships:Away-Coast	30	0.00	0.00	0.00
MEMBC	Memberships:Near-Coast	30	22.17	0.00	600.00
CAMPNC	Camping:Away-Coast	30	0.00	0.00	0.00
CAMPC	Camping:Near-Coast	30	26.67	0.00	200.00
LICNC	Licenses:Away-Coast	30	0.00	0.00	0.00
LICC	Licenses:Near-Coast	30	23.90	0.00	175.00

Private Fishing Summary Statistics for trip and equipment expenditures by Mississippi
noncoastal residents who did't visit an oil/gas structure on the interview date

Variable	Label	N	Mean	Minimum	Maximum
TRANST	Transportation:Total	3	0.00	0.00	0.00
TRANSC	Transportation:Near-Coast	3	0.00	0.00	0.00
RCART	Rental Car:Total	3	0.00	0.00	0.00
RCARC	Rental Car:Near-Coast	3	0.00	0.00	0.00
LODGT	Lodging:Total	3	0.00	0.00	0.00
LODGC	Lodging:Near-Coast	3	0.00	0.00	0.00
GAST	Gasoline:Total	3	20.25	12.00	30.00
GASC	Gasoline:Near-Coast	3	0.00	0.00	0.00
FOODT	Other Food:Total	3	0.00	0.00	0.00
FOODC	Other Food:Near-Coast	3	0.00	0.00	0.00
GROCT	Groceries:Total	3	9.33	3.00	20.00
GROCC	Groceries:Near-Coast	3	9.33	3.00	20.00
FUELT	Fuel:Total	3	13.33	0.00	40.00
FUELC	Fuel:Near-Coast	3	13.33	0.00	40.00
BRNTT	Boat Rentals:Total	3	0.00	0.00	0.00
BRNTC	Boat Rentals:Near-Coast	3	0.00	0.00	0.00
LNCHT	Launch Fees:Total	3	0.00	0.00	0.00
LNCHC	Launch Fees:Near-Coast	3	0.00	0.00	0.00
DOCKT	Dockage Fees:Total	3	0.00	0.00	0.00
DOCKC	Dockage Fees:Near-Coast	3	0.00	0.00	0.00
TREPRT	Trip Repairs:Total	3	0.00	0.00	0.00
TREPRC	Trip Repairs:Near-Coast	3	0.00	0.00	0.00
BAITT	Bait:Total	3	12.00	0.00	28.00
BAITC	Bait:Near-Coast	3	12.00	0.00	28.00
FLICT	Fishing Licenses:Total	3	7.00	0.00	21.00
FLICC	Fishing Licenses:Near-Coast	3	7.00	0.00	21.00
TCKLT	Tackle:Total	3	0.00	0.00	0.00
TCKLC	Tackle:Near-Coast	3	0.00	0.00	0.00
OTHRNTT	Other Rentals:Total	3	0.00	0.00	0.00
OTHRNTC	Other Rentals:Near-Coast	3	0.00	0.00	0.00
CLTHT	Clothing:Total	3	0.00	0.00	0.00
CLTHC	Clothing:Near-Coast	3	0.00	0.00	0.00
GUIDT	Guide Fees:Total	3	0.00	0.00	0.00
GUIDC	Guide Fees:Near-Coast	3	0.00	0.00	0.00
OTHRTT	Other Trip Expenses:Total	3	2.67	0.00	8.00
OTHRTC	Other Trip Expenses:Near-Coast	3	0.00	0.00	0.00
BOATNC	Boats:Away-Coast	3	0.00	0.00	0.00
BOATC	Boats:Near-Coast	3	0.00	0.00	0.00
MOTORNC	Motors:Away-Coast	3	0.00	0.00	0.00
MOTORC	Motors:Near-Coast	3	0.00	0.00	0.00
TRAILNC	Trailers:Away-Coast	3	0.00	0.00	0.00
TRAILC	Trailers:Near-Coast	3	0.00	0.00	0.00
AEQPNC	Electronics:Away-Coast	3	0.00	0.00	0.00
AEQPC	Electronics:Near-Coast	3	0.00	0.00	0.00
BFITNC	Fishing Outfit:Away-Coast	3	0.00	0.00	0.00
BFITC	Fishing Outfit:Near-Coast	3	0.00	0.00	0.00
RODC	Rods:Near-Coast	3	0.00	0.00	0.00
RODNC	Rods:Away-Coast	3	100.00	0.00	300.00
LINEC	Fishing Line:Near-Coast	3	5.67	0.00	17.00

LINENC	Fishing Line:Away-Coast	3	3.33	0.00	10.00
LUREC	Lures:Near-Coast	3	33.33	0.00	100.00
LURENC	Lures:Nonoastal	3	10.00	0.00	30.00
REPRNC	Capital Repairs:Away-Coast	3	0.00	0.00	0.00
REPRC	Capital Repairs:Near-Coast	3	0.00	0.00	0.00
OTHCFNC	Other Fishing:Away-Coast	3	0.00	0.00	0.00
OTHCFC	Other Fishing:Near-Coast	3	0.00	0.00	0.00
BOOKNC	Books:Away-Coast	3	12.67	0.00	20.00
BOOKC	Books:Near-Coast	3	0.00	0.00	0.00
MEMBNC	Memberships:Away-Coast	3	0.00	0.00	0.00
MEMBC	Memberships:Near-Coast	3	0.00	0.00	0.00
CAMPNC	Camping:Away-Coast	3	16.67	0.00	50.00
CAMPC	Camping:Near-Coast	3	0.00	0.00	0.00
LICNC	Licenses:Away-Coast	3	21.33	14.00	25.00
LICC	Licenses:Near-Coast	3	0.00	0.00	0.00

Private Fishing Summary Statistics for trip and equipment expenditures by Louisiana
coastal residents who did't visit an oil/gas structure on the interview date

Variable	Label	N	Mean	Minimum	Maximum
TRANST	Transportation:Total	121	0.08	0.00	10.00
TRANSC	Transportation:Near-Coast	121	0.08	0.00	10.00
RCART	Rental Car:Total	121	0.00	0.00	0.00
RCARC	Rental Car:Near-Coast	121	0.00	0.00	0.00
LODGT	Lodging:Total	121	8.88	0.00	390.00
LODGC	Lodging:Near-Coast	121	8.88	0.00	390.00
GAST	Gasoline:Total	121	5.55	0.00	22.95
GASC	Gasoline:Near-Coast	121	5.55	0.00	22.95
FOODT	Other Food:Total	121	7.86	0.00	350.00
FOODC	Other Food:Near-Coast	121	7.86	0.00	350.00
GROCT	Groceries:Total	121	30.51	0.00	2100.00
GROCC	Groceries:Near-Coast	121	30.51	0.00	2100.00
FUELT	Fuel:Total	121	35.11	0.00	1400.00
FUELC	Fuel:Near-Coast	121	35.11	0.00	1400.00
BRNTT	Boat Rentals:Total	121	0.68	0.00	20.00
BRNTC	Boat Rentals:Near-Coast	121	0.68	0.00	20.00
LNCHT	Launch Fees:Total	121	3.46	0.00	35.00
LNCHC	Launch Fees:Near-Coast	121	3.46	0.00	35.00
DOCKT	Dockage Fees:Total	121	0.12	0.00	4.00
DOCKC	Dockage Fees:Near-Coast	121	0.12	0.00	4.00
TREPRT	Trip Repairs:Total	121	7.15	0.00	560.00
TREPRC	Trip Repairs:Near-Coast	121	7.15	0.00	560.00
BAITT	Bait:Total	121	13.92	0.00	400.00
BAITC	Bait:Near-Coast	121	13.92	0.00	400.00
FLICT	Fishing Licenses:Total	121	1.73	0.00	44.00
FLICC	Fishing Licenses:Near-Coast	121	1.73	0.00	44.00
TCKLT	Tackle:Total	121	4.14	0.00	105.00
TCKLC	Tackle:Near-Coast	121	4.14	0.00	105.00
OTHRNTT	Other Rentals:Total	121	0.00	0.00	0.00
OTHRNTC	Other Rentals:Near-Coast	121	0.00	0.00	0.00
CLTHT	Clothing:Total	121	0.41	0.00	50.00
CLTHC	Clothing:Near-Coast	121	0.41	0.00	50.00
GUIDT	Guide Fees:Total	121	0.00	0.00	0.00
GUIDC	Guide Fees:Near-Coast	121	0.00	0.00	0.00
OTHRTT	Other Trip Expenses:Total	121	0.56	0.00	16.00
OTHRTC	Other Trip Expenses:Near-Coast	121	0.56	0.00	16.00
BOATNC	Boats:Away-Coast	121	380.17	0.00	28000.00
BOATC	Boats:Near-Coast	121	70.25	0.00	6000.00
MOTORNC	Motors:Away-Coast	121	66.12	0.00	8000.00
MOTORC	Motors:Near-Coast	121	82.64	0.00	6000.00
TRAILNC	Trailers:Away-Coast	121	16.53	0.00	2000.00
TRAILC	Trailers:Near-Coast	121	25.62	0.00	1500.00
AEQPNC	Electronics:Away-Coast	121	17.58	0.00	650.00
AEQPC	Electronics:Near-Coast	121	0.00	0.00	0.00
BFITNC	Fishing Outfit:Away-Coast	121	0.00	0.00	0.00
BFITC	Fishing Outfit:Near-Coast	121	0.00	0.00	0.00
RODC	Rods:Near-Coast	121	62.03	0.00	2000.00
RODNC	Rods:Away-Coast	121	27.07	0.00	400.00
LINEC	Fishing Line:Near-Coast	121	10.49	0.00	200.00

LINENC	Fishing Line:Away-Coast	121	4.47	0.00	100.00
LUREC	Lures:Near-Coast	121	38.58	0.00	500.00
LURENC	Lures:Nonoastal	121	21.20	0.00	400.00
REPRNC	Capital Repairs:Away-Coast	121	21.82	0.00	1000.00
REPRC	Capital Repairs:Near-Coast	121	47.55	0.00	2000.00
OTHCFNC	Other Fishing:Away-Coast	121	5.89	0.00	260.00
OTHCFC	Other Fishing:Near-Coast	121	14.82	0.00	500.00
BOOKNC	Books:Away-Coast	121	0.00	0.00	0.00
BOOKC	Books:Near-Coast	121	10.39	0.00	180.00
MEMBNC	Memberships:Away-Coast	121	0.00	0.00	0.00
MEMBC	Memberships:Near-Coast	121	4.82	0.00	130.00
CAMPNC	Camping:Away-Coast	121	0.00	0.00	0.00
CAMPC	Camping:Near-Coast	121	78.00	0.00	9000.00
LICNC	Licenses:Away-Coast	121	0.00	0.00	0.00
LICC	Licenses:Near-Coast	121	11.02	0.00	68.00

Private Fishing Summary Statistics for trip and equipment expenditures by Louisiana
noncoastal residents who did't visit an oil/gas structure on the interview date

Variable	Label	N	Mean	Minimum	Maximum
TRANST	Transportation:Total	9	0.00	0.00	0.00
TRANSC	Transportation:Near-Coast	9	0.00	0.00	0.00
RCART	Rental Car:Total	9	0.00	0.00	0.00
RCARC	Rental Car:Near-Coast	9	0.00	0.00	0.00
LODGT	Lodging:Total	9	26.67	0.00	240.00
LODGC	Lodging:Near-Coast	9	26.67	0.00	240.00
GAST	Gasoline:Total	9	37.50	0.00	90.00
GASC	Gasoline:Near-Coast	9	0.00	0.00	0.00
FOODT	Other Food:Total	9	19.22	0.00	80.00
FOODC	Other Food:Near-Coast	9	3.67	0.00	30.00
GROCT	Groceries:Total	9	30.22	0.00	100.00
GROCC	Groceries:Near-Coast	9	11.11	0.00	50.00
FUELT	Fuel:Total	9	18.11	0.00	60.00
FUELC	Fuel:Near-Coast	9	13.33	0.00	60.00
BRNTT	Boat Rentals:Total	9	0.00	0.00	0.00
BRNTC	Boat Rentals:Near-Coast	9	0.00	0.00	0.00
LNCHT	Launch Fees:Total	9	0.67	0.00	6.00
LNCHC	Launch Fees:Near-Coast	9	0.67	0.00	6.00
DOCKT	Dockage Fees:Total	9	0.00	0.00	0.00
DOCKC	Dockage Fees:Near-Coast	9	0.00	0.00	0.00
TREPRT	Trip Repairs:Total	9	0.00	0.00	0.00
TREPRC	Trip Repairs:Near-Coast	9	0.00	0.00	0.00
BAITT	Bait:Total	9	17.33	0.00	80.00
BAITC	Bait:Near-Coast	9	7.44	0.00	20.00
FLICT	Fishing Licenses:Total	9	0.89	0.00	8.00
FLICC	Fishing Licenses:Near-Coast	9	0.89	0.00	8.00
TCKLT	Tackle:Total	9	1.11	0.00	5.00
TCKLC	Tackle:Near-Coast	9	0.56	0.00	5.00
OTHRNTT	Other Rentals:Total	9	0.00	0.00	0.00
OTHRNTC	Other Rentals:Near-Coast	9	0.00	0.00	0.00
CLTHT	Clothing:Total	9	0.00	0.00	0.00
CLTHC	Clothing:Near-Coast	9	0.00	0.00	0.00
GUIDT	Guide Fees:Total	9	0.00	0.00	0.00
GUIDC	Guide Fees:Near-Coast	9	0.00	0.00	0.00
OTHRTT	Other Trip Expenses:Total	9	1.44	0.00	10.00
OTHRTC	Other Trip Expenses:Near-Coast	9	0.00	0.00	0.00
BOATNC	Boats:Away-Coast	9	0.00	0.00	0.00
BOATC	Boats:Near-Coast	9	1111.11	0.00	10000.00
MOTORNC	Motors:Away-Coast	9	0.00	0.00	0.00
MOTORC	Motors:Near-Coast	9	555.56	0.00	5000.00
TRAILNC	Trailers:Away-Coast	9	0.00	0.00	0.00
TRAILC	Trailers:Near-Coast	9	166.67	0.00	1500.00
AEQPNC	Electronics:Away-Coast	9	66.67	0.00	600.00
AEQPC	Electronics:Near-Coast	9	0.00	0.00	0.00
BFITNC	Fishing Outfit:Away-Coast	9	0.00	0.00	0.00
BFITC	Fishing Outfit:Near-Coast	9	0.00	0.00	0.00
RODC	Rods:Near-Coast	9	22.22	0.00	200.00
RODNC	Rods:Away-Coast	9	11.11	0.00	100.00
LINEC	Fishing Line:Near-Coast	9	0.00	0.00	0.00

LINENC	Fishing Line:Away-Coast	9	2.78	0.00	15.00
LUREC	Lures:Near-Coast	9	1.67	0.00	15.00
LURENC	Lures:Nonoastal	9	7.22	0.00	40.00
REPRNC	Capital Repairs:Away-Coast	9	140.00	0.00	840.00
REPRC	Capital Repairs:Near-Coast	9	0.00	0.00	0.00
OTHCFNC	Other Fishing:Away-Coast	9	1.00	0.00	9.00
OTHCFC	Other Fishing:Near-Coast	9	0.00	0.00	0.00
BOOKNC	Books:Away-Coast	9	4.00	0.00	24.00
BOOKC	Books:Near-Coast	9	0.00	0.00	0.00
MEMBNC	Memberships:Away-Coast	9	4.11	0.00	25.00
MEMBC	Memberships:Near-Coast	9	0.00	0.00	0.00
CAMPNC	Camping:Away-Coast	9	2.22	0.00	20.00
CAMPC	Camping:Near-Coast	9	0.00	0.00	0.00
LICNC	Licenses:Away-Coast	9	14.89	0.00	90.00
LICC	Licenses:Near-Coast	9	0.00	0.00	0.00

Private Fishing Summary Statistics for trip and equipment expenditures by Texas
coastal residents who did't visit an oil/gas structure on the interview date

Variable	Label	N	Mean	Minimum	Maximum
TRANST	Transportation:Total	61	0.00	0.00	0.00
TRANSC	Transportation:Near-Coast	61	0.00	0.00	0.00
RCART	Rental Car:Total	61	0.00	0.00	0.00
RCARC	Rental Car:Near-Coast	61	0.00	0.00	0.00
LODGT	Lodging:Total	61	19.82	0.00	250.00
LODGC	Lodging:Near-Coast	61	19.82	0.00	250.00
GAST	Gasoline:Total	61	11.73	0.00	60.00
GASC	Gasoline:Near-Coast	61	11.73	0.00	60.00
FOODT	Other Food:Total	61	26.48	0.00	300.00
FOODC	Other Food:Near-Coast	61	26.48	0.00	300.00
GROCT	Groceries:Total	61	27.15	0.00	600.00
GROCC	Groceries:Near-Coast	61	27.15	0.00	600.00
FUELT	Fuel:Total	61	34.59	0.00	270.00
FUELC	Fuel:Near-Coast	61	34.59	0.00	270.00
BRNTT	Boat Rentals:Total	61	0.61	0.00	9.00
BRNTC	Boat Rentals:Near-Coast	61	0.61	0.00	9.00
LNCHT	Launch Fees:Total	61	2.56	0.00	30.00
LNCHC	Launch Fees:Near-Coast	61	2.56	0.00	30.00
DOCKT	Dockage Fees:Total	61	0.39	0.00	9.00
DOCKC	Dockage Fees:Near-Coast	61	0.39	0.00	9.00
TREPRT	Trip Repairs:Total	61	1.64	0.00	60.00
TREPRC	Trip Repairs:Near-Coast	61	1.64	0.00	60.00
BAITT	Bait:Total	61	14.59	0.00	90.00
BAITC	Bait:Near-Coast	61	14.59	0.00	90.00
FLICT	Fishing Licenses:Total	61	0.66	0.00	40.00
FLICC	Fishing Licenses:Near-Coast	61	0.66	0.00	40.00
TCKLT	Tackle:Total	61	4.52	0.00	60.00
TCKLC	Tackle:Near-Coast	61	4.52	0.00	60.00
OTHRNTT	Other Rentals:Total	61	0.00	0.00	0.00
OTHRNTC	Other Rentals:Near-Coast	61	0.00	0.00	0.00
CLTHT	Clothing:Total	61	1.97	0.00	80.00
CLTHC	Clothing:Near-Coast	61	1.97	0.00	80.00
GUIDT	Guide Fees:Total	61	9.84	0.00	600.00
GUIDC	Guide Fees:Near-Coast	61	9.84	0.00	600.00
OTHRTT	Other Trip Expenses:Total	61	3.34	0.00	60.00
OTHRTC	Other Trip Expenses:Near-Coast	61	3.34	0.00	60.00
BOATNC	Boats:Away-Coast	61	0.00	0.00	0.00
BOATC	Boats:Near-Coast	61	2.38	0.00	145.00
MOTORNC	Motors:Away-Coast	61	0.00	0.00	0.00
MOTORC	Motors:Near-Coast	61	81.97	0.00	5000.00
TRAILNC	Trailers:Away-Coast	61	62.30	0.00	3800.00
TRAILC	Trailers:Near-Coast	61	32.79	0.00	2000.00
AEQPNC	Electronics:Away-Coast	61	113.93	0.00	3000.00
AEQPC	Electronics:Near-Coast	61	0.00	0.00	0.00
BFITNC	Fishing Outfit:Away-Coast	61	19.67	0.00	1200.00
BFITC	Fishing Outfit:Near-Coast	61	0.00	0.00	0.00
RODC	Rods:Near-Coast	61	104.10	0.00	1200.00
RODNC	Rods:Away-Coast	61	25.25	0.00	600.00
LINEC	Fishing Line:Near-Coast	61	19.75	0.00	200.00

LINENC	Fishing Line:Away-Coast	61	2.62	0.00	40.00
LUREC	Lures:Near-Coast	61	56.31	0.00	500.00
LURENC	Lures:Nonoastal	61	15.74	0.00	300.00
REPRNC	Capital Repairs:Away-Coast	61	68.03	0.00	2000.00
REPRC	Capital Repairs:Near-Coast	61	66.80	0.00	2500.00
OTHCFNC	Other Fishing:Away-Coast	61	5.33	0.00	175.00
OTHCFC	Other Fishing:Near-Coast	61	187.05	0.00	8500.00
BOOKNC	Books:Away-Coast	61	0.00	0.00	0.00
BOOKC	Books:Near-Coast	61	14.26	0.00	120.00
MEMBNC	Memberships:Away-Coast	61	0.00	0.00	0.00
MEMBC	Memberships:Near-Coast	61	12.74	0.00	150.00
CAMPNC	Camping:Away-Coast	61	0.00	0.00	0.00
CAMPC	Camping:Near-Coast	61	27.03	0.00	1199.00
LICNC	Licenses:Away-Coast	61	0.00	0.00	0.00
LICC	Licenses:Near-Coast	61	26.05	0.00	67.00

Private Fishing Summary Statistics for trip and equipment expenditures by Texas
noncoastal residents who did't visit an oil/gas structure on the interview date

Variable	Label	N	Mean	Minimum	Maximum
TRANST	Transportation:Total	20	25.00	0.00	500.00
TRANSC	Transportation:Near-Coast	20	0.00	0.00	0.00
RCART	Rental Car:Total	20	0.00	0.00	0.00
RCARC	Rental Car:Near-Coast	20	0.00	0.00	0.00
LODGT	Lodging:Total	20	95.70	0.00	595.00
LODGC	Lodging:Near-Coast	20	95.70	0.00	595.00
GAST	Gasoline:Total	20	37.22	0.00	181.50
GASC	Gasoline:Near-Coast	20	0.00	0.00	0.00
FOODT	Other Food:Total	20	120.75	0.00	1200.00
FOODC	Other Food:Near-Coast	20	92.20	0.00	1200.00
GROCT	Groceries:Total	20	100.50	0.00	900.00
GROCC	Groceries:Near-Coast	20	94.05	0.00	900.00
FUELT	Fuel:Total	20	31.70	0.00	300.00
FUELC	Fuel:Near-Coast	20	15.75	0.00	120.00
BRNTT	Boat Rentals:Total	20	38.00	0.00	720.00
BRNTC	Boat Rentals:Near-Coast	20	38.00	0.00	720.00
LNCHT	Launch Fees:Total	20	2.35	0.00	30.00
LNCHC	Launch Fees:Near-Coast	20	2.35	0.00	30.00
DOCKT	Dockage Fees:Total	20	7.95	0.00	150.00
DOCKC	Dockage Fees:Near-Coast	20	0.45	0.00	9.00
TREPRT	Trip Repairs:Total	20	0.00	0.00	0.00
TREPRC	Trip Repairs:Near-Coast	20	0.00	0.00	0.00
BAITT	Bait:Total	20	50.85	0.00	360.00
BAITC	Bait:Near-Coast	20	41.35	0.00	360.00
FLICT	Fishing Licenses:Total	20	13.25	0.00	175.00
FLICC	Fishing Licenses:Near-Coast	20	13.25	0.00	175.00
TCKLT	Tackle:Total	20	12.75	0.00	120.00
TCKLC	Tackle:Near-Coast	20	12.75	0.00	120.00
OTHRNTT	Other Rentals:Total	20	0.00	0.00	0.00
OTHRNTC	Other Rentals:Near-Coast	20	0.00	0.00	0.00
CLTHT	Clothing:Total	20	3.00	0.00	60.00
CLTHC	Clothing:Near-Coast	20	3.00	0.00	60.00
GUIDT	Guide Fees:Total	20	0.00	0.00	0.00
GUIDC	Guide Fees:Near-Coast	20	0.00	0.00	0.00
OTHRTT	Other Trip Expenses:Total	20	1.75	0.00	18.00
OTHRTC	Other Trip Expenses:Near-Coast	20	0.00	0.00	0.00
BOATNC	Boats:Away-Coast	20	650.00	0.00	13000.00
BOATC	Boats:Near-Coast	20	0.00	0.00	0.00
MOTORNC	Motors:Away-Coast	20	525.00	0.00	10500.00
MOTORC	Motors:Near-Coast	20	0.00	0.00	0.00
TRAILNC	Trailers:Away-Coast	20	750.00	0.00	15000.00
TRAILC	Trailers:Near-Coast	20	0.00	0.00	0.00
AEQPNC	Electronics:Away-Coast	20	0.40	0.00	8.00
AEQPC	Electronics:Near-Coast	20	0.00	0.00	0.00
BFITNC	Fishing Outfit:Away-Coast	20	0.00	0.00	0.00
BFITC	Fishing Outfit:Near-Coast	20	0.00	0.00	0.00
RODC	Rods:Near-Coast	20	15.00	0.00	300.00
RODNC	Rods:Away-Coast	20	10.00	0.00	200.00
LINEC	Fishing Line:Near-Coast	20	8.00	0.00	50.00

LINENC	Fishing Line:Away-Coast	20	12.75	0.00	150.00
LUREC	Lures:Near-Coast	20	35.00	0.00	350.00
LURENC	Lures:Nonoastal	20	73.25	0.00	1000.00
REPRNC	Capital Repairs:Away-Coast	20	0.00	0.00	0.00
REPRC	Capital Repairs:Near-Coast	20	21.25	0.00	425.00
OTHCFNC	Other Fishing:Away-Coast	20	99.50	0.00	1000.00
OTHCFC	Other Fishing:Near-Coast	20	0.00	0.00	0.00
BOOKNC	Books:Away-Coast	20	8.45	0.00	62.00
BOOKC	Books:Near-Coast	20	0.00	0.00	0.00
MEMBNC	Memberships:Away-Coast	20	5.50	0.00	75.00
MEMBC	Memberships:Near-Coast	20	0.00	0.00	0.00
CAMPNC	Camping:Away-Coast	20	10.00	0.00	200.00
CAMPC	Camping:Near-Coast	20	0.00	0.00	0.00
LICNC	Licenses:Away-Coast	20	24.30	0.00	50.00
LICC	Licenses:Near-Coast	20	0.00	0.00	0.00

. . . .

The Department of the Interior Mission

As the Nation's principal conservation agency, the Department of the Interior has responsibility for most of our nationally owned public lands and natural resources. This includes fostering sound use of our land and water resources; protecting our fish, wildlife, and biological diversity; preserving the environmental and cultural values of our national parks and historical places; and providing for the enjoyment of life through outdoor recreation. The Department assesses our energy and mineral resources and works to ensure that their development is in the best interests of all our people by encouraging stewardship and citizen participation in their care. The Department also has a major responsibility for American Indian reservation communities and for people who live in island territories under U.S. administration.

The Minerals Management Service Mission

As a bureau of the Department of the Interior, the Minerals Management Service's (MMS) primary responsibilities are to manage the mineral resources located on the Nation's Outer Continental Shelf (OCS), collect revenue from the Federal OCS and onshore Federal and Indian lands, and distribute those revenues.

Moreover, in working to meet its responsibilities, the **Offshore Minerals Management Program** administers the OCS competitive leasing program and oversees the safe and environmentally sound exploration and production of our Nation's offshore natural gas, oil and other mineral resources. The MMS **Minerals Revenue Management** meets its responsibilities by ensuring the efficient, timely and accurate collection and disbursement of revenue from mineral leasing and production due to Indian tribes and allottees, States and the U.S. Treasury.

The MMS strives to fulfill its responsibilities through the general guiding principles of: (1) being responsive to the public's concerns and interests by maintaining a dialogue with all potentially affected parties and (2) carrying out its programs with an emphasis on working to enhance the quality of life for all Americans by lending MMS assistance and expertise to economic development and environmental protection.

www.ingramcontent.com/pod-product-compliance
Lightning Source LLC
Chambersburg PA
CBHW051954280526
45793CB00005B/717